PRAISE FOR
Born Trump

"... portrait of the people America thought they knew. . . . Both entertaining and eye-opening, serving up never-before-heard stories on everything from the Trump kids' college fraternity hijinks to a massive blowout fight on the top of Aspen Mountain that could only be described as *Housewives*-ian."
—*Entertainment Weekly*

"Fox's book is not only about Trump's children and his son-in-law and adviser, Jared Kushner. It's also about his marriages and divorces and their impact on his children." —NPR

"In this brisk, highly entertaining volume, Fox, a senior reporter for *Vanity Fair* and an MSNBC contributor, sets out to deliver a 'dish-y' yet 'well-reported' portrait of the Trump family drawn from decades of tabloid headlines and hundreds of interviews with friends, classmates, colleagues, and business associates. This group biography is well-written, occasionally mean-spirited, and rich in gossipy detail." —*Publishers Weekly*

"*Vanity Fair* senior reporter Emily Jane Fox pulls no punches in this dish-y tell-all." —*Glamour*

"Fox's book is a gossipy family study. . . . It will make you weep."
—*The Guardian* (London)

"Fox does not strive to explain politics or policies, but she does provide deep insight into the personal factors that shape the Trump White House." —*New York Journal of Books*

BORN
TRUMP

BORN TRUMP

Inside America's First Family

EMILY JANE FOX

HARPER

NEW YORK ∙ LONDON ∙ TORONTO ∙ SYDNEY

HARPER

A hardcover edition of this book was published in 2018 by HarperCollins Publishers.

BORN TRUMP. Copyright © 2018 by Emily Jane Fox. All rights reserved. Printed in the United States of America. No part of this book may be used or reproduced in any manner whatsoever without written permission except in the case of brief quotations embodied in critical articles and reviews. For information, address HarperCollins Publishers, 195 Broadway, New York, NY 10007.

HarperCollins books may be purchased for educational, business, or sales promotional use. For information, please email the Special Markets Department at SPsales@harper collins.com.

FIRST HARPER PAPERBACKS EDITION PUBLISHED 2019.

Library of Congress Cataloging-in-Publication Data has been applied for.

ISBN 978-0-06-269078-4 (pbk.)

19 20 21 22 23   LSC   10 9 8 7 6 5 4 3 2 1

To my mom, dad, and sister, who gave their unconditional and selfless, protective, and present love so freely and with such ease that I had little inkling of what it would be like to grow up any other way. I am grateful for that now more than ever.

Contents

CHAPTER 1

Inauguration

IVANKA TRUMP and Jared Kushner hustled themselves and their children up to the second floor of the residence in the White House, to the southeastern corner of her father's new sixteen-room home. She was still in the white Oscar de la Renta pantsuit she'd worn all day—through the rain washing over her father's swearing-in ceremony and the parade down Pennsylvania Avenue marking his inauguration—and chilled to her bones. She would soon change into a glittery champagne gown for the inaugural balls. Her hair would be teased and swept and sprayed into an ornate knot at the nape of her neck. She would prick teardrop diamonds into her ears and slather highlighter onto her cheekbones and underneath her eyebrow and onto her bare clavicle, exposed by the deep V of her dress.

All of that would have to wait. The Trump-Kushners sped into the Lincoln Bedroom, where they had stayed through her dad's first weekend as the president of the United States of America. The traditional parade flirted dangerously close to sundown, which, on January 20, 2017, fell at 4:59 p.m. eastern standard time. As practicing Modern Orthodox Jews, Ivanka and Jared needed to light Shabbat candles as day turned into night in order to observe their own tradition, which Jared had been doing his whole life and Ivanka had joined him in when she converted, years earlier, before they married.

She had arranged with the White House usher to have candlesticks waiting in their borrowed room. Usually she would have brought her own, as she typically did for a weekend away, but this weekend, in just about every way, was not typical for the Trumps. She figured the White House must have suitable candelabras lying around. She was correct.

The immediate family of five formed a semicircle around the White House's candlesticks, and Ivanka struck a match to light the wicks. There they were, in a room Abraham Lincoln had once used as an office; which the Trumans had rebuilt in 1945, Jackie Kennedy had spiffed up in 1961, Hillary Clinton had freshened in the 1990s, and Laura Bush had again refurbished in 2004. The eight-by-six-foot rosewood Lincoln bed, with its six-foot-tall carved headboard—the bed that Presidents Franklin Roosevelt and Calvin Coolidge had slept in—was at their backs; a holograph copy of the Gettysburg Address, one of only five signed, dated, and titled by Lincoln, sat on the desk nearby. Ivanka covered her eyes and recited the blessing over the candles: "Baruch ata Adonai, Eloheinu Melech ha-olam, asher kidshanu b'mitzvotav vitzivanu l'hadlik ner shel at." *Blessed are You, God, Ruler of the universe, who sanctified us with the commandment of lighting Shabbat candles.*

It was the first time Shabbat had been welcomed this way in the history of the residence.

SOME FIVE hours earlier, as light sheets of rain fell over Washington, DC, Donald J. Trump had pressed his right hand to two Bibles on the West Lawn of the Capitol and became the forty-fifth person to recite the oath of office, as prescribed by Article II, Section 1, of the Constitution. One of the Bibles he chose was used by Lincoln when he was sworn in at his first inauguration in 1861, as the nation hung on the precipice of the Civil War. The other had been given to him by his mother in 1955, two days before his ninth birthday, just after he graduated from the Sunday Church Primary School at the First Presbyterian Church in Jamaica, Queens. Its cover is embossed with his name and, on the inside, signed by church officials.

After taking the oath, Trump turned his back on the crowd and swung his arms open toward his family, who had encircled him as he made his vow to the American people. He first locked eyes with Ivanka, who had positioned herself directly at the center of the dais, with her brother Eric slightly behind her to her left and her half sister Tiffany next to him. Don Jr. was just to Ivanka's back on the other side, her half brother Barron and stepmother turned First Lady Melania beside him. Ivanka cocked her head at her dad, the president, her lips and cheeks pulled so tightly by her smile that her facial muscles contorted themselves into an aptly bronzed rectangle. She dove forward to kiss him, but his instinct kicked in quick. He had never been on this sort of world stage before, but he had spent enough years with his family life chronicled in the papers to know well enough to greet his wife before his favorite daughter. So before she reached him, he swooped to his left and pecked his wife, and then worked his way through his children—Barron, Donny, Ivanka, Eric, Tiffany—to let them congratulate him, tell him how great he'd done, how much they loved him.

The family soon gathered in a motorcade for the inaugural parade. Ivanka and Jared quickly realized that their infant car seat did not fit in their armored car—an inconvenient, startlingly normal fact that held up the entire motorcade and parade on this historic day. "What's the holdup?" everyone kept asking. At last, they figured it out. Everyone got moving. At a quarter after four in the afternoon—following the custom President Jimmy Carter began in 1977, when he got out of his limousine and walked for more than a mile en route to the White House—Donald, Melania, and Barron stepped out of "the Beast," the armored car the president travels in, in front of the Trump International Hotel. Elsewhere along the route, crowds were sparse and protesters had gathered. But in front of the hotel bearing Trump's name, revelers were packed onto risers, a dozen deep. There were cheers and signs and a sea of red "Make America Great Again" hats. Ivanka and Don Jr. and Eric and their spouses and most of their children followed in cars of their own, and, once he got out of his car, walked alongside their dad, greeting the supporters who'd waited outside for hours in the forty-degree Washington winter.

The family stayed outside for about three minutes before getting back in their cars, which moved along slowly for another half hour, until they arrived at a viewing stand near the White House. Ivanka and Jared whisked inside around sunset.

None of them had expected to be there that day. When their father decided to run—and frankly up until they saw him start winning states on November 8 from the campaign headquarters on the twenty-fourth floor of Trump Tower, a few months earlier—they'd assumed that he would lose and that they would get back to their normal lives and businesses. They would have spent that gray, winter day with the broadcast of the inauguration on in the background as they headed off for weekends at Mar-a-Lago, or at their homes in Bedminster, or Westchester, or the Catskills. It would have been an otherwise normal winter weekend for an otherwise perfectly happy moneyed family, trying to get back into the swing of their old normal. Apart from the fact that it meant that he'd won something, Donald didn't much want to be there. As the reality of the election dawned on him in the weeks leading up to his move, he frequently asked advisers how often he could leave Washington to return to his triplex on Fifth Avenue, and in the weeks after the move he spent most weekends flying on Air Force One down to his private club in Palm Beach.

But it was not a normal weekend, and their old normal was swiftly replaced by an extraordinary new existence—one that they not only didn't predict but also never could have imagined. Nevertheless, that is where they found themselves on January 20. And once they were there, the Trump kids made damn sure that they were at the front and center of everything.

THERE WERE thousands of things to do once the Trump family woke up bleary-eyed and bewildered on the morning of November 9, barely a few hours after Donald gave his victory speech, scraped together with the kids' help just before they all rushed over to the ballroom at the Midtown Manhattan Hilton Hotel. A concession speech had been written in advance. Ivanka had plans to get her fashion line back on track come Wednesday morning. She would lay low for a while and let the rhetoric and rancor die down a bit, so that what her team expected to be strong holiday season sales would speak for themselves, starting a whole new narrative. The manuscript for her book for working women would also require her attention; she had just turned it in, and it was set to go to print around the inauguration. Jared would begin a reputational recovery tour. Friends had told him that would be a feat, now that people viewed him as an asshole; no one would be lining up to do business with him, at least not right after the election loss. Don Jr. and Eric were starting talks with investors and partners about a new, lower-tier chain of hotels in heartland cities that would appeal to the Trump supporters they'd met on the trail, turning their MAGA zeal into Trump Organization patronage. Tiffany would be able to focus on her law school applications. Barron could go to school on Manhattan's Upper West Side without the Secret Service agents who were clogging up drop-off and pickup traffic, enraging the uptown parents and drivers and nannies (to say nothing of back-to-school night, when Melania and her protection locked down the school's only elevator so she could get to Barron's classroom; this left the rest of the parents to hoof it up the stairs, rocketing the school rage-ometer to full-scale fury). There was very little in place for what would happen if Donald actually won.

Now an inaugural weekend had to be put together, which required months of planning and millions of dollars and at least a basic understanding of its history and traditions. Trump tapped Tom Barrack, his friend of three decades, to chair the committee. In a statement on November 15, Donald announced that Barrack—a private equity billionaire who had served as deputy undersecretary of the Department of Interior under Reagan and been one of Donald's cheeriest surrogates and advisers throughout the campaign (and the man who urged Ivanka and Jared to get Donald to hire Paul Manafort)— would be "responsible for the planning and coordination of all official events and activities surrounding the inauguration."

Barrack and Trump had first crossed paths in 1987, when Donald summoned him to Trump Tower. At the time, Barrack was working for a rich Texas family that owned a department store chain Donald wanted to buy a piece of, which he did, thanks to Barrack's help. The family also owned the Plaza Hotel, which Donald could see from his office window in Trump Tower and itched to add to his growing Manhattan empire. The problem was that Barrack's bosses wanted $410 million for the property. It was a bum deal for Donald, but it was a New York institution, the kind of storied figure in New York Donald himself wanted to become. It was a crown jewel. And Donald—a Queens outsider and something of a punch line— wanted it for his crown. So he agreed to pay the price—in cash, no less. And after he'd thrown his kids' birthday parties in the hotel, and later met with Ivana there to hash out the early details of their separation, and later married Marla Maples there, the place dragged him near financial ruin. In 1994 a guy Barrack knew from Chase Manhattan Bank called to tell him Donald was in trouble. He had a $100 million loan with Chase, and a mountain of other debts, and at the very least he needed to unload the Plaza. Barrack persuaded the bank to give Donald a little breathing room to find financing before they foreclosed. In the time that bought, they found a Saudi Arabian prince and a hotel group out of Singapore to take it off his hands. More than a decade later Donald asked Jared, who, in his own Trumpian outer-borough desire to make it in Manhattan, had bought a forty-one-story office tower on Fifth Avenue for what was then the highest price for a commercial building in US history and was struggling to make the loan payments. Jared flew to Los Angeles to ask Barrack for his advice, and Barrack obliged, helping him restructure his debt and holding some of it himself.

The inauguration gig was a high-profile thank-you for Barrack, and a relief for Donald, who'd been saved by Barrack enough times before that he trusted him to do it again. Barrack brought on a team of other billionaires and Trump loyalists, including Sheldon Adelson, Woody Johnson, Anthony Scaramucci, Steve Wynn, Elliott Broidy, and Laurie Perlmutter, to help him out. He asked Stephanie Winston Wolkoff, a former *Vogue* editor and friend of Melania's known around the Condé Nast office as General Winston for the military efficiency with which she planned the annual Met Gala, to serve as an editor-at-large for the inauguration. She took on all the heavy lifting—securing venues and event planners, deciding on table settings, arranging broadcast rights and social media filters, figuring out how to move heavy equipment around Washington, and—perhaps the heaviest lift of all—getting talent to perform at events throughout the weekend. Inaugurations past had been filled with megawatt star power. At Barack Obama's, Beyoncé, Aretha Franklin, Yo-Yo Ma, and Kelly Clarkson performed; at George W. Bush's, Ricky Martin, 98 Degrees, and Jessica Simpson; for Bill Clinton's, Fleetwood Mac got back together again for a rare performance. Virtually no celebrities wanted to perform at a Trump inauguration. That would have been an issue for any incoming president, but it was particularly sticky for Trump, whose fragile ego cracked at the slightest of insults from nobodies.

Wolkoff asked Mark Burnett, the creator of *The Apprentice*, to comb through his Rolodex to convince stars to take part in the weekend—if not in support of Donald, out of patriotic duty. Still, they couldn't get a big name. In fact, everyone whose name was so much as floated as a possible inaugural performer immediately disassociated themselves. When a rumor circulated that Elton John would give a concert on the Mall, his spokesperson quickly threw water on it. Garth Brooks initially appeared open to the idea, since "it's always about serving," but soon afterward declined an offer to appear. The same happened with Andrea Bocelli, Kiss, and Jennifer Holliday. The Mormon Tabernacle Choir, however, did accept the invitation to sing at the swearing-in ceremony. They booked *America's Got Talent* runner-up Jackie Evancho for the national anthem. The Rockettes agreed to perform at the inaugural balls, though some dancers refused to partake, complaining to their union about being asked to perform for what one Rockette described as a man who "stands for everything we're against."

At the same time, millions of people, including Katy Perry, Cher, and Madonna, were preparing to walk in women's marches around the country. In fact, reports stated that DC issued far more permits for city buses for the march on Saturday than for Donald's swearing-in on Friday. And in the weeks leading up to the inauguration, nearly seventy lawmakers vowed to boycott the events to protest the messages Donald had run on and the rhetoric he used during the campaign and after the election.

With protests looming and virtually no one famous set to attend, the inaugural committee's message shifted. As Barrack spun it, with "the biggest celebrity in the world" as president, other stars were superfluous. "So what we've done," Barrack said, "instead of trying to surround him with what people consider A-listers, is we are going to surround him with the soft sensuality of the place. It's a much more poetic cadence than having a circuslike celebration that's a coronation. That's the way this president-elect wanted it."

It was, in a word, a disaster, and they needed all hands on deck. The Trump kids jumped into the planning, though not necessarily to aid in the process or to take on some of the burden. They each wanted to make sure that they individually would be involved in each public event, and took great pains to make sure not only that they would be present but that their seating arrangements were satisfactory. Their proximity to Donald on that day, and thus their presence in photographs that would be telegraphed all over the world that weekend and in history books for centuries, was paramount.

Melania, as the incoming First Lady, tried to organize a weekend that kept them all together. That meant all five kids, all eight grandchildren, would be welcome to stay the Thursday evening before the inauguration at the Blair House, just across the road from the White House, and spend the rest of the weekend in the residence once the Obamas moved out and the Trumps moved in. No one would sleep on couches or double up; Melania made sure that each sibling had his or her own room and determined who would sleep where, though Ivanka did put in a request to stay in the Lincoln Bedroom. Melania arranged enough time for breakfasts and lunches and dinners together as a family, to anchor everyone in the headiest of weekends. She had buffets to be set up throughout the weekend so that no one would go hungry.

Melania was less certain when it came to the parade, which would have the family making the same walk toward the White House on the twentieth of January that presidents have made for nearly half a century. There have been few American political climates so vitriolic and acerbically divided as the one that existed after Donald's election, and she had deep concerns about getting out of the car and marching alongside her eleven-year-old in the open, even with the Secret Service and protection teams that would surround them.

Ivanka was set on the parade. "It's happening," she insisted. It was tradition. It was presidential. It was not something her father and the family were going to miss out on.

There was a sense among those who worked on the transition that the legacy aspect of the inauguration was critical for Ivanka. This was a chance for the Trumps to have their Kennedy moment—

one that looked a lot like Camelot. Melania, in her Ralph Lauren powder-blue suit with matching blue gloves, her hair teased into a bouffant, consciously channeled Jackie on inauguration day. (Initially, she had toyed with the idea of wearing the now infamous red, white, and blue Gucci ensemble that Kellyanne wore and got panned for, but a fashion editor and adviser to Melania nixed it, reminding her of the importance of wearing American designers that weekend.) Ivanka looked to establish the Trumps as the new American royal family. She worked with a stylist and told friends that she wanted a princess moment, particularly for the inaugural balls, for which she chose a sparkly tulle confection. "I told her it's an inauguration, not a coronation," one friend recalled. "The sentiment was that Americans wanted a royal family." (A blown-up photograph of her in that gown, dancing with Jared onstage, hangs outside her office in the West Wing, with a note scrawled across it in metallic Sharpie. "To the most beautiful couple in the world," her father wrote across the image. "I am so proud of you. Love, Dad.") There was less meaning ascribed to the Oscar de la Renta white pantsuit Ivanka chose for the actual swearing-in ceremony. Of course, the choice raised eyebrows. White pantsuits were a Hillary Clinton thing, so much so that Hillary Clinton herself wore one on inauguration day. When advisers brought that up to Ivanka in advance of the day, she shrugged it off. "It definitely was not intentional, her choosing to wear that," one adviser remembered. "She was like, 'oh shit,' not in a stupid way, but she didn't mean to make it a thing. It really wasn't."

THAT IVANKA wanted to harken back to the Kennedys was no surprise. Certainly her mother, Ivana, who had longed for a place in the world of old-money American royalty, played a role in this, at least during her daughter's childhood. For years, Ivana told people that Ivanka's beloved Irish nanny, Bridget Carroll, had nannied for John Kennedy Jr. before moving in with the Trump family, though there is no proof of that, other than Ivana's mentions. She took credit for choosing her daughter's schools, first Chapin, the all-girls private school that Jacqueline Bouvier attended, and then Choate, the boarding school from which John Kennedy graduated. In Ivana's recent book about her children, she noted that the Kennedy family would travel to Aspen for holidays at the same time the Trump family did, engaging in side-by-side slalom races against one another. "It was the Trumps vs. the Kennedys," she wrote, "and Trump always won." At Choate, Ivanka told classmates, particularly when it came up in her political history classes, of her admiration for Jackie Kennedy as a leader. (One classmate remembers that she always took an interest in the Roosevelt family, too, and in Anna Roosevelt in particular. Franklin Roosevelt tapped Anna, his only daughter—who, like her father, had a somewhat sticky relationship with the First Lady—to work in his West Wing after she and her young children had lived with him in the White House during the early years of his presidency. She served as his personal assistant, accompanying her father to the Yalta Conference in World War II, while Eleanor Roosevelt stayed behind.)

Jared and his family had their own affinity for the Kennedys. Jared's father Charlie keenly referred to himself as the "Jewish Kennedy," seeing himself as both a king and kingmaker in the northern New Jersey religious community in which, thanks to healthy donations, many of the buildings bore his name. When it came time for Jared to apply to Harvard as a high school senior, Charlie nudged his senator, Frank Lautenberg, to ask his colleague Ted Kennedy to put in a good word with the dean of admissions in Cambridge. When Jared moved into a corner office overlooking St. Patrick's Cathedral, where the family baptized Caroline Kennedy and eulogized Bobby Kennedy after his death, he hung just one photo on the wall next to his desk. It was a framed Garry Winogrand snap of Jack Kennedy delivering his speech at the 1960 Democratic National Convention in Los Angeles. The shot catches JFK from behind, camera lights creating a halo around the side of his head and contours of his jaw. A television set propped up just behind the desk broadcasts his face again in black and white for the viewer to see. "I love the juxtaposition of him looking that way and seeing him the other way," Jared told *New York Magazine* of the photo in 2009. "I love the glow in his face. I look at it all the time." He bought all the photos in the series, but kept the rest in a box. (Later, once he and Ivanka had married and moved into a Trump building on Park Avenue, Winogrand photographs lined the hallways of their apartment.) After Jared was sworn in as senior adviser to the president at the tail end of inauguration weekend, he and his brother Josh posed for a photo underneath the somber portrait of JFK hanging in the White House.

When Ivanka and Jared got married, they decided to release one photo after the nuptials, in the style of John F. Kennedy Jr. and Carolyn Bessette, rather than selling them to a magazine. When they had children, all the names they chose evoked Kennedy family ties—Arabella Rose, Joseph, and Theodore. Jackie Kennedy unofficially referred to her and JFK's stillborn daughter as Arabella, though the baby was never given a birth certificate, and when she was later moved to be buried alongside her father, her gravestone simply read "Daughter," along with her birthday. Rose, of course, was the name of the Kennedy matriarch.

"I have always loved the name Arabella," Ivanka said in an interview with *The Today Show* a month after her daughter was born. Childhood friends remember her always coming back to the name when they were growing up and brainstorming what they would name their future children someday. They were hardly surprised when she settled on it as her first child's name decades later. "Jared's grandmothers had names beginning with an A and an R. We wanted to pay subtle homage to those two strong and wonderful women while also adopting a name that was very unique. Plus, we thought that the initials, ARK, were cool!"

Joseph was the name of both JFK's father and Jared's grandfather, and Frederick, their son's middle name, was Donald's father's name. Ivanka posted on her Tumblr when her son was born in 2013 that they chose to name him after their paternal grandfathers, "both master builders of their generation and inspiring patriarchs of their families."

"Jared's grandfather, Joseph, was a rock. His indomitable spirit, his sense of family, and his work ethic are the values we hope to hand down to our son. My grandfather, Frederick, was a builder not just of tens of thousands of homes throughout this city, but of a tight-knit family that honors to this day the traditions he established. Both men set the standards that have been passed down through the generations and which we hope to impart upon Joseph and Arabella. They created a legacy for our family that inspires our careers as well as our love and respect for one another. We are honored to name our son after these two distinguished men. We feel so blessed with the newest member of the family!"

Theodore is not as exact a match—Ted Kennedy's first name was short for Edward—but the similarity, after an Arabella Rose and a Joseph, is hard to ignore, especially among those who believe the couple viewed their own gilded, millennialized, social-media-propagated version of Camelot as the end game.

It goes without saying that the clearest and most recent cribbing of Kennedyesque behavior came after the election. Donald chose to tap his son-in-law to serve in his West Wing, and not long after, his daughter joined them in an official capacity as well. Ethics experts sounded the alarms immediately; this violated an anti-nepotism law that had come to be known as the Bobby Kennedy Law, because it took effect six years after JFK appointed his brother Bobby to be his attorney general in 1961. The law was upheld for fifty years, until the Trumps' lawyers found a work-around. The way they read it, the White House is not an agency, and the president enjoys broad executive powers. In the Trump administration, 1600 Pennsylvania Avenue would be just like the twenty-sixth floor of Trump Tower, with a little touch of Kennedy-era nostalgia lawmakers thought they'd banned five decades earlier.

IN THE midst of all the inauguration jostling, Jared and Ivanka decided to move to Washington. Not only would they have to figure out how to divest themselves of portions of their businesses, set up trusts, and figure out who would take over their responsibilities within their family businesses and outside ventures; they'd also need to find somewhere to live and a school for their kids. Melania was having a hard enough time getting the schools to which presidents typically send their young children to even let Barron apply. Ivanka and Jared had two kids who needed to be in school, and they needed to find a Jewish day school. So Seryl Kushner, Jared's mother, took on the task. Jared and Ivanka hired a broker and made a few day trips down to DC to look at houses. Jared's father, Charles, was the one to negotiate the lease. Sometimes dad knows best.

AS PROTOCOL dictated, the whole family boarded a military plane that would take them from New York to Washington on Thursday afternoon. At Joint Base Andrews, Barron made his way down the stairs off the plane first, followed by Don Jr., his wife Vanessa, and their five children, and Eric and his wife Lara. Then came Ivanka, with her little baby boy in her arms, her emerald-green Oscar de la Renta dress and matching coat with its drapy collar blowing in the wind on the tarmac, her big black Jackie O. sunglasses resting on the bridge of her nose. Jared and Ivanka's two older kids trailed behind her. Tiffany came next, followed by Melania and Donald.

The family soon hopped in a motorcade headed for Arlington National Cemetery in Virginia, where Donald and Mike Pence would lay a wreath on the Tomb of the Unknowns. Before her father came out, Ivanka, Jared, and her daughter, Arabella, descended the stairs toward the memorial, in the open plaza overlooking Washington, DC. Ivanka positioned herself closest to the center of the staircase, where her father would later stand, all but ensuring that she would be in almost every frame wide enough to take in the scene. Eric and Tiffany were farther to her left, and Don Jr. and his wife and daughter got stuck behind them.

Then there was the Make America Great Again! Welcome Celebration on the ninety-eight granite and marble stairs at the base of the Lincoln Memorial. The highlight, perhaps, was Lee Greenwood's rendition of "Proud to Be an American," to which the Trump family, who were off to the side of the stage on seats arranged for them, sang along. Donald and Melania sat in the front row, with the two seats next to them reserved for Ivanka and Jared, as they had requested. Her siblings filled in the rows behind them.

That evening they headed over to Union Station for a black-tie candlelight dinner with Donald's cabinet nominees and Republican megadonors. The kids had tables reserved for their friends, where they ate grilled white and green asparagus, roasted branzino with lemon and thyme, and vanilla meringue cakes. They sipped wine out of gilded glasses specifically chosen with Camelot in mind, while listening to their father rehash "this beautiful map" that had emerged on the eve of the election. He thanked Ivanka, who sat next to Wendi Murdoch, wearing a white cap-sleeved Oscar de la Renta column gown with an oversize black bow tied in the back at her waist. He thanked his siblings and their spouses, and boasted that he had a family who actually got along. He then went on to acknowledge his children. "My sons, look at them, standing there," he said, pointing their way. "I say 'Why aren't you campaigning today?' Eric and Don and Tiffany, who was incredible. And Barron is home." He then went on to praise Patriots owner Bob Kraft and tell the crowd that his quarterback Tom Brady, who, a decade earlier, Trump told reporters had dated Ivanka, had called to congratulate him.

Separately, he singled out Ivanka. "We have in the audience a special person who's worked very hard, who married very well. It's my daughter Ivanka. Where is she?" Then, spotting her in the crowd, he said, "I sort of stole her husband. He is so great. If you can't produce peace in the Middle East, nobody can."

After a night's rest in Blair House, the positioning continued on Friday in the swearing-in ceremony, where again Ivanka moved toward the center of the frame when her father approached Chief Justice John Roberts to recite his oath of office. That evening, since it was Shabbat, the Secret Service had to work with the couple to develop a special security plan. Traditionally, those observing the Sabbath do not travel in cars from sundown on Friday to sundown on Saturday. But that would have meant they would not be able to attend any of Friday's balls or the events on the following day— which, for a couple who wanted to be part of everything, was not an option. Walking was out of the question; their detail told them it was not safe, given the vitriol and the protests. Plus, Ivanka had her princess gown and heels on, and the balls were not exactly a hop and a skip away from the White House. So they asked special permission from their rabbi to break the rules of Shabbat, since it was a matter of safety, and what they argued was a once-in-a-lifetime familial opportunity.

They made the most of it. Donald and Melania were meant to share their first dance on stage alone. Planners had no idea that the children would later join them onstage for a family-wide slow dance; Donald, who knew that he was not a skilled dancer and was aware of just how long the song was, asked his children to come out onstage to cut some of the lingering awkwardness. By the second ball that evening, once they'd seen just how uncomfortable he looked the first go around, they joined him out there even earlier in the song. Afterward Tiffany and her boyfriend went back to the Trump Hotel, where they met her mother, Marla, and a few friends from New York. The rest of the family spent the night at the White House.

The next morning, the family attended a service at the National Cathedral. They were all exhausted by that point, especially the grandchildren. They'd patiently sat through the wreath-laying and the concert and the parade in preceding days, but a long, early morning in church was asking too much. Ivanka handed her son Joseph toy cars to keep him occupied, which she quickly regretted. He shot one straight down the aisle, past all the pews, confusing the people gathered there to pray and pay tribute to the presidential rite of passage.

The extended family had settled into the White House by Saturday afternoon. Don Jr.'s son slurped cereal out of a bowl in the dining room wearing his Teenage Mutant Ninja Turtles pajamas. Theodore, Ivanka's youngest, crawled for the first time in the state dining room as they all had a buffet lunch that Melania made sure was set up for them after the church service. Don Jr. and his wife and kids took a spin in the bowling alley in the basement.

By Sunday afternoon there was one official event left, in the East Room of the White House. Donald swore in members of his senior staff, including Jared, who would serve as his senior adviser. Jared's parents and brother Josh tried to keep Jared and Ivanka's kids quiet while their dad recited his oath. Josh handed the kids a container of jellybeans, which they promptly spilled on the floor of the East Room. Josh quietly swept them up, hoping no one would notice.

By Sunday evening Don Jr. and Eric and their families and Tiffany had flown back to New York. So had Melania and Barron, who wouldn't move down to Washington for another five months. When Melania got back to the Trump Tower triplex, it was empty. There was no Donald, no frantic campaign staff or inauguration committees. There was nothing more to plan, at least for the time being. She called one of her closest friends to come over to keep her company. She was now the First Lady of the United States. She was also completely, utterly alone.

Ivanka and Jared stayed behind in DC, arriving at the nearly century-old, 6,800-square-foot home they rented, with six bedrooms,

seven baths, five wood-burning fireplaces, a two-car garage, a sun-
room, a garden, and a terrace off their bedroom. This was their first
night there, and they hadn't yet picked out all of their furniture. So
they ordered in pizza and ate dinner on the hardwood floor. The sun
set on life as they knew it. A new normal dawned.

CHAPTER 2

Campaign/Transition

O<small>N JUNE</small> 16, 2015, Ivanka glided down the gilded escalators into the lobby of Trump Tower, her father's crown jewel in Midtown Manhattan, where she and her brothers had grown up and now worked as executives in the Trump Organization. She slipped past the crowd gathered with the burnished mauve marble walls, adorned on that day with royal blue signs emblazoned with "TRUMP Make America Great Again." Wearing a white sheath dress, her corn-yellow hair parted down the center and swept into a bun, revealing two dangly silver hoop earrings that swayed as she took her place behind the dais, she smiled at the hundred or so people awaiting an announcement and inhaled. Flanked by a half dozen American flags, she began: "Today, I have the honor of introducing a man who needs no introduction. This man," she said, "is my father." The crowd erupted, and her pink-painted lips parted in a toothy grin. Her nose crinkled, and after a particularly raucous shout from the floor above, she let out a little giggle. She went on to praise her father—for his career success, for his negotiating prowess, for his say-it-like-he-means-it candor, for his loyalty to friends. "I've enjoyed the good fortune of working alongside my father for ten years now, and I've seen these principles in action daily," she said. But before she worked for him—in a technical function, that is; the Trump kids have been employees serving his brand in some capacity since they arrived on earth—he told his children they had to work hard and strive for excellence in all that they did, she said: "I remember him telling me when I was a little girl, 'Ivanka, if you're going to be thinking anyway, you might as well be thinking big.'" There was no better person to have in your corner when you were facing tough opponents or making tough decisions. "Ladies and gentlemen," she said, dipping closer to the microphone, "it is my pleasure to introduce to you today a man who I have loved and respected my entire life, Donald J. Trump."

She beamed at the crowd as Neil Young's "Rockin' in the Free World" blasted from the speakers, bouncing off all that marble. For two minutes and forty-five seconds—a full two verses and two choruses of the song and into the bridge—she stood there, nodding and smiling and fidgeting onstage, before Donald Trump emerged from the escalator. Don Jr. and Jared and Tiffany kept staring at her from just off stage right, where they'd watched her introduction, appearing as uncomfortable about her languishing up there waiting as she was. Finally Donald greeted her, gave his speech, and announced his candidacy, which was mostly received as a joke and a branding opportunity by the media and anyone who knew or watched the Donald on television or in the tabloids or around New York for decades.

It was not the first time Donald had flirted with a presidential run. Or the second or third time, either. He did this periodically, when it served his company or stroked his ego, or when he tapped into a message that resonated. And his children had responded in kind each time they were asked over the years about their father's political ambitions. Don Jr. showed up to a town hall in the fall of 1999 on campus at the University of Pennsylvania, where he was an undergraduate at the time. His dad was toying with the idea of running as a candidate for the Reform Party, and he let Chris Matthews interview him live for *Hardball* in front of 1,200 students, including

Don Jr., who was made to stand up in front of the crowd. "He's much better looking than I am," Donald told the audience. Ivanka was also repeatedly asked about her dad's presidential aspirations over the years. In an interview with *Harper's Bazaar* in 2011, she said that her father was "exactly what we need" in the leader of the free world. "He's the best equipped to deal with the most important issues this nation has, which is ultimately that we're suffering under a massive burden of debt," she said. "We need a very acute financial mind to get us out of this mire. America is the largest corporation on the planet. You wouldn't hire a novice to run a similarly sized company in the private markets." Despite their praise, he never made the leap.

This time, though, their father had actually gone through with it. Ivanka reveled in the moment. Don Jr. radiated excitement as he rode up in the elevator after his dad's speech. His phone would not stop dinging. "My Special Forces friend just texted me," he told former Trump Organization employee Sam Nunberg in the elevator going back up to his office. "He loved it." A handful of the people he hunted with sent him similar laudatory messages. "They fucking loved it."

FROM THERE, Don Jr. was dispatched onto the trail. He was perhaps the only real conservative out of the whole lot of them. He had a little bit of red state under the Patrick Batemanesque exterior—the slicked-back hair, the veneers, the big fat tie knots. He went on weeks-long hunting trips and spent time in the middle of the country and somewhat understood life outside of Trump Tower and golf courses and gilded everything. So operatives deployed him to make campaign stops. Ivanka often introduced her father—a tightly wound blond spoonful of sugar leading into his acerbic, rambling speeches. Eric would go on Fox News, as would his wife, Lara. They sat in the family sections at the debates, and participated in town halls, and had dinner at diners in the freezing cold New Hampshire winter. They had a sense that this moment was both fleeting and once-in-a-lifetime, inviting childhood friends and close associates to come with them backstage at debates or other key rallies, knowing full well that this was probably the only time they would get anywhere near this close to the political process, and it would all be over in a flash.

OF COURSE it wasn't. By the time Donald started actually winning primaries, the Trump kids, in part filling in for their stepmother, who loathed the trail and preferred to stay in New York with Barron, took on their roles in the campaign as near full-time jobs.

Donald just about clinched the nomination in early May, winning the Indiana primary. Ted Cruz, one of the last Republican men standing by that point, bowed out that evening. Donald rode those escalators once again down into that mauve marble lobby to give a victory speech. Melania stood to his left, Ivanka and Jared, Eric and Lara, Don Jr. and Vanessa to his right, all closed-mouth smiles and shine.

"I want to start by, as always, thanking my family." Donald leaned into the microphone his campaign had set up on a makeshift stage in front of a cheering crowd in his red baseball hats. "My wife, my kids. They're not kids anymore, but as far as I'm concerned, they're kids. They'll always be my kids," he joked. "It's a beautiful thing to watch and it's a beautiful thing to behold and we're going to make America great again."

He singled out his son-in-law, praising him for the work he had done to get him to that point. "Honestly, Jared is a very successful real estate person, but I actually think he likes politics more than he likes real estate," he told the audience, sending Ivanka into a laughing fit. "But he's very good at politics."

A few days later Ohio governor John Kasich dropped out of the race, making him the sixteenth opponent Donald had put a pin in. As the presumptive nominee, he would soon start receiving intelligence briefings on national security matters and immediately shift to a general election plan. Life beyond the primaries smacked the Trumps in the face. There was a level of planning and organization that the tiny Trump team of novices could not themselves begin to fathom, but they had enough sense and outside advice to start making incremental plans on specific, necessary next steps. That's when Donald put another load on Jared's shoulders. He asked him to come up with a blueprint for a transition team, though Jared himself would not be involved with transition activities should his father-in-law win in November. Jared, campaign manager Corey Lewandowski, and senior adviser Paul Manafort started pulling together ideas for who could join the team and what the priorities should be.

Donald set his mind on New Jersey governor Chris Christie as the guy he wanted to lead the transition. Sure, Christie had been critical of Donald when he ran his own bid for the presidency, but he was among the first former opponents to endorse him in February. The complicating factor was that Jared, assigned to lead the charge here, despised the guy. Christie had put Jared's father behind bars a little more than a decade earlier, after all, and kept him there for twenty-eight days longer than the Kushner family expected. The simmering tension was no secret, and Donald was sensitive to it, particularly because he knew Ivanka would be sensitive to it as well. But it was Donald's campaign, and at least in this instance, no one could talk him out of it.

By May 9 Donald had already made the offer to Christie. He asked the governor to come to his office on the twenty-sixth floor of Trump Tower, where Donald did most of his campaign work when he was in New York, amid a crush of sports memorabilia—Tom Brady's Super Bowl helmet, Mike Tyson's belt, Shaquille O'Neal's size 22 black and white basketball sneaker. A photo of Donald's father Fred shared the desk with stacks of paper, framed magazine covers bearing his likeness lined the walls, and the red leather armless chair he'd sat in as the host of *The Apprentice* was tucked into the room's far end. Corey Lewandowski came, too, and they began to hammer out the parameters of how the transition would work and what notes they wanted to hit in a press release announcing his appointment.

Jared joined them, too, and he tried to pump the brakes. "Well, we don't have to rush this," he chimed in. "Let's take our time with this."

Lewandowski interrupted him. Actually, they did have to rush this. The White House had already asked for the name of a transition head, and it was sure to come up at the meeting scheduled in a few weeks. They needed to decide this and get it out there already. Donald agreed with him. What was the point in waiting, anyway? The choice was made. Let's get on with it.

Unlike Charlie Kushner, whose temper flashed and burned a whole room down in an instant, Jared simmered. The angrier he got, the quieter he became. So when he opened his mouth to respond, he was at little more than a whisper. It was rare for him to talk about his father's stint in prison so openly, but on this day Jared unleashed. What came out was an impassioned monologue that went on so long that his father-in-law ultimately had to interrupt him. "It's unfair," Jared said. "He took advantage of my family members for his own ambition, and you don't understand what he did to us."

Christie, no shrinking violet, either, boiled in his seat. Before he could open his mouth, though, Donald jumped to his defense. "The guy was just doing his job. If you were there, you would have done the same thing," he told his son-in-law. "You really should be mad at your own family here. They are the ones who turned over all that information to Chris." Jared's real problem, he added, was that he hadn't known Donald at the time of his father's trial; Donald and Christie were such good friends that things would have turned out differently. Christie would have taken it easier on his friend's family. "No, no, no," Christie interrupted. "I like you a lot, but I assure you it would not have been any different."

"No, no, no," Donald retorted. "It would have been different." Donald then suggested that Jared, Charlie, Donald, and Christie go out to dinner together, to clear the air. Jared suggested that that might not be the best idea.

"Jared, you and I have talked about this," Donald said soothingly. "Chris is the guy."

"Fine," Jared told him. "If that's your decision, that's your decision." He turned around and walked out. Soon after, Lewandowski asked to be excused, too.

That afternoon the campaign sent out the release announcing Christie's appointment. "Governor Christie is an extremely knowledgeable and loyal person with the tools and resources to put together an unparalleled Transition Team, one that will be prepared to take over the White House when we win in November. I am grateful to Governor Christie for his contributions to this movement," Donald said in a statement.

ONCE THE decision was made, Donald and Jared called Charlie Kushner to let him know about Christie officially heading the transition, both asking for his blessing and making sure that it would not irreparably damage the in-laws' relationship. It was a move out of respect and necessity, and one made with a great deal of anxiety. Charlie's temper was a thing of legend in the tristate area. He would rip into anybody anywhere, burning his victims' eardrums with the volume of his bellow.

Charlie played it cool when Donald called to let him know about the transition choice. He listened patiently to what his *machatunim* had to say. He took a breath. "Listen," he said into the phone. "The most important thing is that you win and that you are prepared." To those who heard the phone call, or how Donald and Jared recounted it, Charlie seemed genuinely magnanimous. Helpful and kind, even. The private father-son follow-up conversation went differently. Those close to the family recalled that Charlie told Jared they could let Christie do his thing now. This would get taken care of down the road. And indeed, six months later, just days after the election, Christie got canned from his gig, after months of working without pay, traveling to the transition offices in Washington every Wednesday, planning for the day when he would be able to execute on all the preparation he and his team had built up. Many believed the decision in large part stemmed from Jared, which they believed had been his plan from the get-go.

THE FIRST conversation between Jared and Christie about the transition role was not a walk in the park. It allayed no concerns over their ability to play nice as they worked to build one of the most complex, consuming, technical, and hugely vital aspects of a general election campaign, and prepare for a potential thereafter. So they talked it out. Don. Jr. was away from Trump Tower for the day they were due to meet during the summer of 2016, leaving his office on the twenty-fifth floor open. Jared asked Christie to meet him there. Across a round table, he admitted that he had not handled their last interaction as well as he had hoped to. He had reflected on it, he said, and come to the conclusion that the most important thing was that Donald win and be as well prepared to be president as he could be. He had put the past behind him, and he wanted them to work together throughout this whole thing.

Christie was skeptical. Just how past it could a guy who carried the wallet his dad made him while he was in prison really be? Christie himself had not totally put it behind him, particularly months later, long after Jared had a hand in firing him from his role, and reports of Jared's meetings with Russian officials and involvement in the firing of FBI director James Comey caught the attention of investigators in the Robert Mueller probe. "Good thing I saved his father's prison number," Christie would joke with friends.

The two would be working together whether Jared and Christie had let it go or not. They were both professionals, who both wanted the transition planning to go smoothly. Neither wanted to spend their time sparring when there was so much daunting work to get done in short order.

A few factors made Christie's eventual ouster a slick operation to pull off. Donald not only declined to be involved in the transition plans but also refused to hear about, read about, or talk about them. He had no clue whether Christie had done a good job getting everything together, whether the team he'd assembled knew their stuff, whether enough of the right materials were produced, and whether the policies and protocols and frameworks they spent months detailing jibed with how he would want to form his government after November 9. He could only rely on what other people he trusted—like, say, his children and their spouses—told him about the process.

Donald's choice to stay removed from the transition had nothing to do with ethical concerns, time constraints, or a mental compartmentalization that pushed him to focus on only one goal at a time. He wanted nothing to do with transition talk because he thought it was "bad karma." When he read in the papers or saw on the news any detail of the transition planning, he'd call his friends and staffers, screaming bloody murder. They would explain to him that, bad karma or not, they were complying with a federal law on the books since the 1960s that required a transition team for an orderly transfer of power between an outgoing and an incoming administration. If he didn't want to have a hand in that, that was fine. But they couldn't just not go forward with the whole thing.

Jared, by contrast, involved himself in the minutia. He ran a meeting every Monday on the twenty-sixth floor of Trump Tower, at which he, Christie, Jeff Sessions, and Rich Bagger, Christie's former chief of staff, who he brought on to serve as the transition's executive director, discussed staffing, policy priorities, and the various aspects of the planning. If for some reason they could not all meet in person, a conference call was set up. Rarely, if ever, did this check-in get canceled entirely. Jared reviewed the résumés and signed off on every staffer transition officials wanted to bring on, from secretaries up to national security and economic team members. All the vetting they were doing on potential Cabinet picks also needed his approval.

BY JUNE, the Trump kids had grown tired of Lewandowski. They thought he appealed to their father's worst instincts; they knew to pull their dad back when he was running full speed toward the deep end and steer him in the other direction, but they felt Lewandowski egged him on to cannonball right in. He was a yes man when Donald desperately needed no guys around him, particularly as the campaign neared the general election phase.

They also hated the fact that Lewandowski was always the first to board Trump Force One with the candidate and travel with him to every rally, every campaign stop, kicking his feet up on the plane and settling in rather too comfortably, as they saw it. Plus, he was a mooch, who would order cases of Red Bull and blow through a full case daily, leaving his breath reeking of the energy drink. It did not sit well with the family that Donald was letting him stay in a Trump apartment. "He was the campaign manager, and all he cared about was the plane and being close to the boss, and he'd constantly take," one associate remembered. "Why wasn't he back in Trump Tower actually running the campaign instead of freeloading off the Trump attention?"

There was also the issue of all the negative headlines Lewandowski generated that spring. First he grabbed a reporter by the arm at an event in Florida and was arrested, but the charges were dropped. Then there was the shouting match with communications director Hope Hicks on Sixty-First and Park Avenue in mid-May, which was chronicled in the *New York Post* gossip column Page Six. Lewandowski was married, and Hope was the Trump family darling—a PR girl who worked on Ivanka's brand before she was brought in-house and, later, got hired by Donald to work in the Trump Organization. That she fell into a romantic relationship with Lewandowski during the campaign became a sore spot between Hope and Ivanka and her siblings, who saw Hope as one of them. That it spilled out into a public spat in the very paper that had published every last detail of their father's affair was unacceptable.

It wasn't just the Trump kids who had problems with Lewandowski. Reince Priebus, then the chairman of the Republican National Committee, bristled around him. So did other key Trump loyalists, who viewed him as both dishonest and unable to pivot to a general election campaign. And so on June 20, before Donald even got down to the twenty-sixth floor, Don Jr., Michael Cohen, and Matt Calamari called in Lewandowski at seven o'clock in the morning. Why have him work a full day if they knew he was going to be out? And why give Donald the opportunity to vacillate and change his mind? "It's over," Don Jr. told Corey. Calamari walked him out.

"Things had to change," Don Jr. said in an interview on *Good Morning America* after the ouster. "No, he didn't see this coming. . . . There was nothing malicious or even vicious about it." He added that his father needed to transition to the general. "I think there's also time to move on. Those are the tough decisions you have to make when you're running for president."

AS THE Republican National Convention in Cleveland inched closer, all the kids wheedled their way into the process of deciding who their father would choose as his vice presidential pick. By July 11, Donald and his team had whittled down the list to three names. Chris Christie was in there. So was Newt Gingrich, the former Speaker of the House turned cable news pundit and Trump cheerleader. Indiana governor Mike Pence, a Christian conservative straight out of central casting, made the short list, too, as the clear favorite of many members of the Trump team, as well as Republican leaders like House Speaker Paul Ryan and Senate majority leader Mitch McConnell. The first two, however, had proved themselves not only loyal friends but people Donald actually *liked* and wanted to shoot the shit with, two of the most valued qualities to Donald. Pence, he barely knew beyond the political boxes he checked and the polling numbers his aides presented him with. They certainly made an odd couple: a thrice-married adulterer who boasted about grabbing women's genitals, and a man who would not even go to a dinner with a woman who wasn't his wife (whom he affectionately calls "Mother").

That Monday started what looked a lot like sweeps week in the VP sweepstakes. On Sunday Donald met with Pence in Indiana. On Monday, Donald told people that the vetting file his team had prepared on Gingrich made Donald look like a saint by contrast, effectively knocking him out of the running. And so by the time Tuesday rolled around, it looked as though there were only two options on the table, though in Trumplandia, nothing is ever really a done deal until it is a done deal. And even then, he could still walk things back or reverse course, without acknowledging that a shift had even happened.

On Tuesday, Pence introduced the candidate at a private fundraiser and public rally in Westfield, Indiana. "We are ready to put a fighter, a builder, and a patriot in the Oval Office," he shouted to the crowd. Trump, ever the reality television host drumming up interest, asked his supporters how Pence was doing in his job as governor. "Good? I think so," he joked. "I don't know if he is going to be your governor or vice president. Who the hell knows?"

By that point, certainly not Donald Trump. That evening he got stranded in Indiana—somewhat of a catastrophe for a man of creature comforts who almost always opted to fly back to New York no matter how late a campaign stop ran or how nonsensical it was in the midst of a jam-packed travel schedule. But Trump Force One had some sort of mechanical problem, so there he would stay.

He rolled through a phone interview with the *Wall Street Journal*, in which he told the paper that he was looking for a "fighter skilled in hand-to-hand-combat" as a running mate. Christie and Gingrich, he said, were "two extraordinary warriors." Chemistry was important, too, which, he said also gave those two men a boost. "You either have it or you don't. I clearly have it with Chris and Newt." As for Pence, he didn't know him enough to judge how much of an extraordinary warrior he could be, or whether they had chemistry or not.

At about 10:00 p.m. Donald called Christie, who was in a hotel in Washington. "Are you ready?" Donald asked his friend. "Ready for what?" Christie asked. "Are you ready?" Donald repeated. Christie didn't want to play coy. He asked if Donald was offering him the nomination.

Donald hemmed and hedged. He said he had not made his final, final decision yet, but wanted to know if Christie was up for it, and if his wife, Mary Pat, would be willing to pick up some slack on the trail, since Melania wasn't keen on campaigning. Donald ended the call by telling him to stay by his phone.

Donald hung up and made a call to his family, telling them that he liked Christie. He felt comfortable with him and knew he'd tear the skin off Hillary Clinton in the general election, and he needed someone who'd willingly, skillfully do that. His kids quickly hung up with their father and called Keith Schiller, Donald's longtime bodyguard. They were all coming to Indiana to stage a vice presidential intervention.

THE NEXT morning, Donald, Don Jr., Ivanka, Jared, and Eric, along with campaign chair Paul Manafort, turned up in Indiana for breakfast at the Pences' home. Jared privately told Pence that he needed to turn on the charm for his father-in-law. Otherwise the gig would slip through his hands before the dishes were even cleared from the table that morning.

The meal went well enough that it buoyed Donald a bit, swaying him slightly from the assuredness he'd felt the night before. Still, that evening, he told Fox News's Bret Baier that multiple contenders—

maybe even as many as four—were still in the mix, though he was debating between two. "I tell you, Chris Christie is somebody I have liked for a long time," he told the host. "He is a total professional. He's a good guy, by the way. A lot of people don't understand that." He added that their meeting had gone "really well." "He has always been very respectful to me and really . . . appreciates what I've done politically," he said. "And we had a great meeting."

At the outset, he said he would announce his decision by Friday. Adding to the pressure, Friday happened to be the deadline for Pence to decide whether or not he would continue with his reelection bid. By Thursday evening, Donald was agitated and uncertain about Pence, chafing at being locked into making a choice under deadline. Jared reminded him that he was choosing a guy who'd make the ticket strongest and bridge the divide within the Republican Party, not a best buddy. Manafort agreed with Jared, adding that he worried Christie wouldn't be as easy to handle and reminding Donald of Christie's own presidential ambitions. He couldn't choose someone who wanted the role for himself. Never mind the fact that very often that is not the case; Donald heard them.

But he was still uneasy. He didn't know what to do, but his family was pushing him in Pence's direction. That evening, a terrorist drove a nineteen-ton rental truck onto the sidewalk of the Promenade des Anglais in Nice, France, after the annual Bastille Day fireworks, killing eighty-six people and injuring dozens more. Out of respect for the victims, the campaign initially decided to delay the announcement. But Donald grew restless, and a little before ten o'clock in the morning, he tweeted out his pick: "I am pleased to announce that I have chosen Governor Mike Pence as my Vice Presidential running mate. News conference tomorrow at 11:00 A.M."

When he talked to Christie, Donald told the governor that Pence just *looked* like a vice president. I have to take him, he said. He told him that if he won, any other job he wanted, all he'd have to do was ask for it.

*　*　*

LONG BEFORE the Republican National Convention in Cleveland, Jared reached out to two speechwriters, Matthew Scully and John McConnell. These guys were the real deal; they worked closely with President George W. Bush in crafting his speeches, including the addresses he gave after the September 11 attacks. Jared wanted them to come up with a bang-up speech for his stepmother-in-law to give onstage at the RNC. Melania was such a reticent campaigner that she hardly ever accompanied her husband on his many campaign stops. She had a young son at home in New York whose life she wanted to keep as normal as possible. She still tried to pick Barron up at school as often as possible, though that grew increasingly difficult as time wore on, given the traffic her Secret Service detail caused at dismissal time. None of this politics stuff had been her idea; she liked their life, and why shouldn't she? Most of it was guarded within their gilded doors and planes and homes on golf courses either bearing her husband's name or at which he was the boss. She was a former model, so the attention wasn't the problem. But she was not a native English speaker, and she saw how the press ripped her husband to shreds every day. No one in their right mind would be happy about throwing themselves to those wolves.

Jared wanted her rare appearance to be a hit. Not only would this boost the campaign, appealing to Americans who might have been turned off by the candidate's multiple marriages and treatment of women, but also maybe if she knocked it out of the park, she would be more willing to jump into the political fray more often. She polled well, and with Trump going up in the coming months against the first female general election candidate, having a woman on the team whom people liked, who softened and defended her husband, couldn't hurt. McConnell and Scully agreed. About a month before the convention, they shot her over a draft. A response never came.

Instead, Melania turned to people within her inner circle to rip the draft to shreds. It did not sound like her. She wanted to essentially start fresh. One of the people who helped was Meredith McIver, a former professional ballet dancer and Trump employee who had helped write Donald's book *Think Like a Billionaire*. A handful of others had their hands in it as well.

None of them stopped Melania from getting onstage on the Monday night of the convention to deliver an address to 23 million viewers that stole entire phrases and themes from a speech Michelle Obama had given years earlier at a Democratic National Convention.

Immediately the Trump campaign spun into damage control mode. It was nearly impossible to understand how this colossal—and entirely avoidable—mistake could have slipped by so many people. How could a gang who couldn't protect the potential First Lady from not straight-up ripping off a former First Lady's speech word-for-word be trusted to run a winning campaign—let alone protect the United States of America? Melania Trump was barely offstage before journalists figured out that much of her speech was borrowed.

It took little more time before the finger-pointing within the Trump campaign began. On Tuesday morning, Ivanka and Jared blew off steam in their hotel gym, as did a number of other campaign officials. Jared walked up to one official who was pedaling idly on a stationary bike as he tried to catch up on the rest of the headlines—as if anyone was talking about anything other than Melania-gate—and for a brief moment forget about the whole thing. "You know, this was all Manafort's fault," he told the official, who questioned why it was Manafort's responsibility or duty to proofread the candidate's wife's speech and make sure she hadn't plagiarized it from Michelle Obama. A month later, Manafort was fired.

IN THE process of figuring out who the campaign should bring in to replace Manafort, members of the team knew they had to find someone who could right a ship that, by that point, was foundering.

The whole tone of the Republican National Convention was dour, downtrodden, and fearful. By contrast, the Democratic Convention felt like the shining city on a hill in which most Americans would prefer to live, regardless of how realistic or euphemistic it was. Donald was entangled in public feuds with a former beauty pageant contestant who said he'd made unkind remarks about her weight and the Khans, a Gold Star Muslim family who criticized the Trump campaign's rhetoric at the DNC.

His poll numbers dipped. They needed a new jolt. Jared started asking his friends and campaign advisers close to his father-in-law for options. Ivanka knew that bringing a woman on might help with the optics, even if, as a fairly obvious political calculation, it would likely be met with snickering. Ultimately, Jared believed no one would run the campaign better than he would—he had been the de facto campaign manager for months anyway—but he agreed with his wife. He started asking around for names of women to whom he could give the title of campaign manager, though, she would mostly just be going out on TV, and talking like the campaign manager. He would still call the shots. The people he asked were gobsmacked. What woman in her right mind would come on board, knowing that she was getting a fake job to make Donald look good while Jared was the one actually running the show? He wouldn't tell her that, he'd reply.

It was under those conditions that, not long after, Kellyanne Conway joined the campaign, officially becoming the first female campaign manager in a general election bid in the history of the United States.

ON MONDAY, September 19, the Secret Service officially started protecting Ivanka Trump and Jared Kushner and their children. Her brothers hadn't yet received protection.

Her father had received his detail nearly ten months earlier, going with the Secret Service code name Mogul. Since the call signs

within a First Family all begin with the same first letter, the rest
of the Trumps fell in line with M names, as well. This naming tradition, which dates back to President Harry Truman, has since its
inception sometimes been a way for commanders in chief to live out
their fantasies—a game of high-stakes make-believe in which the
most powerful men in the world get to try on a name to match the
image of themselves they wished were true. Truman, for instance,
decided to be called General, though he had only been a captain
in World War I. The Kennedys' names all referred to Camelot. The
Obamas stuck with Renegade and Renaissance.

But the point of the practice is much more significant than fantasy fulfillment. The call signs are used in an emergency, when
protection enacts continuity of operation plans. If there is a crisis,
it's safer to say "We have Mogul" than "We have Donald Trump,"
particularly if the Secret Service is operating on unsecure communications lines. But the Secret Service does not come up with these
names themselves. Family members are given a series of names
from the White House Communications Agency from which each
protectee can choose.

Melania settled on Muse. Ivanka landed on Marvel. Her brothers received their details later, but Eric, a spectacular shot, chose
Marksman, and Don Jr., for obvious reasons, picked Mountaineer.
From the start, Ivanka was keen on the idea, of security protecting
her and her young family; part of it had to do with the aura it gave
her as a political power player. In Washington, at least, the presence
of a detail—the men with earpieces and the black SUVs—is a status
symbol. It's the swamp equivalent to a bona fide entourage in Hollywood.

The man assigned to head Ivanka's initial detail, it just so happens, was nicknamed Hollywood by his Secret Service colleagues
and former protectees. He loved to make small talk about designers
and celebrities and what clothes everyone was wearing. Instantly he
fell into step with the family. He had just spent years as an integral

member of First Lady Michelle Obama's detail, so he was not only sensitive to protecting a family managing children not necessarily *of* Washington, but also understood the intricacies of working with a female protectee. It is not exactly comfortable, for either party, to have a male Secret Service member accompany a woman protectee to a gynecologist appointment, for instance, or a Pilates class. Hollywood, though, had spent years learning how to make it more palatable and less intrusive. He understood the importance of keeping his protectees' public and personal lives separate, and immediately deflected attention from them enough so that they were able to take weekend trips or observe Shabbat without cameras snapping photos of them at every turn.

Ivanka, for her part, had spent a lifetime surrounded by live-in help. Many members of First Families past have never had nannies and housekeepers and bodyguards around. But for Ivanka, having people around whose sole job was to serve and protect her was a way of life that had been ingrained in her since she was born. This part of the transition suited her just fine.

It helped that the communication between Jared and Ivanka and their detail was open. From the get-go, they were honest with their detail about the possibility of their moving to Washington, which helped the Secret Service come up with a plan from the beginning. They instantly welcomed the detail into their lives, and members of their detail grew quite fond of the couple. When they visited the Kushner family home in New Jersey to observe the Jewish High Holy Days, Jared would recommend places nearby for the detail to grab a good dinner or a drink at the bar. (He surprised them by picking semi-cool dive bars that none of the Secret Service men could believe Jared himself had actually been to, though he insisted that he had.)

And as the Trump-Kushners gravitated more to the five-star hotel and private-plane end of the spectrum, a place on their detail became one of the more desirable assignments in the administration. In administrations past, the plum gigs had usually been on the First Lady's Detail, known as the FLD. Jokingly, agents have dubbed the FLD "Fine Living and Dining," because most First Ladies make so many trips to so many lovely places, go out to the best restaurants, and take a few vacations with their kids, with their detail in tow. This First Lady stuck closer to home—or homes, in the Trumps' case. She rarely made public appearances or traveled anywhere other than to Trump Tower, Bedminster, New Jersey, or Mar-a-Lago. She didn't socialize outside much, either.

Ivanka, on the other hand, more than made up for it. She criss-crossed the country, flitted about vacation spots at luxury resorts, frequented glitzy parties and hot restaurants, and stayed at several city and beach and country homes. In jest, some agents started referring to Ivanka's detail as FLD Lite. Since the typical FLD didn't exist in Trumplandia. Ivanka's, more than anyone's, was the assignment to get.

IVANKA'S SIBLINGS had a tougher time. Don Jr.—"Marksman"—in particular chafed at the idea of protection, for several reasons. For starters, he was generally more private than his sister. He went to his home in the Catskills to fish and build bonfires and roam around on ATVs with his kids most weekends, and took off for days-long hunting trips in the most remote parts of the Canadian bush, looking for moose, and ten-day boys' fishing trips in Alaska. He wore flannel shirts and baseball caps, sometimes full-camp suits with neon orange vests. He flew mostly commercial, in coach, hopscotching from one flight to a small airport onto a tiny plane into a far-flung town no one on the Upper East Side had ever heard of.

"I have friends that they only knew me as Don," he's said of the people he meets out upstate or in hunting camps. "They find out what my last name is and they're like 'I had no idea.' You see them the next time and they're trying to treat you differently and you're like 'what happened.' Why should that make any difference? They'll say, 'You're right.' It's a great equalizer."

Some of the guys he'd met as just Don more than a decade before at shooting ranges upstate were law enforcement officers. Don, at the time, was just starting off in the business world at his father's company, and these guys were just starting off in the police force, or at the lowest levels of the Secret Service. As Don's role and responsibilities within the Trump Organization grew, so too did his shooting buddies. Some of the guys he'd gone shooting with and hung around with upstate were now assigned to follow him around and look after his family. All of a sudden he went from no-last-name city boy Don to protectee. He was entitled to their service and responsible for pseudo-managing them. For a guy who'd spent years being uncomfortable with them treating him differently because of his last name, this crossed into prickly territory almost overnight.

That Don and his wife Vanessa had five kids living in New York City didn't help matters. That meant that Vanessa had to manage essentially six different details—one for her and her husband and one for each of her children. Her phone lit up with texts and calls from agents, telling her one kid was a few minutes late to meet them on their designated street corner; asking if they would be on the north or south side of the street, what time she planned to leave the house for their drive upstate for the weekend, or who was staying late at school that afternoon. "It is literally overwhelming," a former Secret Service agent explained. "Trying to manage all that with seasoned staff would be mind-numbing. To have someone who's never done it before try and juggle all of that? Well, it would just be horrific."

The head of the detail didn't make it easier. Unlike Hollywood, he didn't instantly mesh with the family. There were some preliminary conversations about a potential move to DC, so they put him in place as a temporary stopgap who might be replaced if the eventual relocation did happen. But it didn't, and they ended up with what came to be a revolving door of agents and shifting dynamics. It was hard for them to get into a rhythm or find a comfortable relationship. "The whole thing has just been sloppy," the former agent said. "The agents have been sloppy. The communication has been sloppy. Don's back-and-forth attitude about them has been sloppy." Hiring someone to help Vanessa coordinate might have made it easier, but the family didn't spend the money.

It was simpler for Eric and his wife Lara. At the time, it was just the two of them. Lara got pregnant in the midst of the campaign, so for months there was no extra detail to coordinate, and they had forty weeks to plan for an eventual detail.

Tiffany's detail was perhaps the laxest of all. One morning at the end of May, she walked in the front door of the Golden Pear in East Hampton, a tiny, teeming see-and-be-seen spot smack in the middle of Newtown Lane, the town's little main street. The Golden Pear is some two hundred feet from the Monogram Shop, a little personalization store that, each year since the 2004 presidential election, has sold plastic cups labeled with campaign logos for each major party candidate, sold for $3 apiece to Hamptonites to display on their marble islands or pass around at their catered beach barbecues. The shop owner starts keeping track after the Super Tuesday primary contests in March, and at the close of business each day, she handwrites the total number of cups sold for each candidate on a piece of paper that she hangs in her store window.

Since this custom started, the cups had accurately predicted the winner—first with George W. Bush, then with Obama, twice. But this cycle, the cups, like every pollster and expert and analyst, got it wrong. Up until the weekend before Election Day, the Monogram Shop sold 4,946 for Hillary Clinton, and just 3,388 for Donald Trump.

Tiffany didn't stop in to buy one of her father's cups that morning, as Chelsea Clinton once did the year her mother ran against Barack Obama in the primaries. She chose to spend her $3—likely four times that, given their prices—on four iced coffees with her boyfriend. She dropped one iced coffee, and no one flinched or helped her pick it up—not even her detail, who was standing at a nearby table noticeably playing a game on his phone.

Most people didn't notice her, besides the brief spill disturbance. She was in a baseball cap, and her security presence was so minimal that other customers readily came in and out both the front and back doors without so much as a glance. At one point someone did approach her, at which point she perked up, expecting some sort of comment—though who knows which way that would have gone. Her detail didn't step in to block the approach, which would have been unnecessary, anyway, since the patron was simply asking if he could steal the extra chair at her table.

One customer that morning had also been in the Golden Pear one day in the 1990s when Chelsea Clinton and her several Secret Service agents walked in. "The world basically stopped," he recalled. "For Tiffany, no one really noticed, and the people who did were intentionally looking the opposite direction."

CHAPTER 3

Election Day

POLICE SHUT down Fifty-Seventh Street between Second and Third Avenues midmorning on Election Day for the Trump motorcade. The cars slid up in front of Public School 59, a school turned polling station for the day, just blocks from Trump Tower. Red and blue lights flashed against silver barricades set up to hold back the dozens of people who'd gathered outside to get a glimpse of the candidate and both cheer and boo him before he cast his ballot. He and Melania stepped out of a black SUV, Ivanka, Jared, and their daughter Arabella following seconds behind. They all went down to the school's gymnasium, filled at that point with agents in boxy suits and earpieces, cameramen clicking away, and reporters shouting questions at the Trumps. The family, in all neutrals, popped against the gym's baby-blue-and-banana-yellow walls. Apart from Donald, who'd walked in wearing only a suit jacket, all of them kept their coats on inside. Melania's Balmain coat, with its wide lapel and gold buttons, hung on her shoulders, leaving her arms free. Ivanka kept her cream trench coat belted tightly over her black turtleneck and pants. Jared's green utility coat remained over the gray V-neck he'd layered over blue button-down, black jeans, and white Common Project sneakers.

Ivanka approached the registration table first. "Here you go," the lady behind the table told her. "What you're going to do is fill out the ballot in one of the privacy booths behind you. When you're done with that, you bring it to the scanner under the basketball net." The woman asked Arabella if she wanted a sticker, and Ivanka smiled and brushed her daughter's hair back as she thanked the woman. She picked up the ballot and showed it to her father. They locked eyes. This was really happening. Melania was next to approach the table, followed by Donald himself. Jared went up last. "Last name Kushner," he told the woman.

Don Jr., his wife, Vanessa, and four of their five kids showed up to the same polling station a little while later.

Election Day happened to be Eric and Lara's second wedding anniversary, and the two voted a few blocks south, at the Fifty-Third Street Public Library. Eric proudly took a photo of his filled-in ballot, and tweeted it out to his followers. It is, of course, illegal to take photos in the voting booth in New York, a fact that many of his nearly two million followers were quick to point out. He later deleted the tweet.

They all wound up back at Trump Tower. Don Jr. did a bunch of local radio hits. They made calls to supporters and took calls from busybodies wondering what the mood was like inside. By around five o'clock, when the first dismal round of returns started rolling in, the three eldest kids started calling in to local stations in battleground states to make a last push. Jared made calls to a few media friends. He asked one high-up executive at a major media organization who'd known Kushner both professionally and personally for years what he was hearing about Florida, which at that point was their last hope for any path to victory that night. The executive told him it didn't look great, but what did he expect? "Did we get your support?" Jared asked. "No," the executive told him. "No you did not." Jared hung up and called Matt Drudge, another *macher* in the media circle he'd accumulated. The media had been off about the Trump campaign the whole time, Drudge told him. Wait until the next couple rounds of exit polls come out, he said. That's when things could start to shift.

Since before five o'clock that morning, campaign officials had been huddled on the fifth floor of Trump Tower—essentially an expansive unfinished utility closet with concrete floors and no heat, which staffers in the early part of the campaign used as a makeshift headquarters. By the time the sun set that evening, dozens of people packed the room as then national field director Bill Stepien zeroed in on the campaign model, mostly focused on Florida, and Jared and Ivanka and Eric and Don began milling about, poring over maps and models and numbers coming in from their guys on the ground and officials in Florida feeding them what they knew. Donald was up in his triplex atop the tower until after eight o'clock, when he called Ivanka, asking where she was. He told her to leave the fifth floor and come up to the fourteenth—the official headquarters— and he would meet her there.

They looked like sardines, the lot of them. Donald, Melania, the kids, Pence, Kellyanne Conway, Steve Bannon, Reince Priebus, Chris Christie, Mark Shot—the whole MAGA mod squad, stuffed into that corporate-looking office, cramped around giant screens and projections and TV screens as campaigners explained the numbers coming in and the *New York Times* prediction needle shifted slightly in Donald's direction. They stayed there until after eleven, when networks and wire services called Florida for him and the tide started turning in other battleground states. They took the executive elevator straight to the triplex—the family, the Pences, Conway, Christie and his son Andrew, Bannon, Stephen Miller, Priebus, Dave Bossie. The rest either stayed on the fourteenth floor or started to make their way a few blocks west to the victory party at the Midtown Hilton.

Miller sheepishly approached a few of them and told them he had prepared an exquisitely drafted concession speech. "What do we have on the victory speech?" someone asked Miller. "Bullet points," he said.

So they pulled out a laptop, and Miller, Pence, Ivanka, Jared, Don, Eric, and Christie started writing. Ivanka pointed out that it would be a great opportunity to reach out to women, who undoubtedly would need it after watching the first female major party candidate lose. Maybe we can mention parental leave or child care credits, she suggested. "Vank," Jared interrupted. "This isn't the speech for that. We have plenty of time to get to that later." The rest of the people around the table exchanged glances and took a breath. If anyone could say that to her, it was Jared. They were just glad he had.

Donald had been watching the returns on the small TV set up in the kitchen, repeatedly calling to check in on the victory speech he would have to give in a few hours. "We're just polishing it!" they yelled to him, though, technically, there was not yet a fully formed speech to polish. "The truth is, we were cramming," one of the people around the table said. "But we couldn't let him know that."

Once it became clear that things were going in his direction, the mood shifted to a mix of giddiness and shock. Jared threw his arm around Christie, saying "We did this." Conway kept repeating, "Can you believe this?" Melania looked shocked, and mostly concerned with Barron, who seemed whip-tired on the couch. It was well after midnight at this point, and she focused on keeping him awake on the couch. Donald remained stoic, and Pence seemed a little more celebratory. Karen Pence, one observer noted, looked as though she were at a funeral.

The ride over to the Hilton took less than ten minutes. There they waited in a tiny holding area off to the side of the main stage. That's when the Associated Press officially called the race for Donald Trump, at about 2:30 a.m. Huma Abedin's name flashed on the screen of Kellyanne's iPhone, which she had on silent. A day earlier, Hillary Clinton's campaign manager, Robby Mook, had emailed

Conway with Abedin's number. If Donald should win, he'd written, they would call him within fifteen minutes of the AP's call. Abedin would be her point of contact.

Pence had already gone onstage to address the crowd, telling them that they were sure they had won, but were waiting for a Clinton concession and an official call. After Donald took the phone and accepted Clinton's concession and congratulations, Pence walked over to his wife Karen and told her that they'd done it. They'd won.

"I know," she told him coldly.

"Well, how about a kiss?"

"Mike," she said, turning to him, "you got what you wanted."

DONALD, NOW officially the president-elect, walked onstage just before the clock struck three in the morning to talk for about fifteen minutes. "To Melania and Don and Ivanka and Eric and Tiffany and Barron, I love you and I thank you," he said about halfway through his speech, after thanking his parents and siblings. "Especially for putting up with all of those hours. This was tough. This was tough. This political stuff is nasty, and it is tough, so I want to thank my family very much. Really fantastic. Thank you all. Thank you all. Lara, unbelievable job. Unbelievable. Vanessa, thank you. Thank you very much. What a great group." Incidentally, and accidentally, he forgot to thank Jared, the de facto shadow campaign manager, a body man meets yes-man, bound to him in law and desire to make their families as rich and powerful, at least outwardly so, as possible.

They got a few hours of sleep before Jared started making calls to close friends and campaign associates. Many of them had told him that November 9 would be a day of reckoning. They'd spent months warning him that people thought of him as a psychopath for supporting this campaign, or at best an asshole. They drilled into his head that no one was going to want to talk to him after the election, and that he'd face a steep uphill climb to rebuild his reputation and that of his family. What they called his "big real estate reboot" would begin on the morning after Election Day. "Prepare yourself," they would say. "You're going to get back to earth, and it's not going to be the same place you left it." His response to all of it was a quiet, repetitive "I know."

That morning played out differently. The big real estate reboot was scrapped. They had all been so woefully wrong. He and Ivanka had prayed for the right outcome in the election, he told his friends, and that his father-in-law was going to be a great president.

Days earlier, on the Saturday before the election, after sundown when they could once again drive, they'd hopped in a car toward Cambria Heights in Queens, a largely black middle-class neighborhood where, on Francis Lewis Boulevard, Menachem Mendel Schneerson, the seventh grand rebbe of the Lubavitcher Hasidic dynasty, was buried alongside his father-in-law in 1994. The site of his tomb is known as the Ohel—the Hebrew word for tent—referring to the structure built around the grave. It is open day and night. Observers and believers have been making pilgrimages up to the Old Montefiore Cemetery in droves for the last near-quarter century because the rebbe, it is believed, will deliver those who visit the Ohel to God. A place to ask for blessings and scrawl prayers on the provided notepaper and toss them into the grave.

It was uncommonly warm that November Saturday, hanging in the mid-fifties even after dark. Jared turned up without a jacket, in a black cashmere sweater, flat-front khakis, and a yarmulke, Ivanka in a slanted black beret, belted coat, and bare legs. In the Ohel, they dropped their prayers into the grave before making their way back home. Friends joked that they weren't sure exactly what Jared meant when he referred to the "right outcome," and whether their prayers had in fact been answered or rebuffed.

AFTER JARED made a round of phone calls, he and Ivanka took their eldest children to school, as they often did, at Ramaz, the Modern Orthodox Jewish day school on the Upper East Side. They were a bit frazzled and tired but buzzing, and more apparent, they were a bit late. The school has a separate elevator to take parents up to preschool classrooms, and because they were running behind that morning, the elevator had already gone upstairs. So they waited. They were sitting ducks in a fishbowl. One by one, parents approached the couple, offering their congratulations. The win had stunned them, they told her. It was remarkable. She must be so happy, so proud. Wow, others offered. "She beamed," one parent remembered of Ivanka. "Graciously, she accepted every last word."

UNTIL THEN, parents at the school and members of their uptown shul had been split on the couple and their involvement in the campaign. On the one hand, the campaign had ignited a new wave of anti-Semitism and hundreds of dog whistles to white nationalists, alarming the Jewish community. After the president tweeted an image of Hillary Clinton with a Star of David and a pile of cash, one of Jared's own employees, *Observer* culture writer Dana Schwartz, wrote an open letter addressed to Jared in his paper, asking him to address the anti-Semitic vitriol spreading in his father-in-law's name that "applies equally to your wife and your daughter."

"Mr. Kushner, I ask you," she wrote, "what are you going to do about this?"

Jared wrote his own op-ed in response, under the headline "The Donald Trump I Know." He defended his father-in-law as "tolerant" and said that "the from-the-heart reactions of this man are instinctively pro-Jewish and pro-Israel." He invoked the story of his grandparents, who survived the Holocaust, as proof that he knew "the difference between actual, dangerous intolerance versus these labels that get tossed around in an effort to score political points."

Some of Jared's own cousins, reigniting a more-than-decade-old family feud that had been punctuated by Jared's father getting sent to federal prison, took issue with this defense. "I have a different takeaway from my Grandparents' experience in the war," Marc Kushner wrote in a Facebook post shortly after, linking to the op-ed. "It is our responsibility as the next generation to speak up against hate. Antisemitism or otherwise." Another first cousin, Jacob Schulder, was harsher. In a comment on Marc's post, he wrote: "That my grandparents have been dragged into this is a shame. Thank you Jared for using something sacred and special to the descendants of Joe and Rae Kushner to validate the sloppy manner in which you've handled this campaign. . . . Kudos to you for having gone this far; no one expected this. But for the sake of the family name, which may have no meaning to you but still has meaning to others, please don't invoke our grandparents in vain just so you can sleep better at night. It is self serving and disgusting."

Jared's parents, Charlie and Seryl, were supportive of the Trump campaign, hosting a couple of open houses at their Long Branch, New Jersey, beach house on Donald's behalf throughout the campaign. It wasn't an option not to throw their support behind Donald; in effect, that would mean not throwing their support behind Jared. They were proud of what he was doing, and whatever he needed, they would do. That their son was effectively running a presidential campaign gave them enough *naches* for them to put their own distaste at some of the campaign nonsense and rhetoric aside.

The *Access Hollywood* tape, for instance, rippled their household. But what rankled them wasn't Donald's language—that he'd boasted about using his special privilege as a celebrity to grab women by the genitals, or kissing a married woman he wooed with furniture shopping. It was that their son had walked to Trump Tower the day after the story broke to help handle the fallout. It was a Saturday, and their son shouldn't have been working. That, they told him, wasn't quite keeping Shabbat.

WHAT DIVIDED the community most unfolded over the summer of 2016. As the campaign worked with the Republican National Committee to put together the schedule for its convention in Cleveland, the Trump-Kushners threw out an idea. Why not ask Rabbi Haskel Lookstein, who'd shepherded Ivanka through her conversion process years earlier and led the congregation the Trump-Kushners attended in New York, to deliver an invocation, an opening prayer to kick off the convention? Lookstein had commanded the pulpit at the Congregation Kehilath Jeshurun, or KJ, for decades, taking over the gig from his father. Israel's Bar-Ilan University had granted him an honorary doctorate in recognition for the "influential role he has played in deepening Jewish values and heritage among American Jewry."

The rabbi agreed, a personal decision that he said he made to honor her request, out of respect for her and their relationship. In the lead-up to the convention, he settled on an invocation that prayed for the welfare of the government, thanking God for translating into reality the biblical command to "proclaim liberty throughout the land for all the inhabitants thereof" and for the constitutional government that fostered "the American ideals of democracy, freedom, justice and equality for all, regardless of race, religion or national origin." He would ask God to help us form a government that would "protect us with sound strategy and strength; which will unite use with words of wisdom and acts of compassion."

By all measures, it was a prayer most Americans, particularly those concerned by some of the campaign rhetoric and policies taking shape and gang-who-couldn't-shoot-straight-ness of it all, would have been heartened to hear. On a subtler level, it seemed almost like a troll of the candidate's position on immigration and concerns over his tolerance for people who looked and lived differently than he did.

Of course, that is not why the Trump-Kushners asked their rabbi to participate. "Jared and Ivanka felt like this was simple, a way to honor their rabbi with whom they had a close relationship," a member of the congregation recalled. But the simple things often turned complicated, in an instant, for everyone attached to the campaign, Javanka included.

The Trump campaign hastily sent a list of speakers, including all four adult Trump children, vice presidential nominee Mike Pence, former NFL quarterback Tim Tebow, former underwear model Antonio Sabàto Jr., and Lookstein. No one told the rabbi that his name would be included on a publicized list, which means he had no time to inform the campaign officials that he was not, in fact, giving a speech at the convention. He was simply offering a prayer.

The distinction may have made a difference to his congregants. Or maybe it wouldn't have, given the immediate backlash he faced once the announcement went public. Congregants started an online petition, signed by nearly 850 people, condemning the rabbi for lending his blessing to Donald Trump.

Lookstein reconsidered. In a letter emailed to his congregants and friends, he wrote that "the whole matter turned from rabbinic to political, something which was never intended." Politics, he added, divide people, and he had spent his life uniting. "In the interest of bringing our community together, I have asked to be relieved of my commitment to deliver the invocation." Some guilt did wash over Ivanka and Jared for the trouble they had caused the rabbi and for the controversy kicked up in their community. At the same time, they felt like they were getting hung out to dry and didn't see this as their fault in the slightest. "An amateur level of organization created a problem that did not need to exist," one person who was part of the planning said. But friends and members of their congregation whispered that they should have known better. "Part of this was that when you've become a bigger fucking deal," one congregant mused, "everything you do becomes a bigger fucking deal, and for some reason they didn't catch on to that."

SOME PEOPLE in the Trump-Kushners' community—KJ members, Ramaz parents, people who went to the Modern Orthodox yeshiva school that Jared attended in Paramus, New Jersey—thought it was a big fucking deal to have one of their own become a big fucking deal. On Saturday mornings throughout the campaign, as the rabbis spoke or cantors chanted, congregants would whisper that it was somewhat of a comfort to have him in the candidate's ear. He was a guy they davened with, who grew up the way they did, with the same kinds of values and priorities they were all taught in school and at home and in temple on Shabbat. "It is still someone who we grew up with, who's close to someone who may be the president," one acquaintance from high school explained at the time. "That is never bad."

Many agreed, however, that if they had their druthers, and it was up to them to choose a guy in their community who would be the one so close to and advising a US presidential candidate, Jared would not have ranked high on their list. The consensus was that, without a doubt, there were smarter, more accomplished guys in his high school class alone who would have been perfect geniuses in that role. With Jared, the feeling was more along the lines of, Well, I guess he'll do.

"He would not be the one who you'd be like, 'Oh, thank God he's there,'" one of his high school classmates said. "He wouldn't be a first- or second- or third-round draft pick. But, great, we have someone there. He's totally solid and fine, maybe more savvy than smart."

IN TERMS of his relationship with Jewish community leaders beyond his own New York, New Jersey bubble, many influential members corresponded with Kushner often, voicing their concerns and urging him to push certain policy positions. They were heartened by his father-in-law's rhetoric when it came to his support for Israel. And for all the attention Steve Bannon got for the alt-right, white nationalist, neo-Nazi agenda pushed on Breitbart News, the website he helmed, he was an unabashed hardliner on Israel.

Jewish organizations could tell that Kushner was overwhelmed and overworked. His father-in-law had tasked the guy, at the time a thirty-five-year-old real estate developer who'd never worked for a place he or his family didn't own, with solving Middle East peace, along with all of his other campaign duties. It is true that he had a close familial tie to Israel; Prime Minister Benjamin Netanyahu stayed at the Kushner family home when he came to the States, sometimes sleeping in Jared's childhood bed during his stays. But years of political know-how and understanding of an issue so complex that it has eluded seasoned diplomats for decades isn't like conjunctivitis. It doesn't rub off on shared pillows, nor is it picked up in conversations with a father's friends over Shabbat dinner.

So Jared frequently relied on feedback and input from these organizations, though it was clear he barely had the time to do so. "He'd reply to emails with letters instead of words, always very short, almost like he was running around on a BlackBerry with one hand tied," one Zionist organization leader recalled. "It was never a substantive discussion. It was more just trying to keep his head above water and get done what he absolutely had to get done."

He did engage with the American Israel Public Affairs Committee, the all-powerful pro-Israel lobbying group, throughout the campaign, particularly after his father-in-law hit the skids with the committee. Donald had particularly strained things when he said he would refrain from taking sides in peace talks between Israelis and Palestinians so he could fairly, credibly serve as a neutral negotiator. That, of course, is a third rail for organizations like AIPAC, particularly for a presumptive Republican nominee to take. The group's nerves were already frayed after eight years of the Obama administration, which many perceived as a dark period of the relationship between the American and Israeli government. They would need stronger assurances of support from the campaign, particularly given its questionable ties to anti-Semitism and white nationalists, if they were going to get anywhere together.

Kushner saw AIPAC's annual conference, an event held at the end of March 2016, as a place for him to both make good and make his commitments to Israeli clear. The initial plan was that Donald would do a question-and-answer session at the event, but it soon got scrapped in favor of a speech. Jared suggested that Donald use a teleprompter, which, given the typical freewheeling, meandering style he naturally gravitates toward, was simple self-preservation. The stakes here were too high to let an ill-informed, breezy throwaway line turn the whole community against the campaign for good. Jared also urged his father-in-law to use the speech to lay out specifics that the audience would eat up. The remarks could be a proof point that Donald would not only charm them and entertain them but knew a little bit about what he was talking about here and, most importantly, in fact, unequivocally have their back.

Jared solicited the advice of Ron Dermer, Israel's ambassador to the United States. Dermer had talked through what could happen with the United Nations after the election with the Clinton campaign, and he wanted to share the Israeli government's point of view with both sides, in language he felt comfortable with. At first he sent over talking points Donald could use for the Q&A, but Jared requested a phone call once he knew the campaign had to plan for a speech.

On the call, Dermer made it clear that he was doing this as a service for all campaigns. He talked for a solid hour about the UN, about Iran, about hard lines and language that was very important to Israelis, and about many people who would be in the audience that day. It was a solid foundation from which Jared and campaign officials could draw in drafting a speech, based on what fit in with their own agendas and strategies and broader foreign policy goals.

The truth was that those broader agendas, strategies, and goals, particularly when it came to foreign policy, were primordial at best at that stage. And so having Dermer spell out a fully fleshed-out policy was like getting your hands on the answer key the night before a final exam that was worth 50 percent of your grade at the end of the semester. As Dermer laid out, piece by piece, bit by bit, the position of the Israeli government and the ways in which they wanted to hear a US commander in chief relate to them and address the rest of the Middle East, someone was clearly taking notes.

The next day Jared sent a draft of the speech to the billionaire casino owner, GOP kingmaker, and major Jewish philanthropist magnate Sheldon Adelson, who promptly sent it over to Dermer. The text Dermer read was like a transcript of what he had told Jared in their phone call, right down to the jokes. It was basically wholesale theft.

Jared continued to polish over the weekend. He loved it. When Jared called Dermer back to give him a preview, it seemed that the campaign had used what Dermer said in their phone call almost exactly, adding a few familiar Trumpian rhetorical flourishes—a bunch of believe-mes and plugs for his *Art of the Deal*. It was Dermer's substance, almost verbatim, put through a Trump Speak machine and fed into a teleprompter for him to read to the crowd.

The speech went through three main takeaways, all of which were very much in line with the AIPAC bent. First, his priority would be to "dismantle the disastrous deal with Iran," which he called "catastrophic for America, for Israel and for the whole of the Middle East." He laid out an uncharacteristically specific plan for what he, as president, would do and the specific problems he said the deal failed to address. Second, he vowed to move the American embassy to Jerusalem. Third, he ripped into what he called "the utter weakness and incompetence of the United Nations," which, he said, was not a friend to freedom, nor to the United States, and surely not to Israel. He vowed to end the discussions swirling about an attempt to bring a Security Council resolution on the terms of an eventual agreement between Israel and Palestine. "The United States must oppose this resolution and use the power of our veto, which I will use as president 100 percent." Next, he told the audience that Palestinians need to stop treating those who murder Jews as heroes and lionizing hatred in textbooks and mosques.

But despite his son-in-law's warnings, the candidate couldn't help himself. He could read an audience—that was his one natural skill—so he threw them some red meat. "With President Obama in his final year" he began, before interrupting himself with a "Yay!" Like any performer worth his salt, he paused to let the crowd applaud and roar. He chuckled to himself, his lips turning upward in a grin, before he turned his head to take in the crowd. This was what he fed off, what set off that little clinking in his brain, like a junkie getting a first taste before opening up wide. He heard the clapping and he wanted more. So he careened off the teleprompter and spiraled straight into rally mode, straight down into the mordancy that played so well to his base. He kept pausing and shaking his head as the rush settled into thought bubbles. "He may be the worst thing to ever happen to Israel, believe me, believe me," he said to more hoots and hollers. "And you know it and you know it better than anybody."

His audience didn't necessarily disagree with these sentiments. But members of AIPAC's executive team started to scramble. Candidates didn't use this event to slam and attack other politicians. AIPAC president Lillian Pinkus opened the next morning's events, during which Netanyahu was scheduled to speak, with an apology for the rhetoric Donald had run off with the night before. Barely swallowing back tears, Pinkus indicated that the candidate had violated the nonpartisan spirit the event tried to retain.

The hubbub around Donald's comments overshadowed the one line he had been sure would get him into AIPAC's good graces. "I love the people in the room. I love Israel," Donald had ended with the day earlier. "My daughter, Ivanka, is about to have a beautiful Jewish baby. In fact, it could be happening right now, which would be very nice as far as I'm concerned."

A WEEK before the election, in the midst of this all, Ivanka turned in the manuscript for her second book, *Women Who Work: Rewriting the Rules for Success*, to her publisher. The book was a marketing dream. The confluence of the company she'd built under her own name and the near-constant attention on her speaking about paid family leave and child care under the glare of the political campaign made a book like this the gold standard for the term "brand tie-in."

Ivanka had spent nearly a decade selling jewelry to women, and then clothes and shoes and handbags and accessories—and later, the notion of a put-together working woman who, if she doesn't "have it all," wants to read about the interview-ready outfits and time-saving tips and recipes and workouts and ways to ask for a more flexible work schedule she'll need to get close to having at least some of it. Her brand website turned into a mecca for that kind of aspirational content, with blog posts about packed lunches and spring looks for the office, most of which let readers shop corresponding looks from the Ivanka Trump brand directly from each post.

She had announced the book publicly in June, in a video message posted on her website. "So last year, I shared some pretty exciting news, that I was pregnant with baby number three, little baby Theodore, and, today, I have some amazing news to share with you as well." She held up a cutout of a white number 4 affixed to a stick, biting her perfectly berry-stained lips, as if the secret would spill out if she didn't physically contain it with her teeth. True Ivanka Trump fans, the kinds of women who religiously read her website or leave comments on her Instagram photos praising her children or cataloging her outfits, would recognize this trick. When she announced her pregnancy with Theodore, again, in a video posted on her site, her first child, Arabella, had held a number 1, her second, Joseph, a number 2, and Ivanka herself held a gold number 3 up to her belly.

"Okay, so I'm not pregnant with baby number four," she said, doubling over her own black-and-white printed shift dress as she chuckled at her own joke. "But I do have another exciting project in the works, and it is also a labor of love. It's a book."

The idea had been born two years earlier, when she launched

her first #WomenWhoWork initiative. "I was advised by many of the top creative agencies to lose the word, 'work,'" she wrote in her announcement. "One after another, they suggested that the idea of 'women and work' wasn't aspirational and wouldn't resonate with a millennial audience. I disagreed. If you ask me, there's nothing more incredible than a woman who's in charge of her own destiny— and working daily to make her dreams a reality.

"Over the last two years, my team and I have been laser-focused on making IvankaTrump.com *the* destination for professional women. Our site is home to inspiring thought leaders, smart content and solution-oriented tips curated for women who work. Today, I'm beyond excited to announce the next evolution of our message—a book!"

When she took the idea to Portfolio, her publisher, half a year earlier, it wasn't a hard sell. At the time, they had no inkling that she would be turning in the pages after more than a year stumping for one of the most polarizing political candidates in American history. None of them believed that Donald would make it beyond a few primaries, certainly not to the general election. To them, he was a fringe candidate who had no shot at winning. They bought her book giving little thought to all of that. They'd market it as a liberal-leaning C-list celebrity version of a career book.

They ran into some bumps even before the prospect of a President Trump dawned on them. Ivanka worked with a writer who the publisher thought was really good, but Ivanka reworked everything herself. She would go through the pages early in the morning, before walking over to Trump Tower or traveling with her father to a campaign stop, typing away on her laptop as she got her hair blown out in her apartment, Jared bringing her coffee as the nannies got the kids ready for school. From the pages they got to read early on, what came through to the publishers was her privileged perspective. For instance, there was no mention of the two women who took care of her own children until the last few pages, in the acknowledgments. After she thanked her agent, the contributors to her book, her sisters-in-law, her mother, her friends, her colleagues, and the two nannies who helped raise her and her brothers, she acknowledged Liza and Xixi, "who are helping me raise my own children," thanking them "for being part of our extended family and enabling me to do what I do."

Mostly, the publishers felt that the book was devoid of emotion. They pumped and pumped her to add personal, relatable details about her relationship with her parents—"to make her seem like she had a pulse," one person involved with the book explained. "Like she was a human and had emotions." They took every shred of what Ivanka and her writer were willing to give, which wasn't much. Ivanka was always unfailingly polite and gracious, though, and so intense in her work ethic that they were surprised every time they visited her in her Trump Tower office (she never ventured to their offices; they always came to her).

The real trouble came once Donald had won the nomination. They had to change their entire marketing calculus, because the demographic they had thought the book would appeal to when they bought it—young women in their twenties and thirties living on the coasts—now staunchly opposed Ivanka's family and everything her father's campaign stood for. So they had to start making inroads into a whole new audience in the middle of the country—an audience that, frankly, the publisher did not know how to reach or market to.

They recalibrated and, once they had their hands on the manuscript, tried bit by bit to turn it into the best book it could possibly be. Ivanka asked Mika Brzezinski, who had her own "Know Your Value" brand already launched, to review the book. At the time, the *Morning Joe* host was on okay enough terms with her father, and she helped Ivanka get his attention on women's-related issues throughout the campaign, to varying degrees of success. Ivanka genuinely wanted to help the cause, she believed; if a few words about her book meant that the future First Daughter would put her efforts there in the White House, then fine.

A week later, Donald won the election, and the entire calculus changed again. Ivanka asked the same favor of Judge Jeanine Pirro, the colorful Fox News host and longtime friend of her father's. Jeanine's ex-husband, the businessman and lobbyist Al Pirro, had served as Donald's power broker in Westchester County in the 1990s, and the three of them would play golf and fly on Trump's plane down to Mar-a-Lago together. (Donald could never get any work done on those flights down to Palm Beach. "I can't pay attention," he'd tell friends traveling with him. "How can you stop looking at her legs? Have you ever seen sexier legs?"). This was before Al Pirro got locked up for conspiracy and tax evasion, a turn of events that went on to haunt Judge Jeanine's career as district attorney in Westchester and her onetime bid for a seat in the US Senate. But it made it so she could staunchly, spiritedly advocate for her old pal in her televised monologues each Saturday night, and say yes to writing a few kind words about his daughter's forthcoming book. "Who knows more about success than Ivanka Trump?" she wrote. "Buy it and learn something!"

ON THE day after the election, most of the staff in Portfolio's offices were zombies. Some cried all day, taking turns wiping their faces in the bathroom. To them, it was a disaster. They were in complete despair about having this book on their hands. But other executives were elated. What they'd bought as a famous-reality-star-meets-builder-meets-fashion-executive-meets-mom-and-wife how-to was now something entirely different. They had the First Daughter's book. By accident. And it was scheduled to come out just about one hundred days after her father would take office. "We never thought of canceling," the person who worked on the book said. "There was the chance for it to be a big hit, and you'd have to be on a suicide mission to cancel the book by a First Daughter, even in this case."

The looming issue was how to do press around the book. Ivanka had not yet determined what her role would be once she and Jared moved to Washington. She would be some kind of an adviser to her father and his administration. That was never the question. What was at issue was how she would describe her position in marketing the book. She hadn't intended to officially join the administration until ethics concerns made it nearly impossible for her not to. So how could she go out before she herself answered those questions and have a book publisher try and field the issue, thorny as it was?

The day before Christmas she called the publisher directly, saying she was not sure what her role would be, whether it was going to be official or unofficial, or how she would describe it to people. She wondered if they could move the publication date from March back to May. As it happened, the book was set to go out the following Monday. The wheels were so far in motion that in any other case, it would have been absurd to try to stop them at that point. But this wasn't another author looking for a favor; it was the incoming First Daughter. They pushed the book back. (Not long after the book was meant to come out, Ivanka announced her official role within the administration, as assistant to the president, advising him on issues related to American families, female entrepreneurship, and workforce development. As an official government employee, she could not market the book herself, which meant no interviews, no tour, no readings, no appearances. Before her attorneys and White House lawyers came down on it, every network had been fighting to get her for the book. "The lineup would have made Princess Diana jealous, had she promoted a book," one publishing executive said. They had to scrap it all, though. And the reviews, one after the next, panned the book—for what it said, for what it left out, and for what people read between the lines. "She didn't ruin the year," the executive said, "but it was a bloodbath.")

IN THE days following the election, foreign leaders and diplomats flooded the switchboard at Trump Tower. There were protocols for how these calls were supposed to be received and made, of course. Many of them were outlined in the dozens and dozens of binders that members of the Trump transition team had put together leading up to November. Few of the transition officials imagined that these binders would actually get put to use. Donald Trump was such a long shot that their work was more of a just-in-case than a these-will-almost-certainly-help-inform-the-next-president. Even fewer imagined that the binders would be picked apart and summarily chucked in the trash once Vice President-elect Pence took over the transition. Ivanka and Jared, along with her siblings and their father and Pence and his allies, had a deep suspicion of any materials put together by anyone connected to Chris Christie. They were also so disengaged from the pre–Election Day transition work that they had their hand in none of the preparation that the professionals—people with real governmental experience, with actual expertise in national security and on the economy and intergovernmental relations and intelligence operations and diplomacy and how the bureaucracy in Washington functions and what all of these areas need to run properly every day—put together. The Trumps, who worked out of their dad's office in a building bearing their last name, knew nothing about any of that. What they did know was that, deep down, they trusted only themselves. Anything prepared without their input, particularly by people who they believed were loyal to Christie, who was not always a friend of the family—well, how could it be used?

Transition officials remember Ivanka coming down to the floor of Trump Tower that housed the transition operations to inspect what was going on. She and Jared seemed paranoid to staffers, worried that officials would be more loyal to Christie than to "the family," which is how, people on the transition said, they referred to themselves—"Like a mafia movie," one joked. People gossiped about overhearing "the family" talking about burning the place down and starting from scratch.

"They came into this with chips on their shoulder and grudges that a little seasoning and worldliness tells you that they shouldn't bring to the party," one transition official who was fired soon after the election recalled. "They brought it to the party anyway."

It became abundantly clear once foreign leaders began to call. Transition officials had prepared a call book, laying out which calls they knew were going to come in, how to prepare for them, and which to prioritize, based on the traditional protocol surrounding these early days of the transition. All of it got tossed aside. It is unclear whether this was totally intentional; perhaps the Trump operation, as it existed after the election, was simply too overwhelmed and understaffed to keep up with all of the high-level international issues and decisions and processes it was suddenly faced with. For all its bluster, the Trump Organization is not a Fortune 500 company, with huge teams of people and sophisticated communication systems and tons of seasoned assistants crisscrossing spanning offices, ticking off to-dos and putting out fires. It's a tiny office stuffed with decades-old magazine covers featuring the boss, and, one floor away, his kids' offices in a sleeker, more modern area. One longtime executive-assistant-cum-gatekeeper, Rhona Graff, who had worked for the company for thirty years, handled all the calls and messages coming in for her boss.

That left Theresa May, the British prime minister, scrambling for a good twenty-four hours to get through to the incoming US president. Egyptian president Abdel Fattah el-Sisi got through earlier, as did Israeli prime minister Benjamin Netanyahu—a diplomatic faux pas deeply reflective of the total chaos within Trump Tower and the transition in the days and weeks following the election. Many lamented that if they had just stuck to the materials the early transition officials put together, this snub of a US ally would not have happened. It is impossible to say, though, whether anything would have really been different; it was Donald Trump who had just been elected president, after all. And Donald Trump, people were starting to realize, was not only unpredictable and erratic but also had a penchant for knocking things off kilter even when trying to stick to protocol. "They all paid for not sticking to what we'd planned," the transition official said. "Because they looked like bumbling idiots."

Japanese prime minister Shinzo Abe was the first leader to make the pilgrimage to Trump Tower, less than ten days after Donald won the election. The Trump team left the pool of reporters on duty that day out of the meeting, as they did with American photographers. No one got the chance to ask questions before or after the sit-down, and no official photos were released, either, apart from a Facebook post on Donald's page that showed him shoulder-to-shoulder with Abe in the foreground, the gilded moldings and marble and cream silk sofas of the Trump residence behind them. "It was a pleasure to have Prime Minister Shinzo Abe stop by my home and begin a great friendship," he captioned the shot.

The Japanese government had a different plan. They handed out more revealing photos of their prime minister's time in Trump Tower to the waiting press. In one, Donald and Abe sat facing each other on that silk cream couch, flanked by two interpreters and a dizzying array of crystal chandeliers and sconces and marble statues and mirrors. Facing them across a gilded coffee table topped with a gold candelabra holding unlit candlesticks, Ivanka Trump sat cross-legged in a beige armchair. Arms crossed at the wrists, she leaned back in her shift dress, black stilettos digging into the cream carpet. In another photo she stood beside Abe and Jared, who wore a slender gray suit jacket buttoned over a slim black tie. In a third shot, the couple stood smiling behind Donald and Abe as they shook hands.

Immediately, alarm bells rang over the ethics and the optics of it all. First, what business did a daughter and son-in-law who had no governmental experience—or even, at that point, a plan to join the government—have at that meeting? Everyone still had faith then that the country would be run as a democracy and not a monarchy, that the First Family would never be a royal family. But these photos were enough to shake that faith. Second, the fact that neither Ivanka nor Jared had security clearances raised some eyebrows. Third, perhaps most concerning, Ivanka was still heavily involved with the Trump Organization and with her own eponymous product line, both of which did deals around the world. The image of her having a cozy meeting, in a diplomatic position of power, with a world leader raised concerns. What, if any, boundaries would be drawn between Trump Tower business and foreign relationships within 1600 Pennsylvania Avenue? Would the family use its newfound political circumstances as a marketing opportunity?

Ivanka's brand had already been hit hard for marketing off her campaign appearances. The Ivanka Trump social media accounts had posted buy links for the sleeveless pink Ivanka Trump dress she wore to introduce her father at the Republican National Convention in Cleveland, and for the gold bangle bracelet she wore on *60 Minutes*, taped alongside her father and siblings two days after the election. Both times, Ivanka made it clear behind the scenes that she herself had nothing to do with the posts. Not only did she know better, but she was so much more focused on the bigger-picture issues she now had a chance to influence. Selling dresses and bracelets wasn't taking up much space in her brain during that period; it was lower-level Ivanka Trump brand staffers who'd thought up the whole thing. Could she blame them? No way. They were just doing their jobs. Was she going to take the blame? Again, no. She had a very different sort of job.

Concerns continued to mount. Soon afterward, the *New York Times* reported that while Ivanka sat across from Abe in her childhood apartment, a two-day private viewing of her collection— including the sleeveless pink dress she wore to the convention—was taking place in Tokyo to shore up a licensing deal with a Japanese apparel company. Talks between the Ivanka Trump brand and Sanei

International had been under way for years, and did not stem from
Ivanka herself. The largest investor of Sanei's parent company happens to be a bank owned by the Japanese government.

The apparatus around Ivanka spun it as a rookie mistake. "Any
meetings she's in is because it's always been a family-focused environment and she has always been invited by her father to attend
every meeting," one person explained at the time. "But she is very
committed to being respectful of different boundaries and it's clear
that it's going to take some getting used to the changes that need to
happen. They all understand that there's a need to evaluate everything, and in the next couple of weeks, we will have a better sense of
how she is going to separate from that."

BUT THE Trump kids did not separate. In fact, despite the months
of preparation carried out by professionals and policy experts, the
Trump campaign's hallmark chaos bled into the postelection process, Donald's three adult kids made themselves at home on the
transition's executive committee. They took seats at the table in the
first official transition meeting in Trump Tower in the days after
the election, alongside Trump loyalist and Alabama senator Jeff Sessions, his chief of staff, Rick Dearborn, and a handful of others. So
began the exercise of trying to fill top agency positions and, most
importantly, decide on Cabinet nominations—a tedious process
for anyone, let alone an incoming president with no governmental
know-how and little to no attention span.

Eric Trump had worked for his father as a Trump Organization
employee for about a decade and as his son for thirty-two years.
He knew that Donald could derail the whole thing if he thought he
could appoint anyone he wanted, including his friends, who had
even less business serving in top agency positions than Donald did.
Nothing would ever get done if Donald believed there were an un-
limited number of possibilities—or worse, if he thought those roles
could go to anyone he thought fit. Eric asked the transition staff

to come up with short lists of potential nominees who had a shot at getting confirmed, and present these to his father. "We have to lead him to believe that this is who he has to choose from," he told people. "He's got to think those are the only guys."

This is where some of the tension between Eric and Jared came from. Where Eric saw Donald's weaknesses, he tried to work around them, filling in for what he lacked and making him stronger. This wasn't entirely altruistic; his success depended almost entirely on his father's, after all. But for the most part, he came from a place of trying to make his father better, and a desire to protect him from himself. Eric didn't feel like that was where Jared came from in his own dealings with Donald. Throughout the campaign, especially, he told people that he felt Jared took advantage of Donald's weaknesses, as opposed to trying to neutralize them.

They put those tensions aside, though, for the initial postelection transition meeting. They had just started working through some of the first steps when Generals Mike Flynn and Keith Kellogg walked in the room. As far as Christie, who was running the meeting, knew, they had not been invited, and this was not a come-as-you-please, anyone-is-welcome affair. "Gentlemen," he said, "we're in the middle of a meeting. Can I help you?"

When Ivanka cut in to say that she had invited both of them, Christie demurred. He told Flynn and Kellogg that since he hadn't known they would be joining, he had not made printouts of the meeting agenda and materials for them. They would have to look on with someone else.

The meeting was getting back on track when Ivanka again interrupted. "General Flynn," she said, turning to him, "you have been so amazingly loyal to my dad. We all love you. How do you want to serve the president-elect? What job do you want?" A few people around the table caught each other's eyes. Jeff Sessions rolled his, pulled his glasses off the bridge of his nose, and sank back into his chair.

There were just a few jobs he would be qualified to take, Flynn responded: secretary of state or secretary of defense, or—if not one of those—head of the president's National Security Council.

Eric jumped in. He asked if Flynn had been retired long enough to head the Pentagon. Flynn said that if he got a waiver from Congress, it would be okay. Eric turned to Sessions and asked how often Congress issued waivers like that to potential cabinet nominees. "Never," Sessions replied.

Later on in the meeting, Ivanka put the same question she had asked Flynn to Kellogg. He would be happy to take on the role of chief of staff, he said.

"To the president?" Eric asked.

Yes, Kellogg told him.

"Well, is there anything else you would possibly want?"

ON THURSDAY the family sat down for an interview with Leslie Stahl, to air on CBS's *60 Minutes* that Sunday. The interview, taped on the first floor of the triplex in which all the kids—apart from Tiffany—had grown up, and together watched news anchors call states for their father a couple of nights before, would be the first time Donald, Melania, and all five children talked about the changes to come.

Earlier that day, forty-some stories down, on the twentieth floor, Bannon called Christie into his office and fired him from his role as head of the transition on the spot. On the one hand, there was a sense that Donald, who out of superstition had not wanted to know anything about the transition, had been sold a bill of goods about where it stood, despite the months of prep done by true experts who'd filled dozens of binders with useful research and delineated next steps. All of that work had been done by people the family considered Christie loyalists, so how could they trust it? They couldn't, they thought, which explains why they made a show of dumping tens of binders in the trash in front of the very people who'd prepared them. Those who believed this was about settling the long-simmering Kushner-Christie score saw Jared's overtures during the campaign—and particularly on election night, when he threw his arm around the governor—as ruthless. Many saw this as an attempt to replace those who'd aligned with Christie to those who aligned with the candidate and his family, which is why the campaign swiftly appointed Pence as its new leader and Dearborn its executive director.

The move to bring in an incoming vice president to head a transition did have a precedent. George W. Bush had done the same when he was preparing to take office. Christie also happened to be mired in scandal in his own state; two of his former aides had been convicted in the so-called Bridgegate scandal, in which traffic lanes on the George Washington Bridge from Fort Lee, New Jersey, to Manhattan were closed as political retribution against a political foe in New Jersey, a week earlier. Dearborn would also be a natural liaison between Trump Tower and Capitol Hill, and as usual, the Trump kids would be there to oversee it all.

But the story that this was just Washington business as usual, without a hint of personal vengeance, became harder to buy as the days went on. Rich Bagger, who'd taken a leave from his job as Christie's chief of staff and temporarily moved from New Jersey to DC to serve as the transition's executive, was waiting for Christie when he came up to the twenty-fifth floor after Bannon canned him. They wanted to keep Bagger on, since he was the guy who knew every in and out. Bagger responded by saying he would quit and finished with a hearty fuck-you.

Bagger still went down to Washington the following day. He had planned a meeting in the DC transition offices in which Bill Palatucci, Christie's former law partner and the transition's general counsel, would go over ethics requirements in front of hundreds of staffers. As he made his way to the stage, Bagger got a call from Dearborn, telling him to stop Palatucci in his tracks. He'd forgotten to tell the general counsel that he was about to be fired. They didn't want Palatucci getting up in front of everyone, and they didn't want Bagger up there, either. Bagger told them to go scratch, and he and Palatucci ran the meeting anyway.

By the next week Dearborn had also fired Mike Rogers, the former House Intelligence Committee chairman Christie had hired to run the transition's national security wing. "I saw this all happening and I said to myself, 'Holy shit, man,'" one high-up transition official noted. "We all knew this was coming from the family, and these were guys who had put their hearts and souls into this, and they treated them like they were something stuck on their shoes. It was just an ugly, ugly bloodletting, and they didn't even have the class to make the call themselves. They had Dearborn do it for them."

Bannon later admitted that the decision to fire Christie and everyone, in the family's eyes, associated with him came from Jared. Donald himself insisted that Christie had not in fact been fired, but simply made a member of a bigger team.

The campaign's statement said it all. "Together this outstanding group of advisors, led by Vice President–elect Mike Pence, will build on the initial work done under the leadership of New Jersey Gov. Chris Christie to help prepare a transformative government ready to lead from day one." Christie would be moved to the role of vice chairman of the transition effort. Jared, Ivanka, Don Jr., and Eric were among the members of the executive committee, along with Steve Bannon, Ben Carson, Mike Flynn, Newt Gingrich, Rudy Giuliani, Rebekah Mercer, Steven Mnuchin, Devin Nunes, Reince Priebus, Anthony Scaramucci, and Peter Thiel.

FIGURING OUT how to untangle everything swallowed up time Jared and Ivanka did not have. Ivanka had to start thinking about whether (or how) to uproot her kids and move to Washington. As she started to seriously consider the possibility, friends urged them not to. There were two camps of people insisting that she should stay in New York—first, those who said attaching themselves further to such a polarizing political environment would ruin their reputations and their friendships and all the little frills and big comforts they'd known and enjoyed for most of their lives; and second, those who worried about what their businesses would be without them. Don Jr. and Ivanka and Eric were the three musketeers within the Trump Organization. People close to the family told Ivanka that if she left and broke up the band, they didn't know if it would ever come back together again. People close to Jared told him that his association with the White House would place tremendous scrutiny on Kushner Companies and scare off investors who didn't want their finances run through by the media and government's fine-tooth combs. There was the added pressure from within the Kushner family, though they fully supported and found great pride in Jared ascending to the West Wing. There were the practical concerns over how the business would run. Jared's brother Josh had his own company. His sister Nicole was a relative newcomer to the business, and while she had been there, Jared very much ran the show alongside his father. As a felon, Charlie Kushner couldn't sign anything. As that reality dawned on him, he would often blurt out "I miss Jared" in the middle of meetings, in front of other Kushner family members and business associates.

Ivanka often responded that she wanted to actually affect change on issues she'd been talking about in the private sector for years, only now with a level of efficacy on a global scale that she could never have imagined before. To close friends, she would add that she couldn't leave her father in Washington alone: "He can't get down there and look around and have no one around him," she'd say. "He needs his people there."

THERE WAS no one on the transition staff close to Jared and Ivanka who could herd them through the process of filling out disclosure forms and security clearance documents. They had dozens upon dozens of businesses and trusts and investments and properties and holdings, all of which they had to somehow untangle themselves from. They had to figure out whether they wanted to fully divest from these, and if so, how to go about that. If they didn't, they faced a whole other set of issues over putting those assets into a trust controlled by someone else—in many cases, by Jared's mother Seryl and his siblings Josh and Nicole. Over time, Kushner resigned from 266 corporate positions, and Ivanka stepped back from 292. In the first six months of the administration, the couple revised its financial disclosure form about forty times—a rate his lawyers called normal, and governmental ethics experts called bullshit.

That the couple was worth hundreds of millions of dollars, scattered so widely and concealed so cleverly, was one factor. Another was a mixture of naïveté and lack of guidance. As one transition official noted, the Trump team was unprepared and woefully understaffed, lacking in the old Washington hands who might have helped Jared and Ivanka avoid the mistakes that would lead them to update their disclosure forms forty times in six months: "If you worked on the Hillary campaign, you'd have Marc Elias explain to you how these things are serious and how you handle them. They had no one. There was no one to say, 'Here is how you need to handle this.' There were just no experts around at all."

The couple's friends intervened. Joel Klein, the former Murdoch News Corp guy who now works for Jared's brother's health insurance start-up Oscar, cautioned him to hire someone who knew their stuff as he waded through the muck of figuring out how he could take a position in the White House, mitigating conflicts of interest and working out how to get around that anti-nepotism law. His recommendation, Jamie Gorelick, had served as deputy attorney general under President Bill Clinton, fund-raised for Hillary, and just gone through the process of vetting potential Cabinet members for Trump's opponent—a rough outline that would never see the light of day. She herself was seen as a likely pick for attorney general, had Hillary pulled it off.

As it was, Gorelick took Klein at his word that Jared would be a necessary voice in the incoming administration, though she did think twice about accepting him as a client. So did her partners at her law firm, Wilmer, Hale—the same firm where now special counsel Robert Mueller worked, and from which hailed a handful of the lawyers he tapped for his investigation into Trump campaign officials, including into some of Jared's activities. Whispers spread around New York's big law firms that some Wilmer, Hale partners worried that with all the reports of and uncertainty over the Trump campaign's alleged ties to Russia, having Jared as a client would open them up to possible legal liability.

Even with help, there were ethical minefields everywhere. The meeting with Prime Minister Abe had normalized the idea of Ivanka not only sitting in on these sorts of meetings but also hosting meetings in Trump Tower with diplomats and thought leaders on her own. On a frigid day in early January, at midday, Queen Rania of Jordan rode those golden elevators up to meet with Ivanka about global women's issues and how to best advocate for them in Washington, though at that point Ivanka had not yet confirmed that she was moving to DC. Queen Rania, an honorary chair of the UN's Girls Education Initiative and founder of an NGO that helps families and children in poverty, had already been doing the kind of work Ivanka had said she wanted to do throughout the campaign. She too benefited from the privileges of inheritance, though by marriage in her case. When House minority leader Nancy Pelosi veered into women's issues while on the line with Donald, he promptly handed the phone over to his daughter. The two of them could talk it out.

A month earlier, in December, Leonardo DiCaprio sat down privately with Ivanka to talk about climate change, presenting her with a copy of *Before the Flood*, a ninety-minute documentary featuring the Oscar winner traveling across five continents to witness the climate impacts communities there already feel. She invited Al Gore to visit Trump Tower, too, to talk about the environment and sit down with her father, who publicly denied the existence of climate change.

"It's an important signal that she's not fucking crazy," a person close to Ivanka said of the meetings at the time. "She gets it. She's normal. These aren't all issues that are going to be part of her advocacy necessarily, but she is interested in learning about them and hearing all sides and to show that."

The couple met with other Washington insiders, tucking into a booth in the BLT Prime setup in the lobby of the newly minted Trump Hotel on Pennsylvania Avenue and meeting with Dina Powell, a veteran of the Bush White House and State Department and a Goldman Sachs insider, who, their mutual friends told the Trump-Kushners, they would be lucky to have as a shepherd. Ivanka had an extended conversation with outgoing First Lady Michelle Obama, the details of which they kept close. Jared continued to take calls and meetings with foreign officials, too. Donald had tapped Jared to be the point person handling incoming requests from the leaders, officials, and diplomats who started reaching out once his campaign gained traction in the primaries, and continued to do so all the way through inauguration and after. It's not that Jared had any sort of diplomatic prowess or experience. He was both a yes-man who complied with his father-in-law's requests and a skilled schmoozer used to being slightly out of his depth in dealing with older, far more seasoned heavy hitters. These officials gamely got in good with a naïve member of the Trump campaign's innermost circle who was bound to the candidate and, later, president, by law and a sense of filial duty. It was a long-haul play that they knew would pay off for months, if not years, to come. Throughout the campaign and transition, Jared, who got hundreds of campaign-related emails a day, including dozens from foreign officials looking to establish some sort of relationship with his father-in-law, talked with somewhere in the neighborhood of a hundred foreign officials from about twenty countries, including Israeli prime minister Benjamin Netanyahu, Jordan's King Abdullah II, Mexico's secretary of foreign affairs, Luis Videgaray Caso, and, rather infamously now, Russia's ambassador to the United States, Sergey Kislyak.

Donald and Kislyak had met more than six months earlier, in April 2016, at a private reception at the Mayflower Hotel in Washington. During a reception before a speech Donald delivered on foreign policy, Jared shook hands with a handful of ambassadors, some of whom mentioned getting together for a lunch that never happened. In the remarks that followed, Donald spoke of "improved relations with Russia" and a desire to "make a deal that's great" for "America, but also good for Russia." Kislyak took it all in from the front row.

A week after Donald's electoral win, the ambassador followed up. His people got in touch with Jared's people a week after the election, requesting a meeting, which occurred in Trump Tower on the first day of December. Michael Flynn—who would soon serve a short stint as the administration's national security director before lying to the FBI about his discussions with Russians and, later, flipping in the Mueller investigation and serving as a cooperating witness—joined them. The way Kislyak told it to his superiors, picked up on intercepts of Russian communications reviewed by US officials, among other topics, they discussed a secret back channel between the Trump transition team and the Kremlin out of Russian diplomatic facilities. The ambassador said he was caught off guard by the suggestion, which would not only raise security concerns for both countries but also break a US law. The Logan Act, a federal statute that dates back to nearly the beginning of the Republic, prohibits citizens from getting involved in disputes or controversies between the United States and foreign governments without authorization.

The act has never been used to successfully prosecute any American citizen, though it does carry a prison sentence of up to three years. Kushner's meeting took place before Donald took office, and without the Obama administration's knowledge or approval.

Jared tells the story of the meeting differently. Kislyak, he said in a statement to Congress months after his father-in-law took office, had asked if the transition had a secure way for Russian generals to communicate to the Trump team information related to Syria, in order to help the incoming administration. Jared had then asked if the Russian embassy had a communications channel already in place through which they could have these discussions about Syria. He contends that he never suggested talking about anything else, or that the conversations would be ongoing. The bulk of the meeting, which he said was not particularly memorable, was taken up with exchanging pleasantries and asking who the best point of contact for Vladimir Putin would be.

Jared declined a follow-up meeting that Kislyak requested, but at the ambassador's urging he sat down with Sergey Gorkov, a Russian banker with direct ties to Putin, in Trump Tower on December 13. The meeting was only twenty-five minutes long—enough time for the man to hand him two gifts, a piece of art and a bag of dirt from the town in Belarus where his grandparents grew up, and to raise suspicions over whether the two had talked about personal, Kushner-related business or public affairs that could impact Russian-American relations.

In one light, the meetings painted Jared as a dewy-eyed novice punching above his weight. In another, he looked like a perfectly soft target, just asking to be struck by an enemy that had spent the entire election cycle repeatedly hitting at the heart of American democracy.

The ethical concerns raised by these hundreds of interactions with foreign officials, so serious in their nature that they eventually played a part in an investigation into the Trump campaign and transition, on top of Ivanka's own meetings, added to the weight placed on the couple. This was on top of the numerous divesting and business decisions they were in the process of making, as well as personal choices over whether or not to uproot their three young children in order to ride this political train down to DC.

Nevertheless, the couple still made time for their family. In December, Jared, Ivanka, their three children, and a babysitter all made their way to the annual Kushner Companies holiday party. That year, at the end of 2016, as the family's heir apparent and his First Daughter–in–waiting weighed taking official jobs that would make them among the most powerful individuals in the world, the Kushners threw their company fête in the basement of Guy Fieri's American Kitchen & Bar—a five-hundred-seat, three-floor restaurant beyond caricature. In perhaps one of the most storied restaurant reviews in the history of the Gray Lady, restaurant critic Pete Wells poses a series of questions to American Kitchen & Bar's celebrity chef and his staff. "Hey, did you try that blue drink, the one that glows like nuclear waste?" he asked. "The watermelon margarita? Any idea why it tastes like some combination of radiator fluid and formaldehyde?" He capped it off with the age-old quandary: "Why did the toasted marshmallow taste like fish?"

None of that mattered much to the Kushners. They owned the building in which Fieri opened his restaurant and, technically, the wall on which he painted his famed "Welcome 2 Flavor Town!" slogan, which meant they got the space for their party on the cheap. They could not purport to have hosted it there because they wanted to dip a toe into "flavor town," even ironically. The restaurant's menu stacked itself with items like mac 'n' cheese in a three-cheese sauce with bacon crumbles, cornmeal-crusted shrimp po'boys slathered in Creole mayonnaise, and slow-cooked pork shank dunked in sweet and spicy General Tso's sauce—a selection of delicacies so flagrantly in violation of every law of kashruth that a rabbi examining the menu might think it a parody. The Kushners, of course, are

Orthodox Jews. They don't eat pork or bacon or shrimp, and they certainly do not mix any of those meats with milk, even within the same meal, let alone in one single dish. To get around that, Kushners brought in their own kosher caterer to handle the food for the party.

A little more than a year later, the restaurant closed its doors; revenues were not enough to keep up with the rent Kushner Companies charged. "From what I understand, it wasn't the right concept for the space in the long run," a Kushner spokeswoman said after the restaurant shuttered on New Year's Eve at the tail end of 2017. "I think he appeals to a more Midwestern aesthetic than a New York [one]."

ABOUT A week later, the Kushners took another break. Charlie and Seryl wanted to treat their kids and their kids' kids to a getaway, as they often did, and so they booked the family a villa at the Four Seasons Resort Hualalai in Hawaii. Jared and Ivanka had gone on vacation a few months earlier, as the guests of Wendi Murdoch aboard David Geffen's yacht, on which they sailed around Croatia while Donald's presidential campaign sank and floundered after his dour convention in Cleveland and his attacks on a Muslim Gold Star family who spoke out against him onstage at the Democratic National Convention. But every day felt like a year in the era of Trump. In 2016, they had welcomed their third baby; traveled across the country and back again and back again and again on the campaign trail; spoken onstage at the RNC; inserted themselves into every major hiring and firing decision; put out some media fires and started others, depending on how it served them; weathered self-inflicted crises in their shul; feuded with media executives and former friends; taken meetings with world leaders and Russian diplomats and CEOs of Fortune 100 companies; decided to move to DC; and tried to shed themselves of assets and positions that any of the thousands of people who wanted their heads could claim as a conflict of interest. With the move away from New York on the quickly approaching horizon—a move that would take them a few states south of the Kushners—and the brutal cold of an East Coast winter only just beginning, the prospect of uninterrupted time away with their family and apart from Donald, who himself was hunkered down in Mar-a-Lago, sounded nothing short of necessary.

The whole Kushner family queued up in Terminal 5 at JFK Airport in Queens and boarded a commercial JetBlue flight en route to San Francisco, in coach, as they always did when the whole family flew together for these sorts of holiday trips. They had billions of dollars, and they flew private when they needed to, but there were two matriarchs, four children, four spouses, and a mess of grandchildren and their help. Billions of dollars do not grow on trees. Coach would do just fine, at least for this leg of the trip. A private plane was waiting for them in San Francisco to take them on the final leg to Hawaii.

Ivanka, in black jeans, a navy zip-up with gray sleeves, and Puma slip-ons, her hair tousled and spilling out of her loosely tied ponytail, looked more like a normal traveler already exhausted before a cross-country flight with three kids under six in tow than an incoming First Daughter. She certainly looked more earthly than she did in the images of her fully made up and in pencil skirts or shift dresses and stilettos plastered across cable news for months on end and her own social media accounts for years.

Fellow passengers recognized her anyway. Of course they did. She was now one of the most recognizable faces in the United States, if not the world—and in New York, which had overwhelmingly voted against her father a few months earlier, one of the most vilified. Dan Goldstein, a lawyer in the city, stopped her after they boarded the flight. Overcome with the frustration built up throughout the campaign and the concern bubbling over since November, he shouted at her: "You ruined our country and now you are ruining our flight!" People around them froze. The flight crew sputtered.

Goldstein continued, "Why is she on our flight? She should be fly-ing private." Ivanka told flight attendants that she did not want to make this a whole big thing, but JetBlue ushered Goldstein and his husband off the flight. "The decision to remove a customer from a flight is not taken lightly," the airline said in a statement. "If the crew determines that a customer is causing conflict on the aircraft, the customer will be asked to deplane, especially if the crew feels the situation runs the risk of escalation during flight. In this instance, our team worked to re-accommodate the party on the next available flight."

They'd brushed it off by the time they arrived in their villa on the 800-acre Four Seasons property, where rooms start in the four figures and the three hundred homes and condos on the adjoin-ing residential community in which they stayed are valued at up to $20 million a pop. There are two championship-quality golf courses with comfort stations stocked with free bourbon and candy bars, a spa with an apothecary peddling herbal remedies made right there before guests' eyes, and attendants by the pool offering to clean guests' sunglasses or present them with chilled towels or spritz them with Evian. Billionaires like Ken Griffin, Charles Schwab, and Howard Schultz own homes there, having paid the $200,000 initi-ation fee and $40,000 annual dues to cover their use of the resort facilities. There, the Kushners were perhaps the poor kids on the tropical block. But they did have something all those other more billionaire-y billionaires didn't have: a First Daughter daughter-in-law and a son on the way to the West Wing. Not everyone there, however, saw that as a draw.

The Trump-Kushners commanded enough attention that other guests snapped photos of them reading under the cover of plush tented lounges by the pool. They caught Jared in a swimsuit with a surprising number of abdominal muscles peeking through his wiry frame, carrying their youngest son to the beach. They nabbed Ivanka in leggings and sneakers picking up breakfast from the resort's café on Saturday morning with her daughter Arabella, though it is unclear how she paid for the meal, given that it was Shabbat. Observers don't exchange money from sundown on Friday through sundown on Saturday. Writing, like signing a name or room number on a receipt, is also prohibited.

The family did celebrate Hanukkah while on the island. "This year is one of the rare and special occasions where Hanukkah and Christmas coincide. As we light the candles, sending love from our family to yours this holiday season! Merry Christmas & Happy Hanukkah," she posted on her Instagram account, under a photo of her, Jared, and their children smiling in front of five lit menorahs—one for each of them. In Jewish tradition, you add to the mitzvah by lighting multiple menorahs in your home. The idea is that the more candles lit, the more people can see the miracles God makes for those who fight for justice and truth. By the end of those eight nights, just weeks before they officially descended onto Washington, the Trump-Kushners lit more than two hundred candles.

CHAPTER 4

Born/Married/Divorced/Married/ Divorced/Married/Raised Trump

I F FATE placed Ivana Zelníčková in the little Czechoslovakian town of Zlín with her grandmother, the president of a shoe factory, and her stay-at-home grandfather, or her parents, an engineer and a telephone operator living in a two-story government compound that amounted to nothing more than a concrete box, it was destiny that allowed her to rocket herself out of it and land in a glittering triplex atop Fifth Avenue in Manhattan three decades later.

Ivana was born in 1949, a year after Stalin's coup. Her family and most others living in those little government-owned boxes were essentially trapped there, burying fruit in their little yards in the summer in hopes of something sweet in the winter. Otherwise, they would wait in line for hours at the grocery store for a taste of anything. Ivana's father, Milos, whom she called Dedo, and mother, Marie (Babi), wanted something different for their only daughter. A daddy's girl, as her own daughter would be, Ivana was taught how to ski by Dedo when she turned five years old. He also pushed her into a pool of freezing cold water and left her to figure out how not to sink. If she was going to make it out of there, she would not only need a hook, she would also have to learn how to quickly adapt and survive, as water rose around her.

By the time she was fourteen, Ivana had become something of a little star, competing in slalom and downhill ski races. She joined the national juniors ski team, which took her to Italy and Austria, and eventually allowed her at seventeen to move to Prague, where she studied at Charles University while she trained. The city soon turned untenable. In 1968 thousands of Soviet tanks rolled in, and Ivana hid out for weeks in Italy. She and her then boyfriend hatched a plan for her to marry an Austrian man they'd skied with for years and obtain an Austrian passport, allowing her to leave Czechoslovakia but return to visit her family when she wanted. In 1971, at the age of twenty-two, she said "I do" in a government building in Prague. It was a politically charged marriage of convenience that would only last long enough to assuage governmental suspicion that the whole thing was a sham—which, of course, it was. She got the passport, and they divorced in 1973. In between, she packed her bags and flew across the Atlantic Ocean to Toronto, moving in with her father's sister and brother before the divorce papers were even drawn up.

Ivana enrolled in English courses, took ski trips to Vermont on the weekends, rekindled her romance with her old boyfriend, and started working with a modeling agent who booked her in little shows in local department stores. By the time she was twenty-seven, she got a break: a runway show for which she and seven other models in town would travel to New York to drum up attention for the 1976 Summer Olympics in Montreal, modeling for Canadian designers. Initially, she turned the job down. Her father Dedo was coming to visit her, and she didn't want to leave him after he had traveled all that way. But the show had already been booked and choreographed for all eight girls. If she didn't go, her agent told her, she'd be spoiling the whole thing for everyone else.

She relented, and arrived in the Americana Hotel on Seventh

Avenue, exhausted and overheated by the July swelter that swallows Manhattan, and a bit homesick for her father. She nearly said no when the other girls pleaded with her to go out for dinner, but again, she gave in, leaving her straight blond hair spilling down over the cherry red minidress she'd slipped on, teetering into Maxwell's Plum on a pair of her high heels.

The eight models stopped in their tracks when they entered the restaurant on First Avenue at Sixty-Fourth Street. The din of voices bounced off the stained-glass ceilings and walls, a treasure trove of Tiffany lamps and ceramic animals and cascading crystals. It was a place where the likes of Cary Grant and Barbra Streisand came to dish over chili and burgers, and twentysomething flight attendants and hungry models looked for a free meal and a rich older boyfriend—of which there were many, all looking for twentysomething flight attendants and hungry models.

Donald Trump approached Ivana, who was standing at the bar with the other models while they waited for a table. He offered to tell the manager to speed the process up. A few minutes later, the models took a seat at a table in the middle of the restaurant. The only catch was that Donald joined them, eating his hamburger in a seat he pulled up right next to Ivana's. He disappeared toward the end of the meal, took care of the bill, and waited for them outside in his black Cadillac limo so that he could drive them back to the hotel. He let Ivana out of the car with a kiss on the cheek.

She returned to her room at the Americana the next day after the rehearsal for the runway show to a hundred red roses and a note that read: "To Ivana, with affection," signed Donald Trump. Moments later, he called to ask her to lunch. She parlayed it into dinner at a private club aptly named Le Club, and, at his request, a lunch the following day at the 21 Club, before she flew back to Canada. He called her most days thereafter, and soon asked her to spend Christmas with him in Aspen. As Ivana likes to tell it, she whupped Donald down the mountain on their first days on the slopes. He hadn't known that she was once a competitive skier. It felt to her like a fun joke, but to him it was a humiliation that sent him storming off in his skis.

He had sufficiently licked his wounds by New Year's Eve, when, less than six months after they'd met, as Ivana recalls in her most recent book, he breezed off what sounded like a mixture of a proposal and a threat: "If you don't marry me, you'll ruin your life." It was not exactly Shakespeare, but not quite Don Corleone, either. They hadn't met each other's families. They'd only met in person a few times. They lived in different countries and essentially knew nothing about each other. But she was inching closer to her thirties, and he was rich enough to pay for a first-class ticket to Aspen and a chalet during peak season, which for many women is the perfect shiny poison apple, impossible to resist. She said yes. They agreed to marry in April, in New York. She flew home to Montreal, gathered her stuff, and got her passport stamped on a one-way trip to Manhattan.

IVANA KNEW no one at first, including the Trump family. Close-knit enough that they shared regular Sunday lunches over Mary Trump's famous meatloaf at Donald's parents' home in Queens and Wednesday-evening dinners gnawing on T-bones at Peter Luger in the shadow of the Williamsburg Bridge in Brooklyn, the family all showed up to meet the soon-to-be Mrs. Trump over lunch at Tavern on the Green in Central Park. Prompt as ever, Donald's parents Fred and Mary took their seats, as did his brothers Fred Jr. and Robert, sisters Elizabeth and Maryanne, and all their husbands and wives and children. It was before noon, and one by one, they went down the line, ordering steaks. Ivana bucked, asking the waiter for a fillet of sole. Fred Sr. interrupted her, telling the waiter that, actually, she would have the steak like the rest of them. Ivana didn't budge. When her fish arrived, she ate the whole thing with her father-in-law's eyes glued to her.

She was less assured when it came to their wedding, having no idea how to find a florist in New York, let alone one suitable for the wedding of a fairly wealthy real estate developer with lofty ambitions. Nor did she have any sense of where they should hold the ceremony or the reception or who to put on the guest list. She invited a half dozen people who attended their six-hundred-person wedding. Donald and his secretary took care of the rest, booking the Marble Collegiate Church, where the Trump family had for years prayed from within the giant slabs of Westchester white marble, beneath the Dutch-style weather vane and the tower bell that had rung after every American president's death since Martin Van Buren passed in 1862. The 21 Club was the natural choice for a dinner reception, where comedian Joey Adams, gossip columnist Cindy Adams's husband, kept the evening running as an MC. Ivana did choose her own dress, created by a Canadian designer friend of hers.

She had never heard of a prenup, either, until Donald slid one her way not long before their big day. He told her she had to sign the agreement, a document designed to protect his family money. She relented, settling for $20,000 for each year they stayed together. At least, that's what the first version of the contract called for.

THE FLORISTS were late on the day of the wedding, though eventually they turned up with a white bouquet for her and boutonnieres for the men. Her fiancé and her father met that morning for the first time. Her mother, who'd stayed behind in Czechoslovakia, would not meet him until after they were legally wed. The church's original swinging doors parted for Ivana and her father to enter. Light streamed through the diamond-patterned stained glass, glittering on the burgundy-and-gold walls of the church as she made her way past dozens upon dozens of mahogany pews filled with friends and business associates of the Trumps, Mayor Abe Beame included. She chose a decidedly un-Ivana dress—stark white and modest, with long sleeves that billowed into little cumulus clouds at her wrists, blousy around her bust until it tapered at her waist, then formed a peasant skirt that pleated and drifted into a slight A-line. There were no great diamonds. None of the collar necklaces or glitzy earrings that would famously define her style in later years—no gold or precious jewels of any kind, really. There was no hint of cleavage. She had very little skin showing at all, in fact.

All of the drama happened north of her collarbones, where her butter-blond blunt bob fell stick straight to her shoulders, held down flat by the weight of her white tulle veil. The veil connected to a froth of a white flower crown at least a quarter-foot high that she stuck to her head. It created something of a willowy arch framing her face, which she'd caked tall with makeup. Cheeks painted a deep rouge, eyes lined on top and bottom, smudged a thick charcoal. Lips smeared an iridescent mauve. She looked older than her twenty-eight years, and scared straight, and like her head did not match her body and her outside was disengaged from her inside. Something about her seemed stunned—the face of Suzanne Somers stuffed into a late 1970s bridal shoppe fever dream. With Donald in his tuxedo and big black bow tie, his longish sandy blond hair parted deep on the left of his forehead, hanging down to the cut of his cheekbones, the couple belonged atop a wedding cake. Or, at the very least, printed across the pages of a New York tabloid.

Donald spared two days for a honeymoon in Acapulco before he jetted back to New York to square away his deal to buy the Commodore Hotel in Midtown, which would become the Grand Hyatt and his first real foray into Manhattan from the outer boroughs his father had already conquered.

Those two days were enough for Ivana to get knocked up. Donald had told everyone even before they were married that he was desperate for kids. Ivana, at twenty-eight, didn't hesitate much either. To be sure, clocks in the 1970s ticked earlier and more often and louder. The pregnancy was somewhat of a medical oddity; Ivana claims that she had an IUD implanted at the time, but she got pregnant anyway.

In fact, all three times she got pregnant, she wrote in her books, she had an IUD in—which, if true, has to make her either a statistical anomaly or the victim of serial gynecological malpractice.

Regardless, merrily along they went, planning for life as a family of three. Ivana took over more work at the Trump Organization, decorating the Trump-owned hotels and turning her attention to their interior. They looked for more space and eventually bought a new apartment in Olympic Tower on Fifth Avenue, which she out-fitted with beige velvet sofas and goatskin tables and a compendium of Steuben glass animals laid out on glass shelves and lit up with little white Christmas tea lights that they kept out all year long. It was hardly what people would call a babyproofed apartment, but that Olympic Tower home was telling of how the Trumps would always view parenthood. Their children would have to learn how to fit into their lives, not the other way around. That, of course, is the prechild fantasy all married couples repeat to themselves and their friends, both out of naïveté and necessity. Otherwise, no one would ever work up the nerve to procreate. But the Trumps, in all their militant self-discipline and self-absorption, actually made it happen for themselves. Their babies wouldn't ruin the white sectionals or break the expensive glass animals. Not if Ivana had a say.

Ivana hated being pregnant. She gained only a dozen pounds, continued to work long days, and wore heels until almost the end of her pregnancy. She made it through Christmas of 1977 before she lost patience. On New Year's Eve, a year to the day from Donald's Aspen proposal, she asked her doctor to induce, and he agreed. Don Jr. would later tell a reporter that there was something of a rush to get the whole show on the road. "My dad wanted to be able to claim me as a dependent on his taxes for 1977, so he told my mom that she had to have me before midnight," their eldest son said to *Forbes* in 2006. "And if she didn't, he'd make her take a cab home." Ivana leaves that bit out of her book. In her recollection, it was noon, and Donald told her to come by the hospital at five that afternoon. She went to a meeting, got her nails and toes done, and checked in with Donald. Within minutes after induction, she felt the urge to push. She kicked Donald out of the room. "Let him witness the birth? Never," she wrote. "My sex life would be finished after that." Twenty minutes later, their son was born.

"What should we name him?" Donald asked. She suggested Donald Jr., which made her husband balk. "What if he's a loser?" he asked. The name stuck anyway, and by eight o'clock he'd left. She threw on her mink and a boa and visited a friend who also happened to be in the hospital. It was New Year's Eve, after all, and as her friends tell it, she had something to celebrate. Donald, they whispered, had agreed to a bonus of $250,000 for each child. Happy 1978 to them all.

ON JANUARY 2 Don Jr., or Donny, as he came to be known, turned two days old. That morning Ivana sauntered into the Grand Hyatt. She felt fine—better than she had through all nine months of her pregnancy. It would be impossibly boring just to sit at home with a sleeping baby, even though that sleeping baby was hers and she had only met him less than forty-eight hours earlier. She wasn't breast-feeding, and would give all three of her children formula from day one. How could she work all day with a kid latched to her chest? And how decidedly unsexy. Nothing about it appealed.

Donald and Ivana did not let things like feedings—and the rest of the tedium that drives new parents to the depths of sleep deprivation and stir-crazy, so stuck in the sinkhole of diapers and spit-up and bottle cleaning and bathtime and witching hours that they hardly find time to wash their hair or heat up dinner—take over their lives. They had work at the Grand Hyatt to get back to. It wasn't like Donald was going to be at home swaddling and concerning himself with diaper rash. As he told Gregg "Opie" Hughes and Anthony Cumia on their radio show in 2005, Donald didn't do diapers. "There's a lot of women out there that demand that the husband act like the wife, and you know, there's a lot of husbands that listen to that," he said, at that point on his third wife and fifth child. "If I had a different type of wife, I probably wouldn't have a baby, you know, because that's not my thing. I'm really, like, a great father, but certain things you do and certain things you don't. It's just not for me." It seemed as though he never learned, because he never had to. After Ivanka had her first child, she told *Redbook* that Donald looked after Arabella all the time, but "he wouldn't know what to do if she started crying or needed a diaper change," although, she added, "I think he'd figure it out."

Donald and Ivana's way of figuring it out when they had their own children was to throw money at the problem and bring in nannies. It is not an uncommon arrangement, particularly among those who can easily afford it and have the space. For two parents working full-time, having consistent, reliable childcare is almost essential—but the Trumps took it a few steps beyond necessity. First they brought in a Swiss nanny to look after Don Jr. The strict sleep schedule she imposed for the baby and the brisk way in which she scolded Ivana for disrupting it lost her the job after a few weeks. In came a German nanny who would last five years, despite the fact that she once left baby Don in a hot bath, alone, while she took their dog for a walk, and put him on the kitchen counter as a toddler while she chopped vegetables, only to have him tumble off and break his leg.

Three years after Donny was born, another IUD mishap led to a little baby girl, whom they named Ivana Marie, after Ivana and Ivana's mother. They nicknamed her Ivanka, the diminutive of Ivana's name. A year and a half later, along came Eric. That pregnancy was not without concern. Ivana and Donald rented a cottage in East Hampton from Michael Kennedy and his wife Eleonora for eight summers. (Years later, Kennedy famously represented Ivana in her divorce from Donald.) Friends remember that Ivana spent those summer days shuffling her children to piano practice and tennis lessons. Donald would disappear, most of the time in white golf shirts, though no one could tell if he spent all that time on the links, and resurface sometime in the late afternoons, or at the least in time for sunset. He was not there when Ivana, four months pregnant with her third child at the time, took out a dune buggy and whipped across the beach, catching air as she bopped over one mound of sand after another. When she got inside, she noticed she had started to bleed, and immediately rushed to the emergency room. The baby was fine, though as Ivana tells it, Eric never let her live it down. "Eric uses it as ammunition when he says I didn't really want him," she wrote in her book. After he was born, she had her tubes tied.

With three new children and a move into the Trump Tower triplex, Ivana got rid of the German nanny and hired two religious Irish women in their place—Bridget Carroll, who instantly took to Ivanka, and Dorothy Curry, who Eric refers to as his "second mother" and who still works as Ivana's personal assistant to this day. They each worked two days on, two days off, giving each other some time to live a life outside of the Trump orbit. When they were on, they shared a little room in the children's wing of the triplex, which happened to take up an entire floor.

THE CHILDREN'S floor, spilling into the entire sixty-eighth floor of Trump Tower, sat atop the family's triplex. Ivana chose to decorate the sixty-sixth floor, the most public-facing of the family home, in a megadose of what is known as the classic Trump aesthetic: beige onyx floors inset with brass; fabric banquettes gilded with twenty-four-karat gold; low-slung ceilings covered in more gold leaf and a Michelangelo-style mural, the latter having caused quite a skirmish between Ivana, who insisted it feature cherubs, and Donald, who much preferred warriors. He ultimately won out, boasting that the painting's quality was in line with that of the Sistine Chapel. The staircase was mirrored, the railings bronze; just about everything else was gold or crystal or lacquered or, at the very least, shiny. And then there were the views—all of Central Park bloomed and the skyline glittered, depending on from where you looked, giving the place the feel more of a dictator's palace than a family home for five plus staff.

The children's floor itself could have fit several normal New York apartments within its walls, but at least it looked like it belonged to a family. There was a little kitchen, off of which was the room where Bridget and Dorothy alternately stayed. There were two guest bedrooms, one suite primarily for Ivana's parents, Dedo and Babi, who spent months each year tending to the kids, and one for anyone else who came to stay overnight. Each child had his or her own bedroom. Don Jr. settled on blue and white for his room, and covered the walls with posters—a Grateful Dead one, another, for *The Terminator*, read "I'm back." His bedroom floor was littered with lacrosse sticks and tangled sneakers and the mess a normal young man accumulates. Ivanka lined her lilac walls with Madonna posters and shots of the cast of *Beverly Hills 90210* and shelves filled with china dolls and delicate glass animals and silver picture frames and stickers stuck haphazardly about. Her white wrought-iron bed backed up into a frilly floral fabric, and a drapy lilac canopy hung above it. The floor-to-ceiling windows put her face-to-face with Central Park as soon as she opened her eyes every morning. Eric's room, yellow and white and bright, did not have his sister's view.

The floor also had a playroom, with stacks of Legos and Lincoln Logs, toy trucks and cars, videotapes and a big-screen TV, a game system and a couch and blankets and enough going on to entice Michael Jackson, their neighbor in Trump Tower, to regularly come over to play video games with the kids. (Ivana's recent book makes clear that her children were never left alone with Michael when he came around; either she or the nannies supervised the visits.) The kids would play in other parts of the triplex, too, raiding Ivana's temperature- and humidity-controlled fur closet, sneaking minks and coats of any little animal off their hangers and back up into their quarters. How could a kid build a proper fort without those, anyway?

* * *

THAT THE kids lived like little princes and princess did not mean they were always treated as such. Ivana, Dorothy, and Bridget kept them on a military schedule: up at the crack of dawn for breakfast, down some forty floors within Trump Tower to visit their father in his office before the nannies took them to school. Afterward Bridget and Dorothy would pick them up and, most often, take them to their scheduled after-school activities. Eric took painting classes at the Museum of Modern Art. Don Jr. primarily stuck to sports and anything that kept him outside or running around in Central Park. Ivana studied piano for a few years, even playing at a party her mother threw for Kathy Keeton, whose husband, Bob Guccione, had founded *Penthouse*. She took up ballet too, before she grew too tall and no longer wanted to miss her family's Christmas vacations to rehearse for the *Nutcracker* performances she would appear in at Lincoln Center, as part of the New York City Ballet's annual production. Twice she was cast in it, first, aptly, as a "party scene girl," and then as an angel, in a long white dress with gold stars sewn onto it, gold trim around the collar and hem, and a round gold halo atop her pulled-back blond hair. Michael Jackson turned up that year to watch her from backstage, which, understandably, caused quite a stir within the company. As soon as the other girls caught wind of his impending arrival, they hatched a plan to each wear one glove as they performed, as a nod to the Prince of Pop's sartorial bent. The adults in the room chastened them, nixing the idea before they got anywhere near the stage.

Afterward the children would come home, stop in for some more time playing on their father's office floor while he rolled calls, and went upstairs to the triplex for an early dinner prepared by the nannies. Ivana and Donald would get dressed for their nights out, with Ivanka sometimes helping her mother choose which cocktail dress to wear that evening or watch her apply her makeup at her vanity, before the children said their prayers with Dorothy and Bridget and were tucked into bed, and Donald and Ivana hopped in the limousine downstairs.

Ivana was strict about her children's daily schedules; she ruled with an iron fist in just about every area, even though she left much of the day-to-day operations to Bridget and Dorothy. "My mother was much stricter than my father when we were growing up," Ivanka once told an *Evening Standard* reporter. "She was the disciplinarian. She is European and a great athlete. You didn't mess with my mother." She recounted how her mother would pull down her pants and spank her in front of her friends until she was about ten years old. "People are shocked but she didn't chase me around with a whip."

None of Ivana's children is shy about the fact that she would spank them from time to time, and neither is she. "Mom was not afraid to spank," Eric wrote in his mother's book. "If one of us messed up, he or she was punished, so we learned to behave." Ivana told a story of Don Jr. misbehaving at a dinner with the whole Trump family—Fred and Mary and the sisters and brothers and children—at Gurney's, the resort overlooking the ocean at the tip of Long Island, in Montauk. Her son was making faces and banging his silverware. For many elementary-school-aged kids, that may be what some parents regard as normal behavior out at a restaurant. For the Trumps, particularly in front of Donald's parents, it was simply unacceptable. Ivana took Donny to a hallway away from the rest of the family and spanked him a few times before telling him to shape up. For the rest of the dinner, he sat stone-faced and quiet.

Around the same time, Don Jr. took another few lashes for no reason at all. His sister Ivanka had been playing a game with her brothers at their home in Greenwich in the glass solarium, which was filled with the kinds of fancy, fragile things many parents with young children remove from their homes. The Trumps' solution to this was to have separate rooms or wings in which the children were permitted to play and eat and socialize, and the rest off-limits, a rule enforced by the nannies when the Trumps were at work or out to dinner or attending parties. The kids found ways around the system, of course. The three siblings decided to toss around a tennis ball inside, and to do so in the solarium, where their mother had chosen two porcelain chandeliers to hang over the informal dining table. When Ivanka tossed the ball a little too hard and a little too high, directly hitting one of these, the chandelier crashed to the ground in tiny, expensive pieces. Ivana came back from work in time to see the mess, and demanded to know who was to blame. Ivanka piped up first. It was Donny, she told her mother. And so Donny, without uttering a word in his own defense, took a few spanks from Ivana. He was a lucky kid, mostly, but no one catches every break.

HOWEVER TIGHT Ivana kept her children's schedules, and however much they came to fear her retribution, there was no question how truly fortunate and overwhelmingly privileged they were, living the way their parents themselves wanted to live. No child is born demanding a silver spoon. It takes a parent or a grandparent or a family to strive for that kind of life and pass it on to unwitting descendants. Those descendants, knowing little else, learn to expect it, and either opt to strive for the same material objectives their parents reached for and pass them along to their own children or actively reject that existence and forge their own paths.

In most meaningful ways, all of the Trump children chose the former, despite occasional minor rebellions. When you consider the sort of childhood the Trump children had, it is not difficult to imagine why they never wanted to wander far. Around the time when Eric was born, in the mid-1980s, the Trumps purchased a home in Greenwich, Connecticut—much closer and with far less traffic than the cottage they'd rented in the Hamptons for years. At the time, Donald was working like a madman, and Ivana was in charge of the Trump Organization's business in Atlantic City. It was an easier trip back to Manhattan for Donald at the end of a weekend away, and a seaplane could whisk Ivana off the backyard dock that dipped into

Long Island Sound and back to the casinos. Donald payed $4 million for the 5.8-acre estate built on a peninsula near the tip of Indian Harbor Point. The house itself, all 20,000 square feet of it, had been built in 1939 by a local superheater executive, and the facade looked much like that of the house Donald would move into with his third wife in early January 2017. The front door of the white Georgian Colonial mansion was buttressed by a grand portico not unlike a miniature version of the one at the front of 1600 Pennsylvania Avenue. The interior was just as grand. There was a three-story rotunda and a sweeping double staircase, where the family would set up a Christmas tree at least twenty feet tall as they celebrated Thanksgiving in the house. Adorning the tree with all of Ivana's Czechoslovakian crystal bulb ornaments took weeks. The formal dining table sat twenty. There were dozens of bathrooms and bedrooms, a bowling alley, and a ten-car garage, though Ivana says she took to driving the family's limousine up to the house from the city herself, with their kids and nannies and pets strapped in the back. Donald never joined them for that.

Once they arrived in Greenwich, the family settled into a routine. Eric and Don Jr. explored the woods for hours on end; Ivanka and her brothers cultivated a few little side hustles to earn some spending money of their own. They once fashioned fake Native American arrowheads that they would bury in shallow ditches they dug in the woods, then pretend to uncover in front of unsuspecting friends, offering to sell them each rare, uncovered treasure for the low, low price of $5 a pop.

Ivana recalled Greenwich as providing them some freedom from their mother's low-grade paranoia and image control. In the city, Ivana would not let her kids set up a lemonade stand on Fifth Avenue, nor were they allowed to do so in the lobby of Trump Tower. (They were not permitted to go trick-or-treating with their nannies alone on Halloween, either; the Trump security team would inconspicuously trail behind as they went door-to-door on the Upper East Side.) In

Greenwich, though, they had the autonomy to sell lemonade at their leisure. It was rich, suburban America, after all, and if young heirs couldn't be free to make even more money off powdered Country Crock, then this was not the nation its founders intended to create. The only trouble, as Ivanka saw it, was that the houses were perhaps *too* sprawling, the neighborhood *too* private at the end of the cul-de-sac on which their own estate stood. "In every other respect, this was a prime spot, but it was a dead zone for aspiring lemonade magnates," she wrote. Here's where their good fortune came in yet again. The family had a bodyguard on staff, and several maids, and all sorts of household help financially indebted to the family. They "took pity on us," Ivanka recalled, though undoubtedly that is not the precise emotion they felt for the children as they "dug deep for their spare change" until the kids had recouped enough money for the day. "We made the best of a bad situation, I guess," Ivana recalled.

The kids shared their home with dogs and parakeets and hamsters and a little white mouse with beady red eyes that Eric and Don begged their parents to bring home from school one summer under the condition that it live in the garage, which it did, until it escaped and bred a teeming family of little white mice with beady red eyes, and the whole lot of them were unceremoniously evicted. They once took in an injured duck they'd found not far from the mansion; it lived happily in Don Jr.'s bathtub for a few weeks, until they released it back into the wild.

GREENWICH WAS close and convenient and august and cozy in the Waspy sense, but the winters were cold and dark, and for New York couples looking to hoist themselves up to a certain rung of society, as Ivana was so keen to do initially, Palm Beach was the great frontier. Like Jay Gatsby before him, Donald set out to find his West Egg manse farther down the Atlantic coast.

Initially he plunked down a security deposit on a place at the Breakers, the historic hotel built by an oil and railroad tycoon and modeled after the Villa Medici in Rome, where society snowbirds take in ocean views and nibble on Sunday brunch under the main dining room's thirty-foot frescoed ceiling. But the resort could not accommodate Donald's desire to combine two penthouses, creating something of a Sunshine State version of his Trump Tower abode. The problem was, he didn't exactly know where to look. As he later recounted it in *Trump: The Art of the Comeback*, he was sitting in the back of a car on the way to a dinner party one evening in the winter of 1985. As he looked out the window at the estates along the way, he asked the driver, "What's for sale in town that's really good?"

The driver pulled up to Mar-a-Lago, the 118-room, seventeen-acre palace that cereal heiress Marjorie Merriweather Post had built in the Gatsby era—a new-money real estate mirage if there ever was one. As its name—Spanish for "sea to lake"—suggested, Mar-a-Lago stretched from the Atlantic Ocean to Lake Worth. Post scattered a potpourri of architectural styles and design themes from a handful of different countries and time periods across the 118 rooms—58 bedrooms, 33 bathrooms, a ballroom, a theater, a dining room—and over 110,000 square feet. The clay roof tiles and some of the marble used inside came from a castle in Cuba. A Persian tree-of-life motif adorned the entrance gateway, inspired by Moroccan souks. Overlooking the water's edge were Venetian arches, and 1920s pastoral scenes were custom painted on the Steinway piano on display inside. Post bought a collection of 36,000 hand-painted fifteenth-century Hispano-Moorish tiles from Spain to use throughout, and commissioned Florence Ziegfeld's set designers to paint Florentine frescos on panels in the formal dining room. The room that originally belonged to Marjorie Post's daughter, Dina Merrill, and later became known among the Trumps as the Ivanka Room, had its own stone fireplace with ceramic cherry blossoms winding around it and all across its walls. An eighteen-year-old Walt Disney painted a castle on the room's rug, as well as the nursery-rhyme-themed story depicted on the tiles bordering its bathroom.

By the time Donald took a walk-through in 1985, the place had been essentially abandoned for a decade and was languishing on the market. Post had willed the estate to the US government when she passed away in 1972, prophetically envisioning Mar-a-Lago as a winter White House to be enjoyed by presidents and visiting dignitaries for years to come. The reality was that the presidents in that era didn't much fancy Florida and that sort of glitz, and the government did not much care for the idea of carrying the property's million-dollar taxes and huge yearly maintenance fees. In 1981 the Carter administration handed the keys back to the Post Foundation, which had even less of an interest in that financial hurdle than the government did. So it listed the estate for $20 million. Until Donald, no one really bit.

The way he tells it, he swooped in with a startlingly low offer they had no choice but to accept. You see, he offered $2 million for a little beach lot in front of Mar-a-Lago, which the foundation had previously unloaded for a fifth of that price. The *Washington Post* reported that Donald said he bought it through a third party and "threatened to put up a hideous home to block Mar-a-Lago's ocean view." The structure, he joked, would be his "first wall," more than two decades before the one he proposed on the 2016 presidential campaign trail. "That drove everybody nuts," he said. "They couldn't sell the big house because I owned the beach, so the price kept going down and down." He didn't actually close on the beach lot until the whole deal went through, but ultimately, the Post Foundation accepted Donald's final offer. He took possession of the estate and all its furnishings for $8 million.

THE TRUMPS' move into Mar-a-Lago was part *Beverly Hillbillies* and certainly all a show. Unsure of what to do with all that space and how to tastefully fill it on her own, Ivana decided to keep much of what Marjorie Post had filled her mansion with, down to the worn fringed sofas and the original Sheraton table in the formal dining room. She sprinkled her touch in the silver picture frames placed around the house, stuffing them with magazine covers on which Donald appeared. Once they had all landed in Palm Beach, a Rolls-Royce would take Donald and Ivana the few miles to their estate. (Donald sometimes insisted they fly on separate planes, fearing that they would all die together in a horrific plane crash.) A second car— usually a station wagon—would be there to transfer the kids, the nannies, the bodyguards, and whoever else came along with them.

"In fifty years Donald and I will be considered old money like the Vanderbilts," Ivana reportedly told the writer Dominick Dunne. A number of her friends noted that the Trumps put on airs as if they already were, and as if the money were far older than that. As Marie Brenner reported in *Vanity Fair* at the time, her acquaintances joked that Ivana suffered from "imperial couple syndrome." She ditched the Hollywood version of rich she'd first adopted when she moved to New York and married Donald, to fit the mold she thought a Mrs. Trump should fill. Once in Mar-a-Lago, "she had become regal, filling her houses with the kind of ormolu found in palaces in Eastern Europe. She took to waving to friends with tiny hand motions, as if to conserve her energy. At her own charity receptions, she insisted that she and Donald form a receiving line."

Ivana claims to have received actual royalty at her own Palm Beach Palace in the late 1980s. Prince Charles, in Wellington, Florida, as the guest of honor at the International Polo Club, on short notice requested a tour of Mar-a-Lago. Ivana says he turned up not long after the request and found himself quite impressed with her home. As she tells it in her book, Don Jr., Ivanka, and Eric all approached him and shook his hand, offering him tea and small talk. (He turned down the former in favor of something stronger, she wrote.)

Donald had a royal vision of his own. He constantly told friends that he thought he and Princess Diana would make a great couple. "This is the way Donald's mind works," one longtime friend recalled.

"He said that so many times that it did not take long for the story to morph in his mind. Soon, it became that Diana had wanted to date him, had been dying to date him. And he believed it. He truly did. He believes his own lies and creates his own realities."

THE KIDS' reality was not much closer to earth. Many of Don Jr., Ivanka, and Eric's winter weekends were spent shuttling back and forth between New York and Palm Beach, particularly in the first few years after their parents purchased Mar-a-Lago, where they always returned for spring breaks and for Easter. Winter breaks were often spent in Aspen. The family flew out before the holidays and took up three suites—one for Donald and Ivana, one for the children, and one for Ivana's parents, the nannies, and security—in the Little Nell, a posh ski-in, ski-out hotel at the foot of Aspen Mountain that stored the Trumps' Christmas ornaments for them and let them drag a tree through the lobby and up to their rooms. Like all true kids of privilege worth their salt—though their competitive skier of a mother and competitive-in-general father also had something to do with it—the three younger Trumps learned to ski almost as early as they learned to walk. Their parents put the kids in the Powder Pandas ski school until they were sturdy enough on their feet to make it down the mountain with a private instructor, and their mother insisted that they stay on the slopes all day, no matter how cold or tired they were or how much they did not enjoy skiing at first. Eric, in particular, hated it. His mother, he wrote in her book, bribed him with McDonald's apple pies if he went through the motions. He loved the pies enough to suffer for them.

Until the start of the 1990s, the family stayed in Aspen to the first of the year, through the kids' whole winter breaks. They would celebrate Don Jr.'s New Year's Eve birthday in a small celebration with family and friends in town and cake before Donald and Ivana left for their own evening out with friends. Once they returned to New York, they'd shut down Wollman Rink—the ice-skating rink in Central Park that Donald owned—for a proper celebration with Don Jr.'s classmates. Sometimes, since Eric's birthday was only a week after Don's, they two would share their party. Ivanka's birthday falls the day before Halloween, so she got to have costume parties, often at the Plaza Hotel. That the Trumps owned the Plaza too—a theme unto itself—made that easy to pull it off and, almost as importantly, free. All of the kids ultimately had birthday parties there, whether in costume for Ivanka's birthdays or in little suits and ties and party dresses for the rest. The staff would transform a meeting room with balloons and an open bar and pass hors d'oeuvres. About a hundred people would come by, watching the mini Trump heirs blow out candles stuck into the multitiered cakes the Plaza's pastry chefs had painstakingly prepared for the occasions.

Well before he started elementary school, Don Jr. spent his summers in Czechoslovakia with Ivana's parents, Dedo and Babi. Ivanka got her own time away, too. Ivana would bring her along to couture shows in Paris, where the small circle of New York women she palled around with would fly twice a year to sit among magazine editors and the people who graced their pages. They would stay at the Plaza Athénée, the storied century-old hotel with a view of the Eiffel Tower out one eye and the Champs-Elysées out the other.

These trips were all dazzle and fantasy and escape, with the added bonus of being an opportunity for Ivana and her little Ivanka to spend time alone together, without the nannies, her brothers, and Donald and Atlantic City and the Plaza sucking up all the oxygen. It was a front-row look at the life Ivanka could choose for herself, both as a model, if she wanted to put in the work, and as a woman who could spend her adult life traveling across the Atlantic to watch hand-sewn confections worth tens of thousands of dollars being paraded down a well-lit runway, if she chose to play the same kinds of cards her mother had to get there.

In the summer of 1991 an airline lost both Ivana's and Ivanka's luggage, meaning that all the designer outfits Ivana had packed for the two to wear to the shows were circulating somewhere in an airport's ether. They were due at a Versace show not long after they landed. Fortunately for Ivanka, her mother happened to have worn a brightly colored blouse on the plane, which she tied and pinned to fit the ten-year-old. It looked good enough to impress the designer himself.

Ivanka did, of course, decide to become a model for a time in the mid-1990s. In the summer of 1997, before she started her sophomore year at boarding school in Connecticut, she cohosted the national broadcast of the Miss Teen USA pageant, which, again, her father happened to co-own. After being introduced as "a young teen who has taken the runways of high fashion by storm, the exquisite, adorable, beautiful Ivanka Trump," she sauntered onstage in a shiny strapless silver snakeskin dress that barely hit a third of the way down her thighs, her curled hair swept up into an ornate, prom-like swirl. Her cohost, the soap star J. Eddie Peck, twenty-three years her senior, took one look at her and mused that "they didn't make them like that when I was fifteen." She told him that she loved modeling but thought she would end up going into business once she graduated from school. "Well, gee, I hope there's someone out there who can help you get your foot in the door," he joked as the camera panned to Donald, sitting front row in a tux alongside Ivana in a white satin gown, a bleached-blond Eric, and Ivana's mother, Babi. Ivanka—with no television experience and all the insecurities of a normal teenager—fumbled through the rest of the live broadcast as the resident "teen expert." She had not quite yet mastered the art of hiding the fact that she was forcing a smile on as she delivered her teleprompter lines, nor the scramble in her brain as she tried to work out, on the spot, whether she should respond to Peck's off-the-cuff jokes. She did manage a few interviews with the contestants, a wardrobe change into a shimmery lavender velvet gown, and a scripted joke of her own after the swimsuit competition. "I can guarantee my brothers were loving that," she said to the camera. "Are any of you up there single?"

Her brothers took on odd jobs that were not nationally broadcast nor as glamorous. But they too wanted to earn their own spending money. All three hustled to learn the tricks of the Trump trade that would ultimately give them a head start on their jobs as executives in the Trump Organization. It is fitting that Ivanka's earliest gigs were on television, as the public face of the family and apple of her father's eye. By contrast, Donny worked as a dockhand at Trump Castle, helping guests on and off the boats and carrying their luggage and doing whatever odd jobs the marina master came up with. He cut grass on the Greenwich property, too. Once Eric was old enough, he and his brother would stay over in the caretaker's cottage on their father's Seven Springs property in Westchester, New York. Up at dawn and at the job site by 7:00 a.m., the two worked on renovating the main mansion under the watchful eyes of the experts who actually had to be there to pay their bills. One of Donald's longtime friends—a golf partner and business contemporary—recalled meeting Donald for a round of golf on the Westchester course one sweltering August day in the late 1990s. He'd never met any of his friend's children before. When Donald asked if he wanted to pop in to say hello to his eldest, Don Jr., he said, "All I remember was how hot and muggy it was out there, and as we walked toward the house, we approached Donny, who was on all fours wearing kneepads, laying bricks down in front of the house. That is not necessarily what I would have thought his kids would be doing on a day like that."

THAT IN 1990 it all unraveled in the winter wonderland Donald and Ivana and their children escaped to each holiday season, on the eve of Don Jr.'s twelfth birthday, is a dark sort of poetry—a coda for the end of the gilded, everything-is-just-perfect-and-we-belong-here-aren't-we-so-lucky Trump family epoch.

In truth, though, it began years earlier, on Madison Avenue. Donald walked right up to a young blonde, a god-fearing small-town Georgia peach who'd turned down a mother-daughter *Playboy* spread when she was a teenager but took home the top prize, bikini clad, in the Miss Hawaiian Tropic pageant. She had moved to New York City in 1985 with dreams of becoming a famous actress. The reality was less rosy; she fell into living with an ex-cop turned broke actor, both of whom might have traded a limb to book a little role on one of the soaps. Marla Maples had seen Donald Trump around town a few times before, and it took not much more than the line-iest of lines—"Don't I know you?"—for her whole world to quake, for all the Good Book's preaching about fidelity and faithfulness to fall away. Donald was charming and handsome, and he really *saw* her. Mostly, though, he was rich. He was famous. He was her way up.

He was also, inconveniently, married. "I never had respect for anyone who didn't honor their marriage vows," Marla told *Vanity Fair* in 1990. But she and Donald started meeting in the pews of the Marble Collegiate Church, the same chapel where Donald and Ivana had exchanged marriage vows eight years earlier. Those vows, though, before Ivana started flying back and forth to Atlantic City to run his hotels there, were a decision he later referred to as a grave error. "I think that putting a wife to work is a very dangerous thing," Donald later told *Primetime Live*. "I think that was the single great-est cause of what happened to my marriage with Ivana." A "softness disappeared," he added, the "great softness" she'd once showed him, once she started taking some of the reins within his company. "She became an executive, not a wife." She was good at what she did, "but when I come home and dinner's not ready, I go through the roof." Ivana's professional schedule grew to irritate him almost as much as her social calendar did. He had not come down with the so-called imperial couple syndrome that her friends joked inflicted his wife. He'd already tired of the social elbowing she was just starting to dig into.

So maybe what Marla's Baptist preacher back home in Dalton, Georgia, could not quite understand was that "Till death do us part" doesn't take into account all the ways money and power and fame and ego can creep into a quickie marriage's cracks. How could he know how a wandering eye and a hot little bottle blonde could light a match with a throwaway pickup line on Madison Avenue and, within months, burn everything down?

"He was there—because he was married and I didn't see it ever being anything more," Marla said in the interview, defending the infidelity every fiber of her moral being had screamed was wrong, until she caught a glimpse of the kind of life it could offer her. "We can't really judge till we're there," she added. "I found that out."

THEY STARTED meeting off Madison Avenue and outside the Trump family church. He snuck her down to his Atlantic City hotels when he knew Ivana wouldn't be around. Donald and Marla tucked into his limousine, his driver making clandestine little circles around Manhattan with them in the expanse of the back seat. In the fall of 1987 Donald put in a cash bid to buy a 280-foot yacht—a vessel with a helicopter pad, five decks, a hundred cabins, room to accommodate fifty-two crew members, a master suite with a tortoiseshell ceiling and a ten-foot-wide bed, a dressing room with a barber's chair leading into a bathroom that boasted a shower with thirteen nozzles in the shape of a scallop shell that a team of guys had spent a year carving out of a single slab of onyx. He renamed the yacht the *Trump Princess*, and on it Marla became something of an undercover queen.

It all seemed like a fairy tale, apart from the fact that there was still legally another queen in the picture—one who knew nothing of the fantasy playing out behind her back, disrupting the version of the fractured fairy tale *she* thought *she* was living out with Donald. The way Ivana saw it, the *Trump Princess* was an extension of *her* kingdom, as was Trump Castle in Atlantic City. She ruled them, owned them, ran them. Certainly to her they were not free zones wherein her husband could stash his southern mistress. So when Donald shoved a foot-tall stack of papers in front of her on Christmas Eve of that year, she had no idea that her husband was asking her to redo their prenuptial agreement because a photographer from Atlantic City was threatening to blackmail him with photos he'd snapped of him and Marla. She was preparing to host the whole family at their home in Greenwich. She had no lawyer there. How could she even think about it at a time like that? But Donald pressed and pressed, and so she relented. He'd later say the revised prenup would give her $25 million and the Connecticut mansion, though the number was closer to $10 million, with an additional $12 million should they sell the Greenwich house before they got divorced. She would also get custody of the three children. It would be years before the number came up anyway, because Donald was able to keep the whole thing quiet, until it wasn't, atop a snowy mountaincap in Aspen on the eve of a new year.

MARLA ANN MAPLES spent much of the summer of 1989 working on her tan on one of the *Trump Princess* decks as Ivana worked in Atlantic City. Occasionally Donald would kick her off when he knew his wife was due to come aboard. He had the same crew catering to both women. As was the case in Atlantic City, too, and at the Plaza, and in the Trump Organization office in Trump Tower, where Donald's assistants toggled between the boss's first wife and his number-one mistress, who often assumed a fake name when she called to speak to her beau. She even joined a few members of Donald's family, including his sister Maryanne and her son David, along with some other friends aboard a helicopter from Atlantic City back to New York. When David, unaware of Marla's relationship with his uncle, struck up a conversation with the young blonde, Donald nearly yanked him away. "That's not for you," he told his nephew. Maryanne had to sit her son down and explain, "Well, that's your uncle for you."

Donald did as much juggling and explaining to both blondes as anyone. Marla grasped the basic outline of the situation: Donald was unhappily married, but the Trumps' tangled finances and the ceaseless attention that followed them, to say nothing of the three children, all under twelve, who would be impacted by any marital disturbance, made things complicated. It was Ivana who was blind to it all, consciously or otherwise. Sure, Donald would throw fits about her priorities and her social climbing, but he never told her just how miserable he was. In his book *Surviving at the Top*, he wrote that he put down the phone with his wife after what he describes as "years of deadlock." She had just run through their plans for another night out in New York. Hanging up, he declared to no one in particular, "My life is shit!" Nor could Ivana know that his distaste for the state of his life was made more bitter by the knowledge that the sweet-as-pie Marla Ann's tanned, uncomplicated twenty-six-year-old arms were open wide, waiting for him. "I have to confess, the way I handled the situation was a cop-out," he wrote. "I never sat down calmly with Ivana to 'talk it out,' as I probably should have."

Unsurprisingly, other people did the talking for him. Ivana first heard whispers of the existence of a Marla in the weeks leading up to Christmas of 1989. Donald by that point wanted to offload the *Trump Princess*. Yachts cost a pretty penny, long after you pay the $30 million to buy them, and he needed the money. He asked Ivana to come with him to Tahiti, where they would show the boat off to possible Asian buyers. She heard murmurs about another younger woman on the trip, but brushed them off. When she got back to New York, the *Post*'s gossip-column stalwart Cindy Adams approached her at a party at the Waldorf Astoria. Adams asked if the rumors about Donald cheating were true. They weren't, as far as Ivana knew.

But everyone else, it seemed, knew better. Donald had been flying Marla to Aspen on his plane or his friends' planes, and Aspen is a small town with a rumor mill always churning. People had seen Donald and Ivana together in town for years, and now they were talking about the new woman he had his buddies shuttling in. Word was that Gary Triano, a real estate developer and serious gambler from Tucson, flew Marla on his plane. (Later Gary and his wife, Pam Phillips, spent time with Donald and Marla, inviting them to a Wildcats game in Arizona, where the four of them were photographed. In 1996 Triano finished a round of golf at his club, got into his car, and was promptly blown into a million little pieces when a pipe bomb placed there by a hit man detonated. The blast was so powerful it sent debris flying some two hundred yards in the air. It took until 2014 to bring the case to trial, but Phillips was convicted of first-degree murder. She is currently serving a life sentence in a federal prison in Arizona.)

Right after Christmas, it was Trump's plane that picked Marla up in Tennessee and headed west to Colorado. He put her up in a three-story penthouse at the Brand Building, with views of the mountain at the base of which Donald and Ivana and the kids would be staying at the Little Nell for a reported $10,000 for the week. They all ran into each other on the ski lifts that week, though they kept enough distance, at least initially, for everyone to keep it together.

The next part of the story is told a few different ways, depending on whom you ask. As Ivana tells it, she and her family were eating lunch at Bonnie's, *the* place for anyone skiing in Aspen that week to stop for a midday meal on their way down the mountain. Out of nowhere, a blonde she had never seen or heard of before came right up to her as she, Don Jr, Ivanka, and Eric waited in line for food. "I'm Marla, and I love your husband," Ivana remembers her saying.

"Do you?" said Ivana, who then told Marla to "get lost," and said that she loved her husband.

The same basic facts appear in Marla's version, though the details diverge. Ivana knew who she was by that point, Marla contends, and laid into Donald once she saw Marla at Bonnie's, shouting loudly enough to raise the eyebrows of everyone who'd stopped in off the slopes. It was Ivana who charged up to *her*, Marla recalls, and started screaming at her, before returning to Donald and continuing to yell.

"She couldn't pronounce my name, but she was asking me if I was Moola or whatever," she said in an interview not long after the fight. "And she just asked if I was the one who had been loving her husband for years."

The way locals and other vacationers retell it is a mixture of both versions, sometimes with the added detail that Ivana told her friend to approach Marla and "give her the message that I love my husband very much" before they directly confronted each other. Stories of this sort and magnitude are sponges. They expand, grow denser, weightier, and start to stink as time passes. They're retold until the witnesses are blue in the face.

Those who witnessed the whole thing that day in Aspen may not be sure who started it, but they do remember what ended it. There was so much yelling that everyone at the restaurant was mortified on behalf of the children. "It was horrible," one local Aspen woman who was there that day said. "The words were flying back and forth so fast, and I felt sorry for the kids. For the whole family, really, I felt so badly." Don Jr. was on the last day of being eleven. Ivanka was eight, and Eric five. When they heard Marla shout, "It's out! It's finally out!" and Ivana bellow at her to stay away from her husband and her family and how happy her marriage was, they knew it was a story they'd have to commit to memory, because everyone would ask what happened that day for years to come.

The fighting continued that night back at the Little Nell, where, again, it was hard for the kids to escape. They didn't leave Aspen, as Ivana initially wanted to do. They kept up appearances, and the next night Don Jr. turned twelve, while his parents left the fact that his family was crumbling around him in a way they could never rebuild unaddressed.

Back in New York, they continued to hold up with spit and phony smiles and quiet desperation. Ivana and Donald went on as normal. Each went back to work. They slept in the same bedroom. They continued to hide what was going on from the children. Marla, meanwhile, reentered the Trump-style witness protection she'd endured for years.

The miracle was that all of those people at Bonnie's, who could barely hold in the gossip as it was happening, were tight-lipped enough that the New York papers could not confirm the story for weeks. Ivana mostly disappeared for a few weeks, returning in time for an event in the Plaza's ballroom looking almost unrecognizable—her face pulled tighter, her chest enhanced, transformed into a tragic blond Jessica Rabbit. No one, even at the event in her own hotel, among close friends, recognized her until she opened her mouth and that unmistakable accent flew out. If there was still anyone in her circle in New York not yet convinced about the tales of a catfight in Aspen between Ivana and Donald's other woman, they fully believed once they caught a look at the work she had done. She looked different and, frankly, sensational enough that the rumors had to have been true.

Donald sat for an interview with *Playboy* at the end of January, and the flimsy wall they'd built around themselves all but crumbled. When the interviewer asked, Donald answered that his marriage was "just fine" and praised Ivana for being a "very kind and good woman," with "the instincts and drive of a good manager." But as a wife, not a manager? "I never comment on romance. She's a great mother, a good woman who does a good job." But is marriage monogamous, to you? He dodged. "I don't have an answer to that."

He went on to say that he never spoke about his wife, "which is one of the advantages of not being a politician. My marriage is and should be a personal thing."

It wasn't so for long. Liz Smith from the *New York Daily News*, who had heard rumblings about what happened on the mountain in Aspen but couldn't quite nail it, caught onto these quotes. Smith had socialized with the Trumps for years, jetting off with them to parties in cities across the country and sitting with them at dinner parties and luncheons. They weren't friends, exactly. She was a gossip columnist teetering on the tightrope separating access journalism and conflict of interest. It was not out of character when she picked up the phone and dialed Donald. She asked outright if the rampant cheating rumors were true. If they were, she said—and by now, she knew they were—she would print them in a way that was sensitive to what was happening to his family. He did not deny the affair. He told her he would think about it and hung up.

After that, Smith wrote to Donald, warning him that it could turn out far worse for him if he didn't let her write the story. It was Ivana who called Smith in early February. It was essential that they meet, Ivana said, privately and quickly, and she gave her the number of a suite in the Plaza and asked her to wait there. "She threw herself, sobbing, into my arms," Smith wrote of that meeting, years later. Ivana admitted that Donald was having an affair, that he no longer loved her, and that he couldn't be attracted to anyone who had a child. Not even the work she had done did it for him. "Mostly," she wrote of Ivana, "she wept." Ivana's other friends at the time remember how hard she tried to keep it together for her children, but every time they saw her, as one close confidant at the time recalled, "Ivana was on the floor, completely devastated. How much of a help could she really be to the children?"

Donald was in Japan at the time, due to fly home on Sunday, February 11. That morning the story ran on the front page of the *News*, with "Love on the Rocks" scrawled across it in big black type. "Ivana Trump Is Devastated 'That Donald Was Betraying Her,'" the headline ran. At the top of the page was a black block in which the paper declared it "Trump: The War." Smith started off her column saying that Ivana still loves Donald and still wants to be his wife. "But the bottom line is—she won't give up her self-respect to do it. That's why, despite the glitz, the parties, the riches, and the preeminence of being one half of the Trumps of New York City, Ivana drew the line."

She continued: "Intimates say she had every chance to continue being Mrs. Trump by allowing her husband to live in an open marriage so that he could see other women. But she had no idea, friends say, that he was seeing any woman at all, this has come as a terrible shock to her."

Donald called Smith from his plane that day, as he flew back to the firestorm awaiting him in New York—though not even Donald, the media genius he and millions of others claim him to be, could have predicted the five-alarm that had only just begun its blaze. He congratulated Smith on the scoop, and gave her a statement of his own. "It is better for Ivana and me to separate at this time," it read. "I am leaving because I want to leave. Ivana is a wonderful woman and a very good woman and I like her. We might even get back together. I can't say we won't. Who knows what could happen?" He denied that his involvement with any other woman was anything but strictly platonic. "Just friends and that's as far as it goes."

Donald and Ivana met for an hour at the Plaza the following day, where Ivana told him she wanted the hotel as part of her settlement. Both sides lawyered up. Donald insisted that the last iteration of their prenup was iron-clad. Her lawyers would argue that it was void, with Marla already in the picture. The *Post* reported that Ivana threatened another suit after she was locked out of her office at the Plaza and his PR folks trashed the work she did for the Trump Organization.

There was a Ping-Pong match in the New York tabloids—one delicious nugget printed across the *Post* one day, an even more salacious headline in the *Daily News* the next. It was the 1990s version of yellow journalism—gold-plated journalism, perhaps—and sales at newsstands went through the roof. "They Met at Church!" one headline read. "Separate Beds," another.

As unrelatable a figure as Ivana had become in her years as Mrs. Trump, it was hard not to sympathize with her humiliation, especially as photographs of Marla started to surface. The coverage, at least from the *Daily News*, started to bend in that direction. "Ivana is now a media goddess on par with Princess Di, Madonna and

Elizabeth Taylor," Smith wrote in one of her columns. Smith was by her side as she exited a birthday lunch Ivana's friends threw her on Valentine's Day at La Grenouille, right off Fifth Avenue in Midtown. All of the ladies who were invited, including Donald's mother, Mary, and his sister-in-law, Blaine, brought heart-shaped gifts for the guest of honor (both Trump women toasted Ivana, who vacillated between laughter and tears in her red dress). As the emotion swelled inside the restaurant, so did the crowd outside. Police cleared cars off the street and held streams of people back as the women left the luncheon arm in arm, cameras flashing in Ivana's face. "Don't forget to smile like Jackie Onassis!" one friend shouted to Ivana as she headed out into the mayhem. She could hardly hear it over the crowd around her cheering her name and yelling "Get the money!" Days later, the *Post* ran its "Best Sex I Ever Had" headline—a quote it attributed to Marla speaking about Donald, though she denied saying anything of the sort. As Don Jr., Ivanka, and Eric made their way to school that morning, the paparazzi who'd started trailing them to get photos held up the paper and asked the children their opinions on the headline. Inside school, some of their classmates reminded them of those words on the front page throughout the rest of the day.

Don Jr. immediately blamed his father. "How can you say you love us?" friends of the family told *Vanity Fair* the twelve-year-old bellowed at Donald. "You don't love us! You don't even love yourself. You just love your money." Donald swore he would stop seeing Marla, but when photos surfaced of the couple at an Elton John concert, Don Jr. burst into tears. Ivana told Liz Smith that all of her kids were suffering. "The children are all wrecks. Ivanka now comes home from school crying, 'Mommy, does it mean I'm not going to be Ivanka Trump anymore?'" As for her six-year-old? "Little Eric asks me, 'Is it true you are going away and not coming back?'" Mary Trump wrung her hands to Ivana: "What kind of son have I created?"

One longtime friend of Donald explained that it wasn't his children's suffering that got to him. He didn't once put up a fight for custody, or actually stop seeing Marla to ease their pain. What got to him, at his core, was that the press had turned so starkly in Ivana's favor. Far worse than taking his children, she was going after his money. The combination was lethal. His animating principles were then, as they are now, being well liked and accepted, or at least respected, and at the very least thought of as very, very rich. The feuding with Ivana, the lawsuit she filed, and the unyielding coverage of both made him crack. Donald raged to anyone who would listen—and even those who had no interest—that it was bullshit. It was unfair. And it needed to stop.

"Why don't we walk down Fifth Avenue together for the photographers and pretend that this entire scandal has been a publicity stunt?" he asked Ivana over the phone, a few weeks into the whole public mess. "We could say that we wanted to see who would side with you and who would side with me."

She never agreed. Instead, she started digging deeper into his soft spots. She charged thousands of dollars for a set of Pratesi sheets to his card—a necessary expenditure for an eight-year-old Ivanka, she explained. "'Why does a seven-year-old need $7,000 worth of sheets?" he blew up at a lawyer. She had her lawyers push forward on a lawsuit contending that their marital contract was void, asking for what friends at the time recalled was somewhere close to $1 billion. "She wants a billion, but we just don't have it," Marla later told *Vanity Fair.*

She was not wrong about that. At that point in time, Donald was leveraged to within an inch of his life. He had millions upon millions worth of personal debt guarantees, on the Taj Mahal, on the Plaza, on the Greenwich mansion, and on Mar-a-Lago and the *Trump Princess* and the Trump Shuttle, along with personal guarantees to Bear Stearns for his positions on American Airlines and Alexander's. The *Wall Street Journal* reported that the total amount he personally guaranteed could exceed $600 million. Thus, in the year of his very public separation, Trump suffered what could have been, to him, an equally gutting blow: *Forbes* slashed his estimated net worth to $500 million, down from $1.7 billion a year earlier. The estimate knocked him out of the so-called three comma club, perhaps the only club he ever cared about being part of.

WHILE ALL of New York tuned its eyes on the former golden couple, the blond mistress who'd exposed the cracks between them had all but vanished. There was little else for her to do. Ivana'd had years to get used to the spotlight, though the glare had never been as blinding and harsh and constant as it was in the winter of 1990. She'd courted the press and befriended reporters and columnists as part of her planned ascent into the circles in which she wanted to run and gossip pages on which she wanted to appear. She cultivated a close-knit group of friends who also understood what that glare could feel like and how to manipulate it to show one's best angles. It helped that she had two nannies who could take her children to school, security and drivers to shield her when she went out, restaurant hosts as friends who'd welcome her despite the hoopla, and—if all those things fell away—a triplex on Fifth and a hotel on Central Park in which to console herself, and three children who needed her there. It is true that she'd never thought she would turn up in the press the way she did after news of her divorce broke. She was dejected, degraded, and in pieces. But she had the blueprint of a system for how to keep things as together as she could, a skin toughened by years in the tabloids, and a stubborn, competitive streak not unlike Donald's that made her not want to shrink away and hide.

Marla had no such conditioning at the time when her image was splashed for weeks on end across the pages of *People* magazine and every paper in New York. She'd made some waves in Dalton, in the rolling foothills of the Blue Ridge Mountains. She was a star volleyball player at Northwest Whitfield High, and she had been elected homecoming queen in her senior year. She dropped out of the University of Georgia after a few years, making her way to Atlanta to pursue modeling. In the meantime, she competed to win Miss Resaca Beach, a local carpet-industry beauty contest in which the winner could take home $2,000 and the chance to host carpet shows for $150 a day. She came in fourth runner-up at Miss Teen Georgia, but snagged the title of Most Photogenic anyway. In 1985, at the age of twenty-one, she entered the Miss Hawaiian Tropic International pageant in Daytona Beach, Florida. Filling out the contest's entry form in a hurry, like the other blondes with bikinis in their luggage and checking accounts counting on a win, Marla scrawled in what she saw as her "long-term goal" for the judges. "I hope to become successful as a screen actress some day and do Broadway," she wrote in her bubbly script. She won the pageant that day, posing with her official sash over her teeny iridescent blue string bikini and white kitten heels, the Farrah Fawcett hair she perfected blowing in the breeze coming off the ocean behind her.

That year Marla made it to New York, landed on a Delta Airlines billboard in another bikini, made a onetime appearance in an episode of *Dallas*, and scored a split-second role in the Stephen King flick *Maximum Overdrive*, in which she was crushed to death when a truck carrying watermelons dumped its cargo on a car she was driving. She'd had no time to develop the thick skin and the support system Ivana had built up over the years as Mrs. Trump before her name and face were everywhere as Mistress Trump. "Trump Mistress Close to Suicide," one headline said. Others promised details of their secret hotel "romps" and rendezvous behind Ivana's back.

Donald shuttled her off to Southampton when the news first broke. His buddy Larry Russo's beach house out there was empty, so she hid out inside the mansion of a man she'd never met (later, once she had met him, and could look back on the whole period as something of a frenetic blip, she joked to friends that he'd renamed the home "Marla Lago"). Once photographers and reporters figured out her whereabouts, she made it down to the Jersey shore, bunking at another one of Donald's friend's houses outside Atlantic City. For two months she lived like a method actor preparing for a role, though this was not some part she would play onscreen. It was her real life, whether she was ready to fully grapple with that or not. She donned a red wig and a straw hat when she went out, though Donald hired a bodyguard to protect her, and she used service elevators and entered buildings through dark garages so no one could see her, anyway. She used her friends' names when calling Donald—a system his assistants accepted with eye rolls.

It was the part of a lifetime for a budding actress, and she gave it her everything. But it wasn't all the coquettish games and self-inflicted wounds that found-out mistresses of powerful men sometimes have to endure. There was real pain in realizing that her newfound celebrity meant finding out how much she was worth to the people she once trusted. Her old boyfriend sold his story to the *National Enquirer* for what she thought was $11,000. Dogged paparazzi started following her family around their small town. High school friends and neighbors blabbed about her to any reporter who would ask—and many did. Marla lost ten pounds from the stress before she flew away from it all, staying for nearly a month with a friend in Guatemala City who had served in the Peace Corps. Finally, she felt at ease. No one knocked on her door. Camera crews weren't peeking through the windows. But her absence didn't help the story die down; perhaps it even prolonged it. By the end of March, Donald told her it was time to come back and face it head-on.

From there, the full-blown public relations romance offense took off like a rocket. They made their first outing together as a couple in Atlantic City—what was once Ivana's domain—at the grand opening of Donald's new Trump Taj Mahal at the beginning of April. By mid-month, Marla agreed to sit down with Diane Sawyer in what would be the highest-rated installment of *Prime Time Live* in its history on ABC News at the time. They taped the interview in the home in which she hid out in Atlantic City before their coming out, Marla in a peach suit, her curls brushed out into a blond 1990s halo, a gold band around her left ring finger—an intentionally far cry from the oiled-up string bikini photos the press had been printing of her in the weeks and months leading up to the sit-down. "I didn't want to bring any more havoc into my friends' lives," she explained of her weeks in isolation. "I knew I had to get away. I knew I needed to turn off the television, not read newspapers, just not be affected by words. I needed to get back to what's real." She had turned down million-dollar offers to sell her story because she felt she had to "keep a bit of dignity," and the story really had to do with other people's problems. "I don't think I would be able to face myself. This isn't the publicity I want. This isn't the way I envisioned my life to be."

As for those "problems," she insisted they had nothing to do with her. "People just grow apart," she said of Donald and Ivana. "I believe that that's a very sad and very serious thing between two people, and I would've only hoped that it could have stayed more private. Everything happened so fast that I wanted to be very careful about the decisions I made."

As for those careful decisions, including the one to make it even less private by talking to Sawyer, she told the anchor that it was Donald who insisted that she do the interview, because "he hated the fact that I felt like I had to be in hiding. I mean, he has a lot of sympathy for how we've been besieged by all of this and I think he wants to see me come out looking okay. He's very sorry." She, too, wanted to stick up for herself and her family. "My family has been so besieged by the press, and I feel like it's time that I step out and I take the heat for a bit for what they've had to go through." She expressed sympathy for Ivana, whom she called an "absolutely beautiful woman."

"I feel like she's gone through a lot of pain," she said of Ivana. "You know, I, I can't lie about it." She blushed. "Oh, I do. I do love him." Would they marry? "I'm taking my life day by day," she de-murred. "I mean, who knows what life is going to bring in the fu-ture."

Marla was reluctant to answer specifics about her relationship with Donald, like how they met and the extent of their affair, which she downplayed anyway. "I don't feel like at this time it's appropriate for me to say," she said, citing "pending litigations" between Donald and Ivana, in which she might be called to testify.

Donald did not give any more answers about Marla in an inter-view he did with Larry King on CNN that week, calling the press "very dishonest" and saying that much of what was printed about his relationship with Marla was lies and made-up stories. As for the attention those stories have gotten, he didn't shy away from that. He recalled that the news of his matrimonial distress broke on the same day that Nelson Mandela was released from prison. Mandela, he said, "is probably calling up, 'Who is this guy? He blew me off the front page.'"

Marla followed her debut by accepting an invitation from *Time* to attend the White House Correspondents' Dinner in Washington. She was red meat to a drooling Washington press corps hungry for a piece of a juicy story that, until that spring evening, they had been entirely left out of. More than two hundred people crammed into the *Time* prereception at the Washington Hilton, an affair where most people typically look around the room midconversation in search of someone better they should be talking to. That night, everyone's eyes were on the doors, waiting for Marla to walk through. Once she did, she was mobbed. Ed McNally, the White House speechwriter responsible for President George Bush's monologue for the event, asked partygoers to introduce him. *Saturday Night Live* comedian Dennis Miller, the headlining entertainer at the annual dinner, brought Marla up in his remarks in front of the 2,500 people sitting in the ballroom. He cracked a joke about Donald before looking out in the audience toward his girlfriend, saying, "Kidding, Marla.

Kidding. I love him too." The crowd erupted as he alluded to her recently aired interview on ABC: "I think she should have asked Diane Sawyer if Mike Nichols was the best sex she's ever had."

There is little question why *Time* wanted Marla as its guest. The better question was why Marla wanted to go in the first place. She had never had to face a live line of press before. Besides, the evening is dry and dull even for people whose whole social calendar revolves around it and never get to dress in black tie or see a comedian and a sitting president poke fun at themselves and people in the room. "It's a very elegant affair," she explained to reporters. "I felt like this would be a chance for me to meet people more one-on-one and express who I am. The president is here. Mrs. Bush. What better environment than this?"

Mrs. Bush, it turns out, was equally as fascinated by Marla. The next morning, she chatted with reporters after attending Sunday worship services with the president at St. John's Episcopal Church across the street from the White House, admitting that she was disappointed not to have seen Marla at the correspondents' dinner. Stuck at the head table with her husband and heads of the White House Correspondent's associations, she never got a chance to "catch a look" at the tabloid curiosity, as she had hoped, she joked.

Donald tried to continue the spectacle once he saw that Marla had turned into a budding media darling. He negotiated a deal with *Playboy*, reportedly in the seven figures, but Marla blew it up. She wouldn't pose nude, and with that off the table, *Playboy* was little interested. Marla had been in itty-bitty bikinis in every other glossy and paper; they weren't going to pay that kind of top dollar for the goods everyone had already gotten for free.

By the end of summer, Marla had started handing some things out gratis. Even with Madonna sitting in the Trump Organization box at the US Open in Queens, Marla was still far and away the story, at least for the New York press, and she was far too busy to much notice. While the pop star took in the match from the seats outside, Marla sat inside signing eight-by-ten photos of herself in a hard hat and cutoff shorts for the hordes of photographers and kids who had lined up asking for pictures and autographs.

BETWEEN WEEKENDS at Mar-a-Lago and in Martha's Vineyard and Atlantic City, Marla managed to meet the Trump family. The way she saw it, things went swimmingly. "It was just like going over to my grandparents'—very solid, very relaxed," she told *Vanity Fair* in her interview that fall. The Trumps saw it somewhat differently. Maryanne, Donald's sister, and Blaine, his sister-in-law, supported Ivana through the spectacle of the breakup and the subsequent divorce proceedings, frequently and openly criticizing Marla. "The Clampetts" became the nickname for the Maples family among the Trumps, in reference to the fish-out-of-water family from *The Beverly Hillbillies*. The Maples had gripes of their own. Publicly, they were all smiles and support and fronts united. To close friends, though, they noted that of course Donald was a narcissist, and the Marla charade was just a symptom of that disease. They made their feelings known to Donald's associates at the time, through not-so-subtle snide comments here and there. "Can you remind your friend to visit his mother?" they would repeat in the jokey, passive-aggressive tone all family members use when they are actually dead serious. In his lucid moments, Fred Trump, Donald's father, who was suffering from dementia, weighed in, saying that he ought to stay with the mother of his children.

The Maples were initially bewitched by the spoils and flash Donald offered their daughter, but once the initial love haze wore off and the reality of the disruption of their quiet little life in Georgia by a brash big-city bigwig more than fifteen years their daughter's senior set in, their tunes changed.

AS TEPID as the rest of the Trumps were toward Marla, Donald's children were, understandably, far colder, both toward their father's girlfriend and their father himself. That Ivana would retain custody of their three kids in the event of their divorce was the one piece of the prenuptial agreement Ivana had signed under great pressure from Donald on that Christmas eve years earlier that neither Donald nor Ivana contested. After their tense meeting at the Plaza, after Smith's scoop about their split in the *Daily News*, after Donald moved tens of stories down from Trump Tower triplex to another apartment within the same building, Ivana sat the kids down one by one to tell them what was going to happen, though she herself did not yet know how it would all play out. To Eric, she told the least. He was still so young, and really only needed to hear that he was very much loved and that his life would change very little. And mostly, that was true. Unlike most children when their parents separate, his mom and dad would continue to live under the same roof within the same building, albeit on different floors. But the Trump kids already slept on a separate floor from their parents within the triplex. Both of their parents already went out most nights, so it was not as though their evening activities would change dramatically, either. Both parents had been working so much and so separately that it was not as if they'd see them less, either. They would still go see their father before and after school in his office, as they had before the marriage fell apart. As far as divorces went, the Trumps was perhaps among the most publicly dissected and salacious. But they had not been present parents to begin with, and their lives would still mostly operate within Trump Tower, as they always had. In terms of day-to-day changes, the split was relatively easy for the kids to digest.

The emotional side—their father leaving their mother for a younger woman, and the confrontation playing out in front of their eyes in Aspen and then relived in gross detail for months in the paper—was a different story, particularly for the two older children. Some of Ivanka's friends had parents who were divorced, so she understood the concept, though she still asked if there was a chance her parents would get back together. It took her quite some time to let go of the idea. A decade after the split, in an interview with *The Mail on Sunday*, Ivanka was still saying that she would not be totally shocked if her parents somehow found their way back to each other. "I know probably every child of divorced parents hopes that they'll get back together, but I'm old enough to have outgrown that whole thing," she said in 2000. "I do think that in lots of ways they were ideally suited. Perhaps it was because they were just too similar and both so stubborn that they had too many clashes, but I reckon if they did get remarried within the next 10 or 15 years, the chances are it would work this time around, because they know everything about each other—the best and the worst."

At the time of the divorce, at the age of eight, Ivanka clung to her father even more. She's admitted that she sees any other woman in her father's life as competition, and the fear that he might replace her or not always be around for her led her to visit him more in his office, call him more when she was at school. "I got angry with him," she told the *Daily Mail* in 2006, but she did not turn her back on her father—not necessarily because she forgave him or felt as though he deserved her attention, but because she couldn't help herself. "I'm such a loudmouth that giving him the silent treatment would only seem to be punishing me, rather than him," she said.

Don Jr. had more willpower, and more anger toward his father too. Perhaps that is because Ivana told him the full truth: his father had a mistress, and the divorce was Donald's fault. Without hesitation, he stopped talking to his father. He beat up a couple of classmates at Buckley who brought up some of the headlines about his mother in school. Ivana kept the kids away from the papers—as much as she could, at least, in an environment in which photographers would hold up the front pages to get their reactions as they made their way to and from school—but they would sneak looks when she went to her friends' houses. Even some of Eric's little friends knew enough to bring it up in class.

No containment strategy could keep them from the pandemonium after the "Best Sex I Ever Had" headline ran. Within days, Ivana instructed her staff to start packing the family's things, and asked the kids' teachers to start forwarding their schoolwork. Donald's plane was fueled and ready for them by the time Ivana, Don Jr., Ivanka, Eric, Babi, Dedo, Dorothy, and Bridget came down the elevator in Trump Tower and into the waiting limousine, into which their suitcases had already been loaded. They flew down to Palm Beach and pulled into Mar-a-Lago, where they would stay for three months—the three months in which Marla started making her way back from Guatemala to New York and into the public eye. Each day, the children would do the homework assignments their teachers dutifully sent each morning; they'd take tennis lessons and go swimming and fish with Ivana's father and splash around on the beach. Helicopters would fly overhead sometimes to catch photos of the family who'd fled the chaos in New York, but mostly, they found peace in Palm Beach, in the middle of what would have been a constant barrage had they stayed in New York. Ivana made sure of it. Even now, away from the bedlam that had followed her out of La Grenouille for the Valentine's Day luncheon, the paranoia those weeks had instilled in her lingered in Palm Beach. She kept the staff at the mansion as bare-bones as she could manage—though that's not to say she went without the maids, security, nannies, landscapers, and maintenance crews she'd become accustomed to—to limit the number of people who could sell stories about the family.

They stayed there until May, returning in time for the kids to finish up the school year in New York. Though Don JR. still wanted little to do with Donald, they had to spend some time with their father, since Ivana agreed to let him take their children on some weekends.

Eventually, that meant spending time with Marla, too. "I hated Marla initially," Ivanka admitted in an interview years later. She lost it when she saw Marla put her hair up in the sort of golden twist her mother fancied, and the photographers, seeing her from behind, took her for her mother. "Ivana! Ivana!" they yelled, to get her attention for a snapshot. "She's *not* Ivana," Ivanka growled at them. Together the three siblings would spy on their father's girlfriend, a mini Nancy Drew and Hardy Boys trying to collect evidence of her betrayals and misdeeds to present to Donald, in hopes of turning him against her and getting her out of their lives for good. "We'd spend hours spying on her, trying to catch her on the phone saying something awful about my father," Ivanka told the *Mail on Sunday*. "We thought that if we could catch her being nasty, we could report back to my father . . . and he'd get back together with my mom." The kids played the same game with Ivana, pressing their little ears to doors to overhear her conversations with friends and lawyers, try-ing to glean more about what was going on with the divorce.

With so much in flux, Ivana inconsolable, and Donald consumed with himself, the kids leaned on Babi and Dedo. They'd flown back to Czechoslovakia once the kids returned from Mar-a-Lago to New York in the spring, but Ivana took her children to stay with them for a few weeks in July. They came back in time for Don Jr. to move to Pottstown, Pennsylvania, to start his first year of boarding school at the Hill School.

IT IS not hard to understand why Don Jr. wanted to get away from it all. In one year, his parents had blown up at each other on the mountain in Aspen on the day before his birthday, their marital discord then playing out so publicly that he got chased to school by gossip hounds and teased by his schoolmates to the point where he felt like he had to throw punches. For a Trump, being sent away for school was not so novel an idea; after all, Fred and Mary had sent an unruly Donald to military school as a kid, and Ivana had left home as a teenager to escape an oppressive regime in Czechoslovakia. But for much of his life, Donny had always seemed to get something of a raw deal within an otherwise undeniably lucky life. His first nanny had left him in a tub of water alone, and on a kitchen counter that he tumbled off, breaking his leg; his sister had blamed him for breaking the precious chandelier in Greenwich, leading to a few strikes on his backside at the hands of Ivanka; his parents' public spat played out over his birthday.

Until Don went to boarding school, his only experience with life outside his gilded bubble was with his Dedo. In Greenwich, they'd set up a tent on the edge of the Long Island Sound and cast lines to reel in fish. At their grandfather's suggestion, Don and Eric would venture into the woods and disappear for hours. At Mar-a-Lago they'd catch tuna and mini sharks straight from the Intracoastal Waterway at the edge of the club's property. Since he was a young kid, Don had been spending about half of his summer break at Ivana's parents' home in Czechoslovakia—speaking to them in their native language so much that when he returned, especially in his youngest years, other mothers at his school often wondered who the little boy in Sears clothing with a Czech accent was, until they realized that he was the eldest Trump boy and simply spent too much time with his mother's parents abroad. With Dedo, Don learned how to hunt, fish, shoot an air rifle, aim a bow, climb rocks, and appreciate the beauty of getting lost in the woods for hours alone, not returning until well after dark.

"My grandfather was a blue-collar electrician from what was then communist Czechoslovakia," Don Jr. told a hunting publication in the early stages of his father's presidential bid, noting that his grandfather saw the charms of growing up in an affluent family in New York City. "While he recognized clearly some of the benefits of that he also probably recognized a lot of the downfalls of that." Don came around to his grandfather's way of seeing things once he hit his early teenage years and the stress within his nuclear family and the reverberating chaos started to weigh on him. "It was sort of a mess, reading about that every day as a young kid growing up, in that stage where you think you are a man but you're not really yet," he recalled. "So it would be great to get out of New York."

That Buckley, Don's prep school in Manhattan, counseled him

out of the school, telling his parents he would be better suited else-where, made the decision even easier. He could leave the ghosts haunting him in Trump Tower—the media scrutiny, the simmer-ing contempt for his father and the new blond model who hung on his arm—for the peace and quiet and relative normalcy that a fairly low-key boarding school would allow.

The Trumps settled on the Hill School, located in the steel-country sticks in Pottsville, Pennsylvania, a town of 22,000 about 40 miles outside Philadelphia and 120 from Trump Tower. The school, founded as the Family Boarding School for Boys and Young Men in 1951 before it changed its name to Hill a quarter of a century later, sits on two hundred acres. In its first years, it charged students, some of whom boarded and some of whom came for English, Greek, and Latin courses, $200 per year. Today, it costs boarders nearly 285 times that. It is now co-ed, and male students are required to wear coats and ties to class. Twice each week, students must attend nondenominational chapel services. The school colors—blue and gray—were chosen as a symbol of reconciliation between the North and South after the Civil War. All students operate under the motto "Whatsoever things are true."

This was a fresh start for Don Jr., who, for most of his twelve years had been regarded as the rich son of a rich father with a flashy mother and a flashy apartment and a well-known last name that, at least in New York and Palm Beach, stood for a comically public and opulent way of life. None of that brought him happiness, and all of it is what he wanted to leave behind in New York and scrub as clean as he could at the Hill School.

His parents brought him to school in a limousine, which didn't exactly set him up for that kind of clean break. Hoping to get them off campus and away from his new classmates as quickly as possible, Don Jr. suggested that they have dinner as far away from Hill as possible. There weren't many options in and around Pottsville in the early 1990s, but the Trumps obliged as best as they could. When the local Taco Bell broke it to Ivana that they did not, in fact, have the Chablis she ordered with their tacos, she took it in stride, as she did when the register did not have change to break the hundred-dollar bill she tried to pay with. Luckily, their driver agreed to find another store that would make change for them. As much as Don Jr. hoped all of this would be the end of Page Six following his every move and chronicling his parent's foibles as they related to him, they somehow caught wind of the fact that Ivana had to make a stop at a local Kmart to get her son some items she'd forgotten to buy him, things like sheets and towels and shampoo—things a kid moving into boarding school dorms might need, yet inexplicably got overlooked. They ran a photo of the superstore on the cover. The story spread as wide as the *Houston Chronicle*, which reported a week later that the family "stopped at a Kmart and filled two carts with items for their son." As for their behavior, Donald and Ivana were "very civil" to each other in the store, and "when the items were totaled, Donald handed the woman behind the register an American Express card but was refused." At the time K-Mart apparently did not accept American Express, so he offered cash instead. According to the report, "an assistant store manager would not say what the Trumps spent."

Don Jr. had learned his lesson by the time he arrived on campus at the University of Pennsylvania years later. Former classmates remember him driving up in a dirty pickup truck. "Talk about trying to come off as the anti-rich kid," one Penn friend joked. "It was very much a statement, not that anyone couldn't see right through it," another recalled.

That October, about a month after Don Jr. moved to Hill and his siblings started back in classes, Dedo had a heart attack, followed by a second one a day later. He died at sixty-three in Ivana's hometown. She hopped on Donald's plane with her shell-shocked children, and after the pilot dropped them off, he turned around to New York to pick up Donald and his mother Mary, who would fly right back to meet them in time for the funeral. Paparazzi hid in the cemetery to snap shots of them at the gravesite—the boys with blond bowl cuts and suits and ties, Ivanka with her hair swept back in a braid, standing in height order beside their parents and a priest, all holding flowers and weeping. The anguish hung from the baby fat of their cheeks as they placed their wreaths on Dedo's grave, honoring a man who had been far more a dad to them in the conventional sense than their own father. For the moment, Donald draped his arm around Ivana, but he would soon be back in Marla's grasp in New York. Dedo *had* done things with them. He'd taught them things. He'd sat with them for dinner and let them know that if they grew up to be kind and appreciative and unspoiled by all of their spoils, they would be loved not because of their money but despite it. For the second time that year, a man they idolized left them, and nothing would ever be the same. For the second time, too, the leaving spoiled one of their birthdays. Just as the Aspen showdown had played out just before the celebration of Don Jr.'s twelfth birthday, Dedo's funeral took place on Ivanka's ninth.

A LITTLE more than two months later, in a Manhattan dressed up in its Christmas best, with millions crowded around department store windows and hundred-foot trees with their thousands of lights and crystals, Donald and Ivana's lawyers met in front of New York State Supreme Court justice Phyllis Gangel-Jacob. After thirteen years of marriage, and just shy of a year after the Bonnie's incident in Aspen, the judge granted the couple a divorce, citing cruel and inhuman treatment by Donald as grounds. Donald wasn't in the courtroom, but his attorney, Jay Goldberg, said that the grounds for divorce were based on his very public year with Maples, and that was the real cruelty in the situation. "It caused Mrs. Trump to have anxiety and sleeplessness. The claim was that media attention to the relationship supposedly between himself and Miss Maples in

1990—that's important, 1990—caused Mrs. Trump to endure pain and suffering that amounts to cruel and inhuman treatment."

Judge Gangel-Jacob said that unless the couple could come to an agreement about the equal division of property and the validity of the premarital and postmarital agreements, the two would be forced to head to trial, where these things would be decided for them. The two sides were so far off that initially a trial seemed likely. Ivana's lawyers were pushing for half of what Donald said he was worth, at the time upward of $5 billion. The truth, of course, was that he was worth far less, and the year around his divorce had nearly brought his business to its knees, forcing him to ask his lenders for money to help pay off his bills. There was no gussying up Donald's financial reality. You can squeeze only so much out of a cow with no milk. Short on cash and with miles of debt, Ivana realized that she'd do better to take what money was there now than wait for more that might or might not come. And there was the danger he could file for personal bankruptcy, which would put her in line behind Donald's many hungry creditors.

On a Saturday in late March 1991, they reached a settlement. Ultimately, what they agreed to that day did not afford Ivana much more than she'd agreed to when she signed the redone prenup Donald presented her on that Christmas Eve years earlier. She ended up with $14 million—$10 million in cash and a $4 million housing allowance—along with the Greenwich estate. Donald also had to pay her $650,000 a year, broken down into $350,000 in spousal support and an additional $100,000 to support each one of their children. It also spelled out that Ivana was entitled to one month out of the year at Mar-a-Lago. Donald got the Trump Tower triplex in the agreement, though Ivana and the children stayed for another few years before Ivana moved out to a townhouse of her own and Donald moved back in with Marla. Donald was so cash-poor that he reportedly needled his bankers for the $10 million to cut Ivana the check, but was promptly turned down. He got it sorted, and everything was signed and delivered on that early spring weekend day.

Ivana was in Palm Beach the day she signed the papers, not far from where Donald was also staying. She was preparing to host one of the ladies' weekends she'd started hosting after the divorce—a small group of coiffed women doing their best Jane Fondas in Lycra and leg warmers, sweating by the pool during the day, swigging something harder as the afternoon rolled along. Ivanka would go along with her mom, crafting place mats out of seashells or construction paper for each guest. In her mother's book, Ivanka recalled getting up on the stage in the Mar-a-Lago screening room dressed up like Madonna, belting out "Express Yourself" and "Vogue" to a round of applause.

While Ivana toasted her girlfriends as the ink dried on her divorce settlement, Donald held a scheduled press conference announcing his plan to liquidate his ownership of Trump Plaza of the Palm Beaches, upward of sixty condominiums that he'd bought for $40 million in 1986. He borrowed $60 million to finance improvements—all of it cash he needed and needed now. At the end of April, he unloaded all sixty-three of the stalled waterfront apartments he had on his hands. He said at the time that he walked away breaking even.

OFFICIALLY SINGLE, Donald spent a good deal of time with Marla in an apartment in Trump Park, another building with his name on it on Manhattan's East Side. With Ivana legally out of the picture, they could freely be together for the first time in six years, which certainly had to be a relief. It also had to make it feel real, and real is often not what draws a fortysomething married man-about-town to a wide-eyed twentysomething aspiring model. Once the real sets in, well, where's the fun in that?

Donald and Marla knew that, which perhaps is why they would pick at each other and push each other away. They would not settle into the dull, steady rhythm most couples do, because Donald saw what that did to his first marriage, and Marla was living what happened when the man she loved got bored by that and strayed away. So they fought. They teased each other. She knew enough to grow paranoid about what he would do behind her back, and he didn't much care to give her peace of mind. It was all about him. He made her a star, and she was lucky, and if she didn't act as such, she could and would be replaced. Add the self-destructive tendency that made Donald almost want to get caught, and they had all the makings of a perfectly toxic pairing. On that, they both got off.

They broke up and got back together within the span of one issue of the *New York Post* going to press and the following day's paper going to bed. There were promise bands and diamond rings worn and rejected. And then there was a phone call from someone called John Miller that threatened to end it all for good.

On June 26, the *Post* splashed a photo of Marla and Donald smiling next to each other under the headline "It's Over." "The Donald boots Marla from his East Side Condo," the bold text below the photo read. Donald had apparently dumped Marla in favor of an Italian model named Carla Bruni. Word started spreading that Donald felt caged in. He had been married for so long, and the pressure he felt from Marla and her family to settle down didn't feel right. It was too soon. Plus, in his mind, Bruni and every other model and actress in town was after the new bachelor, and who was he to turn their advances down? As long as they complied with one request Donald reportedly made, that is. The known germophobe was scared straight of sleeping around for fear of what he could contract. All of his dates, he told people, would have to go to his doctor and submit to an AIDS test.

A reporter from *People Magazine* reached out to Donald to get in on the Carla-for-Marla swap, and within minutes, a man calling himself John Miller phoned back. Miller, of course, was Donald himself, posing as his own spokesperson. The voice was unmistakable, and all of Donald's friends and everyone within the Trump Organization knew he did this kind of thing. So Donald, as John Miller, unleashed on the *People* reporter. He truly didn't care what Marla had to say. As for other lovers, his light was on. "Beautiful women call him all the time," he said of himself, and if it were to come to marriage, "then that will be a very lucky woman." Bruni wasn't the only one he claimed to be dating at the time, creating something of a woman-on-woman fight club for his attention and affection. "Competitively, it's tough. It was tough for Marla and it will be tough for Carla."

Bruni flatly denied the rumor in the months after. "Trump is obviously a lunatic," she said. "It is so untrue and I'm deeply embarrassed by it all. I've only ever met him once, about a year ago, at a big charity party in New York." To this day she denies it (she would go on to marry Nicolas Sarkozy, becoming for years the First Lady of France).

People played the tapes for Marla, who immediately identified the voice as Donald's. She was no longer taking his calls. "I'm shocked and devastated," she said, listening to Donald speak that way about her and fessing up to seeing other women. Doubts about Donald had been festering as she went through the motions as his mistress, publicly living the improbable happy ever after. This stomped all over whatever delusions she had left. "I feel betrayed at the deepest level. My friends and family have been praying for me for a long time, and this may be the answer to their prayers." In response to him, she mustered up a southern, "Baby, you're on your own."

She herself started praying after she fled the Trump Park apartment to the Connecticut home of Frank and Kathie Lee Gifford. Donald couldn't take being shut out that way. And so he caved and gave Marla what he knew she was after. He turned up in Connecticut when the Giffords were at the White House for a state dinner and handed Marla a little box from Harry Winston with a big 7.45-carat emerald-cut diamond, set in platinum, with sixteen graduated channel-set baguette diamonds along the band. Marla said yes, yes, yes. (In 1999, she sold the thing for $110,000. It was resold to a private collector in June 2016, weeks before Donald was officially named the Republican nominee in the general election, for $300,000.)

The next morning Gifford broke the news on her ABC show *Live with Regis and Kathie Lee*, and Donald called in to dish. "She's something special. It worked out great," he said. "We've decided this is the thing to do."

The reality was that the ring was a shiny, expensive guarantee of absolutely nothing. Even after their engagement, Donald felt wishy-washy toward a second marriage and toward Marla in general. She hardly let him get away with it.

Donald would dump her, go out, make certain he was photographed that night with a pretty young thing, and make even more sure that it would wind up in the paper. He would publicly pick on her. A friend who sat with them for dinner at Mar-a-Lago one evening remembers Donald turning to him and saying, "Don't you think Marla looks terrible tonight?" The friend froze. Marla was beautiful inside and out, the friend managed to get out, and Donald was lucky to be with her. "Yeah, yeah, yeah, but you have to admit, she looks really terrible." Donald was partly joking in the dry way he tended to, but, in part, he meant it. Marla had lost weight, hoping that shedding a few pounds might kick-start her fledgling acting career and finally land her a part. That meant she lost some of her chest, which, the friend remembers, Donald took as a personal affront. "Donald is the most transactional person you'll ever meet, and the most possessive, too," the friend said. "He was with her for her body, and she changed the way her body looked in a way he didn't like, and so he thought, 'How could you do that to me?' He's a narcissist, and a narcissist like that is incapable of understanding that saying something like that might not make for a great partner." Marla ended the dinner in tears.

Marla's tongue could cut, too. She'd deride him in front of friends, calling him fat and out of shape. One colleague remembers carpooling with Donald and Marla on the way to an awards dinner one evening. It was during the week when the United Nations convenes in New York, which turns the city's gridlock into an impassable mess. Stuck in traffic for an age, the car grew quiet. Donald and Marla never made much chatter, because, as friends noted, they had little in common. What would they talk about? So the friend commented on Marla's new haircut. She'd lobbed off a good few inches days earlier, and he told her that it suited her just fine. "Thank you," she said, beaming. "It's been three days and the man I sleep with hasn't even noticed."

Donald struck back. "Well, I dyed my hair and *you* didn't notice." The rest of the car fell silent.

This level of distrust rotted the relationship from the inside, too. Marla had for years watched the ease with which Donald lied to Ivana, making her somewhat of an expert witness. She knew how he would cheat on her, and, armed with that knowledge, she acted as the first line of defense. Donald would often tell Ivana that he was going out for a day of golf when actually he was going to the Midtown hotel where he took all his other women—a nothing of a place where no one who knew him would ever go, certainly not in the light of day.

Donald had developed a system with which Marla was intimately familiar. If he'd told Ivana that he was hitting the links, he would often remember to run his socks under water before he returned home, in order to make it seem to her as though he had, in fact, spent his day out on the course and not in the hotel room or house or limousine or helicopter where he had actually passed the day with Marla or someone else. By the time the divorce was finalized, Marla decided that she would tag along any time Donald said he was going out to play golf for the day. Friends and golf buddies remember having to pair up with her, driving around the course with her in the passenger seat of their golf carts. "The only reason Donald put up with it is that she knew well enough to turn up in a pair of Daisy Dukes and one of her very tight tops," one friend who partnered up with her on a number of occasions said. "She knew that's all he cared about, and she was absolutely right."

Marla also knew how territorial Donald could be. She saw it in the way he reacted to his nephew making small talk with her on the helicopter from Atlantic City to New York, back when he was still married to Ivana. When any of his friends would make a comment about her, even in a friendly way so as to compliment Donald, those remarks drew him closer to her. So when she needed to, she took a page out of Donald's book. He might go out and have photos taken with models or actresses when they fought. She'd go out and make a younger, more handsome or famous guy go completely gaga over her.

Donald would often tell the story about how, during one prolonged breakup with Marla, Michael Bolton fell head over heels for her. Bolton asked to take her out, she agreed, and, as things like this do, it got back to Donald. In one sense, this was validation for Donald. It was *his* Marla this rock star at the peak of his fame was after. That a guy like Michael Bolton would take his leftovers boosted his already outsize ego. But on the other hand, if a guy like Michael Bolton was after his castoffs, why had he left her in the first place? If she was good enough for Michael Bolton, surely she would do for him, at least for the time being, right? His self-congratulation quickly spun into a blinding, jealous rage. "I say to myself, Wait a minute. I don't like this. Michael Bolton—he's got the No. 1 fucking album in the world, *Time, Love and Tenderness*, and what that does to a guy like me, a competitive guy, it's like an affirmation that the girl has to be great, because the No. 1 singer has fallen for her. There's nothing wrong with what she's doing. I left her. Not only that. I left her like a dog," he said at the time.

"So what happens is, I say, 'What the fuck is going on?' I do a

Trump number on her. All-enveloping. I call her. She says, 'How could you have left me the way you did?' She decides to go to Hawaii with me instead of to Europe with Michael Bolton. In Maui, this guy finds out where we are, and starts sending flowers. Yellow roses with a note: 'I've got Georgia on my mind. Love, Michael.' She's torn. I've left her twice. But she drops him and comes back to me."

IN THE meantime, Marla got to work with a coach to prepare for an audition for the role of wealthy showman Florenz Ziegfeld's sexy girlfriend in *The Will Rogers Follies* on Broadway. Marla was perfect for the role. She was already playing it, to a degree. The ledes for all the New York papers wrote themselves. It would have practically been malpractice for any producer not to cast someone as white-hot as Marla was in that role at the time, a year into the show's run. They knew that her name in lights would pack the house with Donald's pals and every critic in town and every lookie-loo who'd never get an up-close look at the woman who tore the 1980s golden couple apart if they didn't buy a ticket to see her.

Marla rehearsed for a few weeks, and on opening night, in the dog days of the summer of 1992, Donald invited some three hundred friends and associates to watch his fiancée's Broadway debut. He told friends that he was astounded by Marla's ability to handle herself under all the pressure leading up to that night. Donald, on the other hand, was cracking. He got up from his seat in the theater shortly after the house lights dimmed, pacing back and forth, his chin bowed toward the ground. Marla rose from a hydraulic lift in gold glittery cowboy boots and a matching gold cowboy hat under which her matching golden locks flowed out. According to The *New York Times* review of her opening night, a financial consultant who knew Donald whispered to his wife that the little gold hot pants Marla had on were too tight. "That's the idea," his wife replied. Everyone was in on the joke, Marla included. And so when the show's directors specifically put back in an original line in which one of the other actors asked Marla's character, "How did you get this part?" they knew the audience would immediately laugh in an on-the-nose moment of art imitating life. They roared at it on opening night, a reaction Marla anticipated, rolling her eyes as soon as it was uttered.

She didn't flub a note or forget a line or screw up in any of the ways revelers expected, or perhaps hoped, she might. Donald slung his arm around her shoulder at the Western-themed after-party in the ballroom at the plaza to which he'd invited five hundred guests, including Mike Wallace, Maury Povich, La Toya Jackson, Regis Philbin, and Kathie Lee Gifford. For the moment, they were full on again. They'd been off not long before, and on not long before that. They'd soon be off again, then back on and off and on and off and on like a ratty old fuse that they loved to see blow almost as much as the tabloids did.

But by the following spring, they made an even greater spectacle at the theater. It was the first week in April, and the two arrived before Marla's performance, a line of cameras there to meet them, Donald in a suit, Marla in a white one-shouldered gown, her lips painted cherry red. He leaned over, in full view of the cameras, and put his palm on Marla's stomach, confirming speculation that she was pregnant. It was true—a new little Trump would arrive the following October.

As gamely as Donald celebrated the news in public, he did not immediately take to the news in private. In an interview a decade later with Howard Stern, he said that he had assumed Marla was on birth control, and he had been stunned at the news. "At the time it was like, 'Excuse me, what happened?' And then I said, 'Well, what are we going to do about this?'" he told Stern, obliquely suggesting he'd pushed her to get an abortion. Marla, he said, replied, "'Are you serious? It's the most beautiful day of our lives.' I said, 'Oh, great.'"

Donald later admitted that he was "not the kind of guy who has babies out of wedlock and doesn't get married and give the baby a name. And for me, I'm not a believer in abortion." But he still couldn't wrap his head around the idea of getting married again. It wasn't about Marla, though his family still was not open to the idea of her legally binding herself to the clan, even with a baby Trump on the way. Mary Trump reminded him that Ivana still loved him, and that she would likely take him back. It wouldn't be the worst decision he could make, she'd tell him. Donald knew that. He still called Ivana regularly, and he loved her still, too. But Marla had stuck by him. She had been loyal and patient and, mostly, nothing but kind and forgiving of his many sins. "It was a wrong time for me to have a relationship," Donald said then. "At the same time, it was great to know somebody was there, and she was there like nobody I've ever seen."

He knew that it was the right thing to do, and that Marla wanted it more than anything. He polled his family, his friends, anyone who would feign interest and pick up the phone, for what he should do. He'd repeat that he only had one option, which perhaps made him want to go through with it less. Being put in a corner may be the quickest way to make some people cave, but for Donald, it's the surest way to make him chew himself out of the room instead. He started referring to marriage as "the M word" and the "monster." Publicly, he would say the phobia came from his battle with Ivana over the prenup, and the resulting trauma and legal bills. Marla found a way around that. She told him over and over again that she would sign anything, if that made him feel better. In an interview on *The Today Show*, she said that Donald had "a little freak out" when the subject came up, but she'd figure out how to tame "the fear monster." And just in case she found him in a moment of weakness, she started carrying a wedding gown with her whenever they traveled. "I've always told Donald that I will do whatever I need to do," she said on *Today*.

While he sweated over the decision and Marla started planning for new baby Trump, Donald's three children had their lives rattled again. It was the Friday of Memorial Day weekend of 1993, and Don Jr. came home from the Hill School for the long weekend to be with Ivanka and Eric at the house in Greenwich. Ivana was in Tampa, taping a segment for the Home Shopping Network, where she'd started shilling goods after she left her job at the Trump Organization. Ivanka had gotten into bed and was waiting for Bridget to tuck her in and say their prayers together, as they did every night, but she never came. The phone started ringing, and Bridget didn't answer it as she usually had, swatting away reporters who'd sometimes call the house. Ivanka went to find Donny and Eric, who were watching TV together, and asked if they knew where Bridget was. The boys volunteered to go look for her, eventually running down to the basement to see if maybe she was down there, unable to hear the phone ring. Bridget was unconscious by the time they found her there. After an ambulance came, they told the family that she had had a heart attack and passed away immediately. Ivanka was devastated. They all were. Within three years, the kids had seen their parents' marriage publicly unravel, their grandfather, who was much more their father figure, die of a heart attack at sixty-three, and Bridget, their nanny, who was much more their mother figure, die of a heart attack at sixty-seven. Their dad's sex life was thrown in their faces, and his mistress, whom they didn't much like at all, was now expecting another baby, while the press hounded them throughout.

A WEDDING date still had not been set by the time Marla went into labor in October 1993. It was her first, Donald's fourth, but different for him in every imaginable way. Don Jr. came into the world before Ivana even had time for an epidural. Ivana had time enough to shoo her husband out of the room, for fear he'd never want to sleep with her again. Donald had not protested much, given the profoundness of his germophobia. Much was the same when Ivanka and Eric were born; he stayed clear until they were all cleaned up and Ivana had time to make herself look presentable again.

Second wives often have the benefit of a softer version of the man the first wife married—a man beaten down by vows kept and those deserted, who's reflected on what he missed the first go-around and how he'd do it over again if he could. If the man is successful, and the woman younger and more beautiful, as tends to happen, particularly in New York, the women have leverage. Sure, the men have the outward-facing power, but the women, in their own way, own their husbands, too. Marla was not yet a wife, despite that traveling wedding gown and Donald's own internal pressure cooker ticking away, but when she went into labor, she knew full well Donald was going to be there, whether he wanted to or not. And Donald, who'd missed out on the births of his eldest three kids, complied. He was in New York when Marla's water broke at Mar-a-Lago at two o'clock in the morning. An hour later he boarded his plane, bound for the hospital Marla had chosen in Palm Beach. By six o'clock he was by Marla's side in the delivery room.

Perhaps he should have chosen Don Jr.'s light-speed delivery instead. Marla was in labor for ten hours, and as someone who prided herself on her spirituality, she turned the birthing suite into a full-blown New Age wonderland. Candles were lit all around the room. New Age music played softly in the background. She invited her manager's fiancée, a Native American who called herself a "nurturer," to give massages and send prayers to help make the birthing process more peaceful for mom and baby. "Pray for me now," Marla would shout as a contraction neared. Donald was a wreck. Marla's mother Ann and her closest friend were in the room, too, trying to settle things down, to keep things as calm as possible for Marla and make sure Donald did not run away or blow all the candles out in frustration. "He could not stand all the hippie-dippie stuff Marla was into," one longtime friend of his remembered. "It infuriated him, particularly when it came to his child. You have to remember this is a man who ate steak and potatoes and heaps of ice cream and fast food and can after can of Coke. You think he cared about his kid being brought into the world with Native American prayers in candlelight?"

What he wanted was the ob-gyn to give Marla drugs. Strong drugs. Drugs that might make her stop all that screaming, because all of it was freaking him out. "I was very nervous, because she was in a lot of pain," Donald said. "I tried to convince her to take something, but she wouldn't. I asked the doctor to convince her, but he knew Marla was determined not to take any drugs. She's so strong, such a strong woman. I'm amazed." Marla added that she and Donald "did a lot of kissing while I was delivering," and once the baby was born, it was Donald who cut the umbilical cord.

The other thing about a second wife, or mother of your child, in this case, is that this go-around, you may get to name your child something your first spouse rejected. Donald had built his beloved Trump Tower after he secured the air rights over Tiffany and Co., the famed jewelry store next door, for $5 million. "Everything involved with Trump Tower has been successful," he told the *Times*. "And Trump Tower was built with Tiffany's air rights. But I've also always loved the name." Tiffany was the name Donald tried to give Ivanka when she was born, but Ivana shot down his suggestion immediately.

Tiffany Ariana Trump, a seven-and-a-half-pound blue-eyed, blond-haired little girl, was born in the early afternoon of October 13 at St. Mary's Hospital in Palm Beach. Donald called a reporter at the *New York Times* twenty minutes after Tiffany was born. "We have a perfect little girl, a combination in looks of both of us, to go with my three other wonderful children," he said.

With Marla relenting to his long-favored name, would he relent to Marla's request that they get married, especially with a new little baby Trump in the picture? Donald paused at the *Times* reporter's question. "That is something being seriously contemplated."

He was being quite honest. Even after Tiffany's birth, he had his doubts and his moments of conviction, neither of which stuck around for very long, each of which could easily replace the other in his head. Marla had been loyal, but his family wasn't crazy about her. Tiffany deserved to have her father and mother together, but he couldn't go through the kind of divorce battle and near financial ruin he'd just barely crawled out of again. The should-I-or-shouldn't-I indecisiveness that plagued Donald Trump—that continues to plague Donald Trump today—would have gone on forever if not for a red line drawn by Marla, a second line drawn by his business advisers, and, to a lesser extent, a mass shooting close to home that finally pushed him over.

Marla, who'd settled into life at Mar-a-Lago with her mother as a doting nanny and Marla whisperer for Donald after Tiffany was born, delivered her man an ultimatum: either he married her by Christmas, or she would take his daughter and move out. She'd had enough. She was not going to spend another Christmas with Donald, at Mar-a-Lago or anywhere, without a wedding band on her finger. Marla wasn't even living with Donald full-time in New York; he lived part of the time in his Trump Tower apartment below the triplex, sometimes staying with her in the Trump Park apartment. It wasn't the way she was going to raise her daughter, with a sometimes daddy who refused to marry her mother out of fear of losing his money and a desire to chase tail around town.

Ann, who wanted the wedding perhaps even more than Marla, did what she could to assuage Donald's concerns with the financial side of things. Marla was resisting signing a prenup a month after Tiffany was born. Forget the money—which, of course, she couldn't; she knew full well that with a premarital agreement like that came a subsequent nondisclosure agreement. She didn't want to let go of the power that came from being able to tell the secrets Donald most cared about keeping close. Without that, what power could she wield over him? But it was a nonstarter for Donald to marry Marla without one. "A prenuptial is a horrible document," he told *Vanity*

Fair. "When you're a believer in positive thinking, it isn't good. But it's a modern-day necessity."

By late November, Marla relented. Donald wore down further under pressure from his advisers. They had a plan in the works to take his casinos public early the next year, and they didn't want Donald's personal life bandied about in the tabloids, as they knew it would be if he didn't give Marla the wedding she wanted. No sane investors would put their money into a company whose CEO's sex life made front-page news for weeks on end. "We had to tell him over and over again to settle down," one adviser said. "He would say, 'I know. I know I had to do it. It's the right thing to do,'" but they all knew that only made matters harder.

When a New York man pulled out his Ruger P89 9-millimeter handgun on a Long Island Rail Road train as it pulled into the Garden City station at about 6:00 p.m. on December 7, walking backward down the aisle and staring passengers in the eyes as he fired thirty shots, Donald knew what he had to do. In the days that followed, authorities said six people had died and nineteen were left injured. "I figure life is short," Donald said in the aftermath, which it is, though it is unclear why this tragedy struck so close to home. It's hard to imagine that Donald himself ever commuted at rush hour on an LIRR train. Nevertheless, on the morning of December 10, Donald told the New York papers he would marry Marla in a ceremony before Christmas.

Marla sprang into action. She had been furiously trying to lose the baby weight for weeks, just in case. Carolina Herrera was making her dress, and she had the first fitting for the gown exactly two months after Tiffany was born. At five feet ten inches, she weighed 151 pounds by the middle of October, and knowing that just maybe her ultimatum and the internal and external pressures on Donald might make him cave, she started a strict diet to slim down to wedding shape as quickly as possible. It was all seeds and vegetables and raw nuts and greens and fruits all the time. "Nothing in excess," she told *Vanity Fair.* Breastfeeding helped, too. She fed Tiffany just about anywhere she pleased around Mar-a-Lago—in the dining room for breakfast, by the pool in the afternoons. One longtime guest of the private club remembers Mar-a-Lago staffers delivering Marla a breast pump on a silver platter as she bronzed herself on a lounge chair tilted toward the sun. A few days before her fitting, she was down to 127 pounds. If she was extra strict, she would reach the 125-pound mark she had stuck in her head by the time she walked into Herrera on December 13.

The wedding was set for December 20, which gave the designer less than a week to come up with a dress worthy of a Trump wedding and the circus this Trump wedding in particular would command. It was not going to be the dress she'd lugged around in her suitcase over the last year. That dress was immediately discarded after she got the official green light, Donald's credit card, and an appointment with Ms. Herrera, who made clothes for British royals and American ones (namely, the Kennedys). Marla waltzed into her salon and chose double-faced satin from the famed Maison Bucol—a luxe fabric house in Lyon that's been spinning its yarns for nearly a century—in bright white, belying the fact that their baby Tiffany would herself be there for the wedding (in a mini designer dress of her own, inlaid with pearls). The sleeves were cut off-the-shoulder, with a slight sweetheart neck and bodice fit close to her chest, leaving little of Donald's favorite feature to the imagination. Down the back ran little traditional fabric-covered buttons leading to more white satin that fell in a removable train, which she could take off after the ceremony for the reception. She chose a very of-the-moment, vertically voluminous tulle veil that she found in the Carolina Herrera shop. For shoes, she went with Manolo Blahnik.

Donald's tuxedo was sorted; he would wear Brioni, as he always did. He was far more concerned with who would actually show up to see Marla in white. There was no time for proper engraved invitations. There was no time for an official invitation at all, in fact.

On the day Marla went to fit her dress, Donald's assistants started working the phones. It was a week before the big day, which would take place just before Christmas in New York. The A-list celebrities and bigtime moguls Donald wanted there to watch his soon-to-be second wife walk down the aisle were busy or simply turned off by the spectacle of it all (some would call it more on the charade end of spectacle, which enticed some of the more gossip-minded members of the Trump Rolodex to come anyway and steered the more discerning away). Michael Jackson, Liza Minelli, Whitney Houston, they all declined. So did his three older children. Don Jr., Ivanka, and Eric opted to stay with their mother, who, as usual, was spending the final weeks of the year in Aspen, where they'd watched their parents' marriage unravel and caught a glimpse of their father's bride-to-be for the first time four years earlier. In a statement a representative faxed to media, they said, "In discussion among ourselves, we decided to stay in Aspen with our mother and grandmother." On the night before his big day, it was Ivana he sent a dozen red roses to. Ivana, however, had brought her younger Italian boyfriend along for the trip. Together, they spent December 20 with Donald's children while Donald and Marla entered the Plaza Hotel, the place once managed by Ivana, to say "I do."

With a week's notice, Donald got 1,100 people to file into the Plaza on that Saturday evening, from New York mayor David Dinkins to Senator Al D'Amato, Bianca Jagger and Robin Leach, Howard Stern and Rosie O'Donnell, O. J. Simpson and Susan Lucci, Carl Icahn and Randall Cunningham, Don King, Evander Holyfield, and Joe Frazier. Some made a quick entrance out of professional courtesy, like billionaire Ron Perelman, who was spotted arriving at the last second and calling for his car a few minutes later. As Donald feared, the final guest list lacked the heavy hitters he and others at the affair had expected. "It's just like I was afraid of," Howard Stern told reporters that evening. "I'm the biggest name here. I don't see any big stars."

The ceremony took place in the hotel's mezzanine, where they'd constructed an altar covered in white orchids and birches, from which cut-glass teardrops cascaded. As the *New York Times* Vows column the following day noted, other than those teardrops, "as the writer Julie Baumgold remarked after the ceremony, 'there wasn't a wet eye in the place.'"

Though perhaps no one else felt it, Marla radiated in what she called "all the warmth in the room." For her, it was about "looking out and seeing our friends and family that have been there through everything with us. Reading from 'The Prophet.' Just holding his hand tight and knowing we were home."

Fred Trump, Donald's father, who'd never much cared for Marla, served as Donald's best man. Janie Elder, whose name Marla had often assumed when she was in hiding as Donald's mistress during the chaos following his divorce from Ivana, was the maid of honor. A singer from the Metropolitan Opera sang throughout the ceremony, and the reverend from the Marble Collegiate Church, where Ivana and Donald were married and Marla and Donald flirted during their affair, performed the traditional vows.

After they promised to be there for better or for worse, in sickness and in health, for richer and for poorer, till death do them part, the thousand people looking on broke into a round of applause. It was all a big show, after all, and everyone there had a prime seat witnessing a moment in a very specific sort of modern American history. "He's our P. T. Barnum," longtime *Spy Magazine* and *Vanity Fair* editor and Trump foe Graydon Carter said of Donald that evening. "This is the triumph of romance over finance." Mayor Dinkins had a rosy view of what he'd just witnesses to share with reporters. "The bride was a vision in white," he said. "Donald just beamed. It was a lovely, lovely ceremony." Once it was all said and done, Fred Trump lifted up Marla's veil, revealing her baby face and a $2 million tiara she'd borrowed from Harry Winston, all of its 325 diamonds flashing in unison. Donald winked at Marla, his wife, before planting a faint little kiss on her cheek.

The following morning, every New York paper put the affair on its front page, including the *New York Times*, all with the same raised eyebrow and snark in their tone that revelers had adopted the night before. "The bride is taking her husband's name," the Gray Lady said in its Vows column. "The bridegroom is keeping his name, The Donald, a legacy from his former wife, Ivana."

The snark was not unnecessary. Marriage is no great healer. It's not even a Band-Aid. So the wounds from their courtship continued to bleed long after they said "I do," or perhaps because they had. Donald never wanted to be married; he'd been pressured to marry a woman he lusted after but didn't truly love. As his one longtime friend reminded, the only person Donald ever really loved was Donald; and the rest were just accessories who, for a period of time, piqued his interest or served his needs. Marla expected the kind of loving husband and doting father Donald never had been and never would be. The gaps between what they each wanted had led them to break up and make up ad nauseam before the wedding. But legally bound as they now were, they instead just fought—about everything.

Marla's New Age inclinations irked Donald to no end. Tiffany's birth was just the start. Friends recall that Marla would take her Jeep—her car choice alone annoyed her husband—up to a property he owned in Westchester to be one with nature. "She would tell him she was going up to gaze at the stars and look at the moon and spend the night out there, and he fucking hated it," one friend recalled. "Part of him maybe didn't trust that she was going up there alone, but part of him just despised the fact that that is how she wanted to spend her time." Donald, all steak and potatoes and meatloaf and fast food, balked at Marla's habit of mostly ordering things in various shades of green when they went out to dinner. At Mar-a-Lago, she would brew a special tea that Donald looked at with disgust. "I would never drink that," he'd seethe at her. That she was passing that on to their daughter sent him into a rage. "She didn't even like Tiffany to have whole milk, and she was married to my dad, who's like the biggest pig ever—a real McDonald's guy," Ivanka said in an interview in 2000. "I remember once he bought a Big Mac for Tiffany, and Marla said, 'Don't give her that, she likes carrots.' So my dad ended up waving the Big Mac and a carrot in front of Tiffany and asking her which one she wanted, and she picked the Big Mac." The Trumps intervened when Marla hesitated to get Tiffany vaccinated. Donald's sister Maryanne went ballistic. She called Donald's closest friends, begging them to talk sense into him. "The baby's health is at stake," she fumed into the phone. After that, Donald took Tiffany to get vaccinated behind Marla's back. (By the time Donald started campaigning for the 2016 election, he had been swayed more in Marla's direction. "I am totally in favor of vaccines but I want smaller doses over a longer period of time," he said in a Republican primary debate in 2015. "We've had so many instances, people that work for me. . . . [in which] a child, a beautiful child went to have the vaccine, and came back and a week later had a tremendous fever, got very, very sick, now is autistic.")

Donald grew frustrated by Marla's mother, Ann, whom he told friends he found overbearing and always around, which she was. She doted on her daughter and her granddaughter and gave Marla some company, which she desperately needed, since her husband was off working most of the time. Donald told people he felt like he had no space from his mother-in-law, who'd butt in and give her opinion when Donald just wanted his space. He told his friends that she was a mooch and that she needed to worry about her own life and get out of his.

His work schedule weighed on Marla, too. "Why can't you be home at 5 o'clock?" Donald recalled her asking in *Art of the Comeback*—a request Donald viewed as "very selfish." On the flip side,

Marla's acting career, which she tried to restart over and over again, with frequent trips to Los Angeles and auditions on both coasts, got under her husband's skin. "He really has the desire to have me be more of a traditional wife," she said in an interview—an expectation he'd had with Ivana, too, once she started working for him in Atlantic City and at the Plaza. "He definitely wants his dinner promptly served at seven, and if he's home at 6:30, it should be ready by 6:30."

That Marla didn't much trust her husband did not help matters. There were only so many golf games she could tag along to, especially with a little daughter in tow. Donald did little to reassure her that he'd changed, because the reality was that he hadn't. He once took a New Yorker writer on a tour through Mar-a-Lago, stopping in its Spa. He introduced the writer to the resident physician—a woman named Dr. Ginger Lea Southall, who'd recently graduated from a chiropractic college. Donald wasn't sure where she got her degree. "Baywatch Medical School?" he joked. "Does that sound right? I'll tell you the truth. Once I saw Dr. Ginger's photograph, I didn't really need to look at her résumé or anyone else's. Are you asking, 'Did we hire her because she'd trained at Mount Sinai for fifteen years?' The answer is no. And I will tell you why: because by the time she's spent fifteen years at Mount Sinai, we don't want to look at her."

A year and a half into their marriage, Marla had a dalliance of her own, which Donald never really forgave. The *National Enquirer* ran a story detailing how a cop caught Marla and her bodyguard, Spencer Wagner, who was more than six feet tall and fifteen years younger than Donald, huddled behind a lifeguard stand in the middle of the night while her husband was back in New York. On April 16, at four o'clock in the morning, a police officer happened upon a car parked next to a stretch of beach twelve miles south of Mar-a-Lago. The way Marla tells it, she had been out to dinner in Fort Lauderdale with friends and then on to a jazz club. When they were headed back to the mansion, nature called. She couldn't make it the extra few minutes, and instructed the bodyguard to pull over so she could relieve herself on an empty beach. The officer didn't see Marla initially when he walked onto the sand to investigate. Wagner insisted he was alone, until the cop spotted Marla, in spandex and a sports bra, crouching behind the lifeguard chair. The *Enquirer* reported that she tried to sweet-talk the cop initially, saying there just had to be a way to make this go away. She resorted to pleading with him not to put her name over the police radio. He let them go with a couple parking tickets and a warning to get on home. Donald called the story garbage once it came out: "Along the lines of Elvis sightings and Martian invasions, the *National Enquirer* has once again fabricated a wholly unreliable cover story for this week's issue," he said in a statement. But privately, he didn't trust Marla's story. The validity of what she told him, though, mattered less than a public perception that Marla was running around on him. "It made him look like a cuckold, and that really disturbed him," a friend noted. "Their relationship, and everything, was always supposed to be all about him, about how adored and wanted he was, and when it wasn't, he couldn't stand it."

The simple fact of the matter was they did not much like each other. Everything they each were individually, the other wanted the opposite. They had nothing in common, apart from their daughter. But the ultimate undoing of their marriage, as with all things related to Donald, came down to money. A few years into his marriage to Marla, Donald finally had some. By the mid-1990s, as Donald neared his fiftieth birthday, the "Trump is back" storyline started permeating newspapers and magazines. *Forbes* once again put him on its list of the 400 richest Americans in 1996, ranking at no. 376. (He insisted that he was owed a position much higher up on the list, claiming that the $450 million that the magazine had estimated was about one-eighth of what he was actually worth.)

The remainder of the Welcome Back Donald stories were prompted in large part by the windfall Donald got from selling his interest in the Grand Hyatt Hotel—his first big splash in Manhattan, and the deal he had rushed back from his honeymoon with Ivana to close—to his business partners, the Pritzker family. The vast majority of what the Pritzkers paid him went to people he owed and toward various commissions, but he nevertheless walked away with about $25 million.

It was a novelty for Donald. He could tuck himself in his oversize bed in his Trump Tower triplex and doze off without the thought of creditors and debts and all the financial mires that had encumbered him year after year. Something else started weighing on him. The prenuptial agreement he'd convinced Marla to sign in 1993 guaranteed her somewhere in the range of $1 million to $5 million if they were to split up before their fifth wedding anniversary. After that, it would balloon into a sum many, many times that. The fixed amount that accounted for a portion of his fortune could become a large chunk of what he'd just got back.

Once again, Donald got lucky with the timing of his marriage unraveling. With Ivana, the conflict in Aspen had unfolded when he was broke enough that Ivana couldn't push for more than she'd agreed to in their prenup; and now he was fed up with Marla just a few months before the milestone that would guarantee her much more of what he had. "I remember him pulling me aside in the lobby of Trump Tower one day and telling me all these reasons he was considering filing for divorce," one friend recalled, "and I just looked him dead in the eye and told him to cut the crap. I knew it was about the money, and he knew he couldn't hide it from me. I just reminded him that he should do what he wanted, but he needed to do it with a little dignity this time."

Marla had an idea of what was coming, though she tried to hide it as long as she could. She had just gotten off the wild ride that is a Trump divorce. She knew full well what she was about to face, and if she could head it off, she would. At the end of April 1997, Marla and her mother Ann and a three-year-old Tiffany traveled back down to

Dalton for a celebration in honor of her hometown's 150th birthday. Speaking at the bridge club in town, Marla brushed off her husband's obvious absence from the event. "He works all the time," she said, smiling at the curious women she'd left behind to live in that gilded triplex and sweeping oceanfront mansion. "That man!"

Less than a week later, she and Donald released a joint statement announcing their separation. "After a $3^{1}/_{2}$-year marriage, we have decided to separate, as friends," the statement read. "For the sake of our family, we ask that the members of the media will accept this statement, respect our privacy and move on to coverage of more important issues." The sentiment from a man who dipped his bride-to-be nearly a half dozen times in front of a hundred flashbulbs at their wedding, who phoned in stories to court the press after his first divorce, dripped with irony. Although paparazzi started to stake out some of the exits in Trump Tower and flew helicopters over Mar-a-Lago, the coverage paled in comparison to that of divorce number one. Outwardly, there was no other woman or man in the picture, which made this separation far less delicious for gossip columnists from the get-go. There was no trail of affair bread crumbs for them to follow, and no months of whispers about a looming split, either. "I hadn't heard any rumors of a breakup," said Liz Smith, who chronicled Donald's split with Ivana down to the second. "I wish I had. It's a great story."

Inherently, though, a second divorce is less great a story than a first, even if this particular second marriage was recorded as if it were a sordid royal courtship. The Trumps may have dominated headlines for weeks and months straight in the early 1990s, but no one is particularly shocked when the quintessential Other Woman becomes just another woman in Donald Trump's storied history of them. Stern called it, on their wedding night, no less. This relationship always had a shelf life. But with a young child in the picture, no one really reveled in the I-told-you-so and karmic retribution of it all, either.

This did not mean that the tabloids didn't extract whatever juice they could out of the split. "Donald wants out. He's looking for his freedom," the *Post* reported. "Marla's Beverly Hillbillies' family drove Donald crazy," one source told the paper. Another suggested that the whole breakup was all a ploy to get more eyeballs to tune in to the Miss Universe pageant, which Trump owned and was scheduled to air two weeks after the announcement. It took only a few days for the papers to cast new leads in Donald's romantic melodrama—including Dr. Ginger Southall, the Mar-a-Lago staff chiropractor he'd lauded for her fictitious degree from the Baywatch Medical School. "I've heard Sharon Stone's name mentioned," he boasted to friends of the rumors. "I have heard Princess Di!. It's wild!"

Like Ivana, Marla initially contested the prenup she'd begrudgingly signed to quash "the little fear monster" keeping Donald from agreeing to "the M word." She claimed she agreed to it under duress and extreme pressure, and it went against all the things her husband promised to provide her and her daughter in their three-odd years of marriage. Neither Marla nor Donald showed up to the Manhattan Supreme Court hearing on July 8 of 1999—two years into a legal tug-of-war between the two sides. Trump's attorney had called the agreement iron-clad, and contended that Marla knew exactly what she was giving away and getting herself into when she signed it. Marla disagreed. "After giving Donald two years to honor the verbal commitments he made to me during our 12-year relationship, I decided to walk away completely under the terms of our prenuptial agreement that had been placed before me just five days before our 1993 wedding," she said in a statement. She was in Los Angeles at the time, once again auditioning all over town to land herself an acting gig. What she got after two years of fighting was something close to a reported $2 million, along with more support to take care of Tiffany. It wasn't nearly enough to keep up the lifestyle she and her five-year-old had grown accustomed to. The way he saw it, that wasn't Donald's problem. In a statement of his own, he said that he was happy that the split worked out "so amicably" and that he wishes his now ex-wife well.

THOSE WELL-WISHES came ten months after Donald Trump spotted a twenty-eight-year-old Slovenian model in a Midtown nightclub, whom quickly turned into what his friends considered "the next hot flavor of the month." Donald had already been dating twentysomething models and socialites about town for months, barely taking a breather following his initial separation from Marla. He took out model Kara Young for a time. Norwegian cosmetics heiress Celina Midelfart made the rounds with him, as well. She turned up with him to the Kit Kat Club—a joint on Forty-Third Street named after the club in the musical *Cabaret*—one night in September of 1998. It was the middle of fashion week, which meant the club was flush with more models than usual. Among them was Melania Knauss, who'd moved to New York two years earlier from Milan to see if she could make more money doing commercial work. Paolo Zampolli, an Italian-born businessman who owned ID Models at the time, met her at a casting call years earlier and secured an H-1B visa for her, typically reserved for high-skilled workers like engineers and computer whizzes with advanced degrees but sometimes copped by models who have not even graduated from high school, let alone college. (On the campaign trail, Donald would deride the use of such visas, calling out "rampant, widespread H-1B abuse," saying that they are for "temporary foreign workers, imported from abroad, for the explicit purpose of substituting for American workers at lower pay.") She moved into an apartment in the Zeckendorf Towers near Union Square, with a roommate and rent mostly footed by her agency, but work wasn't as easy to come by as Zampolli made it seem. She'd found more success in Paris and Milan before she moved to New York. In Manhattan, models a decade younger beat her out for the tobacco and alcohol ads she got called in for. She found some jobs doing ads for a watch company, some lingerie shoots, a Panasonic spot that aired on TV, and a billboard for Camel, which got mounted in the middle of Times Square, not far from the Kit Kat Club.

Melania was toying with the idea of moving back to Europe as her bank account tipped toward empty when she went out in Midtown that September evening, which she typically did not do. Usually she went to the movies or to the gym. Sometimes, she'd spend an evening sewing clothes for herself in her apartment. She'd always been somewhat hermetic and studious growing up. She was born in Novo Mesto, what was then in Yugoslavia, in 1970, and lived with her parents and sister in a Communist apartment block in the riverside town of Sevnica. The family had more than most. Her mother, Amalija, worked developing patterns at a textile factory, and her father, Viktor Knavs, was a chauffeur for the mayor of a nearby town who later became a car salesman for a state-owned company (he allegedly was suspected of having evaded taxes when Melania was in elementary school, though his daughter has since denied the reports). When she was young, Viktor would spend weekends washing his antique Mercedes—a ritual he took great pleasure in—and Amalija would bring back fashion magazines from France and Germany, where she traveled for work, for her daughters to flip through. By the time Melania turned twenty-two, she landed herself in a Slovenian magazine as part of an annual Look of the Year contest. The magazine promised that the top three women would get contracts in cities across Europe. Melania was furious when she was named runner-up. She later claimed to have won the competition, a small white lie that became one of a number of fibs she told of her upbringing. She changed her name, of course, from Melanija Knavs to Melania Knauss; she dropped out of the University of Ljubljana to move to Milan to model after a year, though throughout the 2016 presidential campaign her website still claimed she'd graduated with a degree in design and architecture.

Despite the white lies, friends describe Melania as unfailingly sweet and unwilling to look for any kind of trouble. In an interview with author Charlotte Hays, one former model friend likened Melania to "strawberry ice cream." "Sweet," she said, "and smells nice." She hardly dated, hardly went to bars or clubs, but Zampolli was throwing the Kit Kat Club party, and his parties were a thing of legend at that point. He'd bring in tiger cubs and fashion television cameras and, once, an alligator, and men like Donald Trump who'd come with one blonde and leave lusting after another. That night, when Midelfart got up to go to the ladies' room, he moved toward Melania. "I went crazy," he'd later tell Larry King in an interview about seeing her for the first time. "There was this great supermodel sitting next to Melania. I was supposed to meet the supermodel. But I said, 'forget about her. What about the one to the left?'" The one to the left had a vague sense of who Donald was—he was rich and well known—but anyone with any sort of gut sense could tell that by looking at the way he carried himself. "I had my life. I had my world," she later said of their introduction. "I didn't follow Donald Trump and what kind of life he had."

The legend they like to tell is that when Donald asked for Melania's number, she suggested she take his instead. It was a test, she says. If he gave her his office line, she'd know it wasn't for real. She had no interest in doing business with him, though ultimately that is what all of Donald's relationships—romantic or otherwise—become, transactional. He gave her his office line, along with his home phone for the triplex and his number in Mar-a-Lago. Melania told friends she had no interest in Donald, especially knowing he'd cozied up to her after coming to the party with another woman. Zampolli's girlfriend at the time, a Hungarian model who lived in the same apartment building as Melania, told reporters that she was "turned off" by the whole thing and that the idea of her friend actually calling Donald was "absolutely out of the question."

She did call, though, after she went on a photo shoot in the

Caribbean and came back to New York. Donald took her on a date to Moombah, the downtown club of the moment, and soon after, on his jet down to Mar-a-Lago for the weekend. It didn't take long for Donald to introduce her to his children, who were older now and less stung by this relationship than they had been with Marla. Melania hadn't come between their parents, nor was she the first, second, or tenth pretty young thing they'd seen him with around town. "It was much more difficult getting along with my dad's girlfriends when I was younger, because almost every woman who came into the house was somehow a challenge to me," Ivanka admitted to gossip columnist Chaunce Hayden years later. That she and her brothers could see how plainly they were after her dad's money also didn't sit well, coupled with the fact that they tended to be half Donald's age. "As long as his girlfriends never get any younger than my oldest brother, then it's fine," Ivanka joked in an interview with the *Mail* on Sunday, adding that with Don Jr. getting into his twenties at the time, "it's starting to cut down his options." The only thing that bothered her about her dad dating younger women was that she could so clearly see their intentions. "There was one girl he was seeing, and I knew she wasn't a good person and was just after his money, so I said it to her face on several occasions," she said in the interview, adding that she "managed to get rid of her," though they still ran into one another because they were both modeling at the time.

Ivanka didn't worry about gold digging as much with Melania. She could tell she had "a good character," and she'd known her father long enough now that she would have left if it were just about the money. "Dad's too much of a pain in the ass to stick around with for too long if your motives aren't genuine." Plus, she added, "You can be a money-grabber at 45. So if that's the real problem, then the age doesn't matter." Melania sat rows behind the children and Ivana in the Marble Collegiate Church when Donald's father Fred passed away in June 1999, where Mayor Rudolph Giuliani eulogized him,

and the likes of Joan Rivers and Al D'Amato sat in the pews. Paparazzi caught Melania, in a low-cut lacy black slip dress barely
covered up by a black cardigan and a silver cross around her neck,
leaving the church alone. Marla did not attend the ceremony in
the church in which she'd secretly meet Donald, with the reverend
who'd married them half a dozen years earlier. Ten days after the
funeral, their divorce was finalized.

That's about the time that Donald started toying with the idea
of running for president as a member of the Reform Party. It was
serious enough that he let Chris Matthews interview him live in
front of 1,200 students that November for an episode of *Hardball*
taped at the University of Pennsylvania, where both men had spent
their undergraduate years. Matthews opened with a question asking Donald what life, liberty, and the pursuit of happiness meant
to him. Donald immediately brought up people who were going to
do great things in the world, and pointed to his own son, Don Jr.,
in the audience. Matthews urged him to tell his son to stand up for
the cameras. "He's much better looking than I am," Donald joked.

Matthews mentioned that he had another special guest in the
audience. "My supermodel," Donald said, smiling. "Where is my supermodel? Melania. That's Melania Knauss. Stand up," he ordered.
She did, cameras catching the whole thing.

"One thing that's safe to say about you, Donald, is that you know
the difference between Slovakia and Slovenia," Matthews teased.

"I do," Donald mused. "I do. Absolutely."

As Donald mulled what came next for his political future, he
nudged Melania forward in her career. He was keen on his girlfriend
posing for a photo shoot in the January issue of British *GQ*—a special edition emblazoned "Naked supermodel special!" on its cover,
alongside a cover line reading "Sex at 30,000 feet: Melania Knauss
earns her air miles." Donald lent them his Boeing jet, which was
parked at LaGuardia Airport in Queens, for the shoot. The concept
was to make Melania into a sort of Bond girl meets could-be First

Lady. As the story accompanying the photos suggestively said, Melania is "an expert in the art of in-flight entertainment. And as his personal hostess, [she] might just end up as the next First Lady." It continued: "Miss Knauss is relishing the prospect of a future pressing the flesh on state occasions. 'I will put all my effort into it, and I will support my man.'"

Melania showed her support in the nude, or barely covered. In one photo, she splays out completely naked, apart from a diamond choker and thick diamond bangles on each wrist, on a tan fur blanket, where she is handcuffed to a locked briefcase. In another, she digs into the briefcase, which is filled with more diamond bracelets, spilling out of the gold sequined negligée that just barely remains tied on. In one shot she stands on the wing of the plane in a bright red python-print push-up bra, matching thong, and black knee-high boots, pointing both her bare backside and a silver pistol in the direction of the camera. She also posed sitting with her legs spread on the captain's chair in the cockpit, a silver chain-linked body suit barely hiding her chest, but a silver headpiece covering most of her head. In all of the photos, what she lacks in clothing, she makes up for in avant-garde eyewear. It was not exactly a traditional spread for a potential First Lady, though it did presage the unconventional nature of the role she'd unwittingly fall into seventeen years later. Donald was not on set the day of the shoot, but he insisted on the photos being delivered to his office. The magazine framed the cover and a few other shots and sent them his way as quickly as it could.

Friends remembered that he could not have been more thrilled to have his girlfriend looking the way she did in a photo shoot in a major magazine. "It was his dream come true, to have her looking like that, getting more and more famous," one friend remembered. This was a man who constantly boasted about his ability to make stars out of both Ivana and Marla, even if the attention was often of the negative variety. Even still, the pair broke up around the time the issue hit newsstands. On January 11, 2000, the *Post* ran a story under the headline "Trump Knixes Knauss." As the tabloid reported, Donald thought Melania was great, but the same little fear monster that had reared its head once he divorced Ivana for Marla appeared again. "Donald has to be free for a while. He didn't want to get hooked," a source told the *Post*. "He was still reeling from his split from Marla, and he needed companionship, and then Melania came along and she was beautiful and available." As the paper told it, she was also now completely and utterly heartsick. Two days later, Donald posed for cameras at One 51, a club in Midtown at which he was throwing a party for his Miss USA pageant. Asked about the split, he told reporters, "Melania is an amazing women, a terrific woman, a great woman, and she will be missed."

Melania's friends told the story of their breakup differently. She, like Marla, didn't trust him. He was up to his old ways, and she wasn't going to have it. She got over it soon enough, and he did not miss her for long, because the pair got back together a few months later.

Melania retreated further into his world, away from her friends and deeper into the sinkhole that can swallow anyone close to Trump. She had not been back to visit her parents until the summer of 2002, when, after a stop in London, Donald and Melania took his plane to Slovenia, where a pair of black Mercedes and both of her parents awaited their arrival. They landed in time for a late dinner, for which they drove a half hour from the airport to the Grand Hotel Toplice, where they were seated at a table overlooking Lake Bled. Melania had to translate everything; Donald, of course, did not speak Slovenian, and her parents did not speak English well (Melania, on the other hand, spoke five languages). The whole trip lasted only a few hours. It was enough for Donald. They boarded the plane back out of town a few hours after they'd touched down. "I was there about 15 minutes," he told Larry King of the visit a few years later, laughing at the abrupt nature of it. "A beautiful country," he added. "I landed, said: hi mom, hi dad. Bye!"

In the winter and spring of 2004, *The Apprentice* premiered on NBC. Donald often showed off his girlfriend—when he brought contestants up to tour his triplex; when winners of a contest got to dine with the couple at his father's table at the 21 Club; in the finale, when they took a helicopter to the Trump Taj Mahal in Atlantic City (a contestant mispronounced her name, and in the entirety of the hour-long episode, she said six words: "It's so cute. It's really cute").

Two weeks after the finale aired, to record ratings, at the end of April, Donald proposed to Melania. It was five and a half years after they first met at the Kit Kat Club and his third official proposal. By that point, he knew what he was doing. He surprised Melania before he left to attend the annual Costume Institute Gala at the Metropolitan Museum of Art—the coveted event attended by megawatt stars and fashion insiders that takes place the first Monday in May each year. It was the first time Melania had scored an invitation, and she would arrive with a fifteen-carat emerald-cut stone with tapered diamond baguettes on each side, all set in platinum. When she showed up to the event, the ring sparkled against the black strapless corseted dress she chose to go along with that year's theme—aptly, "Dangerous Liaisons"—as she posed with her soon-to-be stepdaughter Ivanka, who wore a peach silk-and-lace slip dress, on the carpet. No one much noticed at the gala. The next day, they shared the news with the *Post*. "How Trump 'Iced' the Deal—$2 Million Sparkler for His Fiancée," the headline read. "It was a great surprise," Melania told the tabloid. "We are very happy together." Donald later told Larry King that they "were together for five years" and "literally never had an argument. I said, 'you know what? It's time. It's time.'"

The *Post* headline got something slightly off. Donald later told the *Times* that the truth was, he paid half as much. Graff Diamonds—Oprah Winfrey's jeweler, he reminded King—had offered him a steep discount. "Only a fool would say, 'No thank you. I want to pay a million dollars more for a diamond.'" The deal paid off for the London-based jeweler, which noted an uptick in its stores from all the publicity Melania's ring received when news of their engagement broke. (In early 2018, Graff's chairman told *Forbes* that Donald was given no such "favors.")

Donald's previous marriages had been all about money in their own ways. Ivana had threatened to bleed him dry by fighting their premarital agreement, though at the time he had no blood to give; Marla was around while he made something of a fortune back, but fought him for years for a larger portion of it than she'd agreed to in their prenuptial agreement. As for the ceremony and receptions themselves, Donald had spent hundreds of thousands of dollars—if not more—to entertain guests who didn't truly care for the newly-weds or the idea of watching them say their vows or cut their cakes under canopies of imported white flowers.

In his third go-around, Donald of course again demanded a pre-nuptial agreement, but this time, he figured out a way to make the wedding about money coming in to him, rather than flowing out. After he said he took the special price from Graff, and Graff, in turn, made it back so quickly, other wedding vendors raced to cash in on the latest Trump nuptial spectacular. Once the couple had decided to wed in Palm Beach, the offers started rolling in. Donald told the *Times* that he'd turned down offers from a handful of high-end florists who offered to flood the Versailles-like ballroom in Mar-a-Lago with a cascade of whatever flowers the couple envisioned for their day. A half dozen top chefs raised their hands to prepare the dinner that evening. One private jet company agreed to hand glasses of champagne to those arriving at the airport for the wedding, and another company said they would be more than happy to provide a grand fireworks display—gratis—during the reception. Lest he risk turning into Star Jones—the former host of *The View* who'd turned her wedding into a freebie wonderland and earned herself the moniker Bridezilla—Donald turned down the fireworks, and Melania nixed the idea of having the whole thing filmed and televised for all the world to see. "Literally anything you can imagine from photos to flowers to food to jets to airports to diamonds," Mr. Trump told the paper. "And for every item, there's five people who want to do it. In all cases they don't want anything, but they want recognition."

Initially both Donald and Melania contended, at least publicly, that they wanted the wedding to be small and simple. "Who needs a big hoopla? I get enough of it," Donald said to *Us Weekly*. "I like private and intimate," Melania told *People*. This was Donald's third, after all, and the first two had been such big to-dos, with hundreds of people, and thousands of flashbulbs, honking big wedding cakes, elaborate gowns, crystals and caviar and critics nastily gossiping about the couple barely out of their earshot. But it was Melania's first wedding, and so many things were going to be free this go-around. His kids would be there this time, too. "I'm so excited for my dad," Ivanka told the *Palm Beach Post* about the upcoming wedding. "When he's happy, I'm happy," she said to Chaunce Hayden.

Donald also had a show to promote. He was now a national household name, as opposed to just a tabloid regular. This wedding, if he did it right, wouldn't be just a gossip rag sensation like the last two; it could be an American royal wedding, on the cover of the most regarded magazines and talked about the world over. It would feed his ego, sure, but it would also line his pockets. You can't pay for that kind of publicity, particularly one that branded him as a fifty-eight-year-old landing a stunning model twenty-four years his junior in a lavish affair fit for a king. As soon as that thought dawned on him, small and simple dissolved in an instant. Big hoopla it would be.

This time around, Donald had time to send out proper invitations—engraved, from Tiffany's. They requested the honor of the presence of hundreds of famous friends and acquaintances and anyone with a name fit for a public guest list they'd ever come across at the Episcopal Church of Bethesda-by-the-Sea, where they would participate in a traditional wedding ceremony, and a reception to follow at Mar-a-Lago on January 22, 2006. While in his first wedding, Donald and his assistants planned the whole thing while Ivana got her footing in New York, now Melania had a hand in every detail. On the night of the wedding, in fact, a *New Yorker* reporter overheard Donald in a men's room during the reception telling someone that it was time to make an honest woman out of Melania, and this night was her night, not his.

FOR ALL the A-listers who'd turned down an invite to Donald's wedding to Marla in New York, they sure did file into Palm Beach to bear witness to lucky number three. Just around 7:00 p.m. on January 22, they made their way into the pews at the Episcopal Church of Bethesda-by-the-Sea, breathing in the gardenias and roses that dozens of refrigerated trucks had driven from New York to Florida for the affair. There were politicians—Hillary and Bill Clinton, Chris Christie, Rudy Giuliani, George Pataki, Steve Wynn. There were those from the sports world—Derek Jeter, Shaquille O'Neal, Don King. There were those in the music universe—Billy Joel, P. Diddy, Paul Anka, Usher, Simon Cowell. And there were media heavy hitters—Jeff Zucker, Barbara Walters, Katie Couric, Matt Lauer, Kelly Ripa, Chris Matthews, Kathie Lee Gifford, Les Moonves. "If someone had dropped a bomb on that place, it would have wiped out an entire generation of famous Americans," the bandleader's wife told a reporter.

Tiffany had handed out all of her programs before she took a seat beside her half sister. Don Jr. and Eric took their places at the altar. A soloist from the Metropolitan Opera—in fact, the same soloist who had performed at Donald's second wedding—began singing "Ave Maria" after Donald joined his sons at the front of the Gothic-looking church, lit by gleaming lanterns hanging from the pointed ceiling. The doors at the back of the church swung open, and Melania walked through. Or, she tried to walk through. She hadn't practiced moving around in her gown, which likely weighed more than half as much as she did. It would have taken her down in front of

all those famous guests staring directly at her, had it not been for a few quick-on-their feet minders, who steadied the bride and sent her on down the aisle. She didn't stop when a guest's cell phone rang from the pews. She fixed her eyes on her soon-to-be husband, who looked almost humbled—if not by the woman he was about to marry, then by all the genuine stars who had turned up to watch the woman he was about to marry say her first "I dos." Melania carried a set of rosaries that had long belonged to her family, and as part of the traditional ceremony, the couple lit a candle she asked her mother to bring from Slovenia. She'd lit it only once before—at her baptism, decades earlier. Ivanka read from the Bible, Donald and Melania exchanged their vows, and their guests broke into a round of applause and rowdy cheers, throwing white rose petals in the air. Whereas Donald had only offered Marla a peck on the cheek at the conclusion of their ceremony, he kissed his newest wife a hearty three times in a row. "It was quick but beautiful and perfect," Cowell told a reporter afterward. "I give it a nine."

About a hundred limousine drivers were on hand to transport guests back to Mar-a-Lago for the reception, where forty-five chefs were at work preparing mountains of caviar and hors d'oeuvres covered in edible gold leaf.

Both Eric and Don Jr. offered toasts to their father and new stepmother. "I know this is the last time I'll ever have to stand up here," Eric said. "I look forward to spending many years annoying both of you," Donny joked. Donald gave a toast of his own, telling the crowd that his years with Melania had "been the best six years of my life in every way." Unquestionably, one of those ways was that they happened to be the years in which he had become a figure of enviable outward success and status. Billy Joel, Paul Anka, and Tony Bennett serenaded the crowd before the couple cut into their cake after midnight. It was a seventy-inch, seven-tiered gold and white classic yellow sponge cake flavored with sprinkled zest, soaked with Grand Marnier, filled with buttercream, and covered with two thousand

sugar flowers. The whole thing weighed two hundred pounds and was held together inside all that butter, sugar, and flour by an intricate construction of hidden internal wires—so intricate, in fact, that it couldn't actually be cut into enough to serve to the hundreds of guests. They baked a bunch of backup cakes to serve instead, and Mar-a-Lago staffers dug into the real cake after the party was over.

The party itself went well into the evening. Melania changed into a second dress—a far lighter Vera Wang ruched silk tulle gown with a slit well up her knees, the whole thing hugging close to her body. A DJ played by the pool for guests to dance, until Donald carried his third wife into his suite in his club at around four o'clock in the morning.

The couple stayed at Mar-a-Lago for their honeymoon. "Why are we going to leave our beautiful house and venture out to some tropical island where things aren't clean?" he explained to Larry King a few months after the wedding.

MELANIA TOOK to the role of being the third Mrs. Trump immediately. By April, she chaired the Martha Graham Dance Company's season-opening fund-raising gala at Tavern on the Green, to which she showed up in a strapless cream Dior gown, embroidered with little pastel flowers and cut on an empire waist. It was an uncharacteristically flowy silhouette for the model, which immediately sent the gossip mill churning out rumors that she'd chosen the looser dress to cover up what could be a growing baby bump. She was not pregnant, at the time. But by the summer, a little more than half a year after their wedding, Melania had news to share with her new husband. "He came home one day in August and I told him he'd be a daddy," she told *People* months afterward. Of course, he was already a daddy four times over. All three of his children with Ivana were into their twenties, and Tiffany was a preteen. His reaction, as Melania described it, was about at the excitement level you'd expect for a fifth-time father who would be nearing his sixtieth birthday by

the time the new addition came into the world. "At first, he needed to take it in," she said. "It was a real surprise, and then, he was very happy." Donald interrupted her, saying that the news didn't totally take him by surprise. "I expected we were going to have children, but I was surprised by the speed of it. It happened very quickly."

They announced the news to the *Post* at the end of September. "Baby Trump," the headline ran. "A baby Donald is due in the spring." In the meantime, Melania started waking up at seven o'clock each morning to oversee construction of the nursery they would build in the Trump Tower triplex. Donald didn't do much to help his wife prepare, which was just fine with Melania. She'd already hired a nanny by the beginning of 2006, months before the baby would arrive (she later denied in an interview with *Harper's Bazaar* that she ever had a nanny—a notion that Donald later corrected in an interview of his own, conceding that they did indeed have someone to help with their child). She knew what to expect of her husband as a father, since she'd seen him with his four older children. "I don't expect him to walk down Fifth Avenue with a stroller," she said. As for the birth, Donald would revert back to the role Ivana put him in—outside the delivery room. Seeing Tiffany's birth in Marla's hospital séance scene had been enough. "I think it's easier for Melania if I'm not there," he told *People*.

He did turn up for a sonogram to find out whether they were having a little boy or a little girl—the one thing they kept hidden from the press in those nine months. And he made it to the baby shower as well. In February the couple reserved the famed Fifth Avenue toy store FAO Schwarz to celebrate the new baby Trump. Ivana's friends commissioned a cake with "Trumpette" scrawled across it in frosting while combing through the store's many aisles and floors—all the towering stuffed animals, the bright pink Barbie wing, the Lego section, through the art projects and board games and dress-up costumes. Donald and Melania already had everything they needed for their little one on the way—all the gifts guests chose in the store that

day would be donated to children at the nearby New York Presbyterian Hospital. Melania, in a gender-neutral yellow sleeveless dress,
said that her husband "loves the baby" already and is "very excited"
by the whole thing.

What seemed to excite Donald as much as the baby itself was
the fact that NBC had recently signed him for two more seasons of
The Apprentice. What the pregnancy was doing to his wife's figure
wasn't so bad, either. In December, he described to Howard Stern on
his radio show how Melania had changed since she'd found out she
was expecting. "You know, they just blow up, right?" he said on air.
"Like a blimp, in all the right places." In *her* case, he qualified, it was
in all the right places. Later in the show, he said he no longer found
model Heidi Klum, who'd been a guest at his wedding to Melania,
attractive since she gave birth to her two kids. "I looked at her the
other day and it's off," he said of Klum.

But Melania was different, special. "I mean she really has become
a monster, in all the right places." Catching himself, he explained
that he meant "monster in the most positive way." He continued
to dig: "She has gotten very, very large, in all the right places." The
whole world got to judge for itself a few months later. A seven-
month pregnant Melania posed for a photo shoot by Annie Leibo-
vitz for the April *Vogue*, wearing only gold body paint drawn on
in the shape of a string bikini and towering gold pumps. She stood
on the stairs of an airplane parked on a tarmac, her body tilted just
so, giving a profile view of her belly, which, even at that stage in her
pregnancy, was hardly blimp-like. Donald was off to the side of the
frame, sitting inside the silver $600,000 Mercedes SLR McLarren
he'd given his wife a year earlier. "I think it's very sexy for a woman
to be pregnant," she told the magazine, which came out close to
her due date. "I think it's beautiful, carrying a baby inside." As for
how she planned to discipline her child, she thought she would be
the sort of mother who was "strict, but not too strict, and I think
grounded. Very grounded."

Melania wasn't due until the tail end of March, which meant that on March 18, Donald thought he was in the clear to spend another weekend at Mar-a-Lago, while Melania stayed put in New York. He had talk show host Regis Philbin and his wife Joy fly down to keep him company. Not long after they left, Melania called Donald and told him he needed to fly home. She checked into the hospital on Sunday evening, and on the morning of Monday, March 20, after eight hours in labor, Melania delivered an eight-and-a-half-pound baby boy, nine days early. They hadn't yet settled on a name by the time Donald called into MSNBC's *Imus in the Morning* show to share the news with the world. Philbin was shocked when his producer told him that a baby Trump had arrived when he was on air filming *Live with Regis and Kelly* that morning, so he picked up his phone and dialed Donald, who promptly answered the call. "She gave me a nice son," Donald told his friend. He continued to gush that day to the Associated Press, the wire service—only about himself. "I continue to stay young, right?" the fifty-nine-year-old said. "I produce children. I stay young."

They eventually settled on a name—Barron William Trump (Barron was one of the pseudonyms Trump sometimes took on when pretending to be a member of his press team, planting stories and leaking tidbits about himself to reporters). Two weeks after giving birth, Melania appeared on ABC's *The View*, telling the ladies that the birth was "great" and "very, very easy." Had she gotten an epidural? Joy Behar asked. "Of course," Melania said, laughing, in a decidedly un-Marla-like way.

Three weeks later they invited *People* into their triplex for an exclusive look at the little heir, or, as the magazine nicknamed him, the "Billion Dollar Baby." "I like to spend every minute with him," Melania said. "I feed him. I change him. I play with him." Sometimes she let him sleep in a bassinette in her room with Donald, though he has an entire floor for himself—and the nanny, of course—right above his parents'. The couple had transformed the floor that Don Jr., Ivanka, and Eric grew up in for the third iteration of Donald the new daddy. Barron would grow up looking out of those same floor-to-ceiling windows his siblings did when he woke up on the sixty-seventh floor each morning. Donny's Grateful Dead posters, Ivanka's lavender canopy, Eric's nautical bedroom, they were all gone by now. Ivana had fled the triplex with her kids more than a dozen years earlier; Marla and Tiffany packed their bags and moved west nearly ten years before. It was Melania and Barron's turn now, and she filled his nursery with a mink coverlet presented to the littlest Trump by furrier Dennis Basso and a floppy, feet-long dog from FAO Schwarz, courtesy of Barbara Walters.

Donald seemed to be just fine with it—in front of the cameras and a reporter, at least. "I don't sleep much anyway, so if he cries, that's fine. I love to feed the baby, not because I have to, but just because I love it," he said. "A lot of times, early in the morning, I'll take care of him." That stopped short of diaper changes, which he said his wife was fine with, too. "Some women want the husband to do half the chores," he said. "That's not Melania—fortunately for me." They posed for an official portrait all together—Melania in an ultra-low-cut black satin cocktail dress, Donald in his typical boxy black suit and cobalt tie, clutching his son, who'd fallen asleep in a white onesie in his arms. Neither of the parents is smiling or looking toward the baby. They stare intensely into the camera, as if the child does not exist and they are posing for an ad for a Trump casino or the new season of *The Apprentice*. Barron fell into the background of most of the other photos too—like the one in which Melania is posed in front of the apartment's gilded front doors, under its gilded ceiling, pushing a golden pram with its own chandelier, which Ellen DeGeneres had given the baby a few days earlier. She holds Barron in her other arm, though he's mostly out of view. He is at the center of a photo shot in his nursery, in which Melania feeds him by bottle on the floor, though the gigantic stuffed dog Walters gave him and the even bigger stuffed lion and elephant and polar bear and teddy bear surrounding mom and baby are the clear focal points—artfully arranged in front of the Central Park view to tell a story of all the spoils this child, not even a month old, already enjoys. In a final photo, however, he is the star. This one was to be of just the baby, wrapped in a Burberry robe, his tiny toes covered by slippers with floppy bears hanging off the top of each foot. As he got changed out of his clothes and into the robe, Donald hovered nearby. "Come on, Barron," he told his new son. "You're going to make your debut."

CHAPTER 5

Meet the Mini-Voltrons

A BOUT A decade ago, Donald's three eldest children piled into one of their offices on the twenty-fifth floor of Trump Tower. They had just finished up their weekly sibling lunch date, for which they meet outside their glass-doored offices, which are all in a row, and travel down the elevators into its puke-pink marble and down the corridor to the Trump Grill.

The three were finishing up a conversation as other people in the office popped in, when out of nowhere, Don Jr. zeroed in on his sister. He clotheslined her, tackling her to the ground, in the dress she had been wearing to meetings all day. Then he plopped down and sat right on top of her head. "I used to do this all the time when we were kids," he said. "All the time."

Too stunned to speak, colleagues looked at Ivanka's beet-red face, which was growing redder by the second. Eric chuckled in the corner before he, too, flew to the ground toward his sister. He started in on tickling her, while Don kept his perch on her blond ring of hair.

"I'm going to kill you both when you get off me," she barely got out through her laughter. One colleague told the boys to knock it off by the time she'd reached a deep crimson. "It was funny, and I guess it was sweet," a colleague recalled recently. "I'd say it was definitely not something you'd see in every office, but this wasn't every office."

This was an elevator ride away from their old childhood bedroom, a floor below their dad's office. They were the heirs apparent. If they wanted to turn the office into a sibling Summer Slam, so be it.

THAT THE siblings are so close is largely the product of the bunker mentality they adopted during their formative years, through Page Six and the Mar-a-Lago sequester, through Marla and Melania and more tabloid mayhem than any children need witness. No one else understands what that was like. Nor does anyone understand quite as well what it's like to work for their dad. They were handed a set of golden keys, and with them, golden handcuffs.

It is hard to believe that this bond, this shared mentality, is what Donald imagined when he decided he wanted a big family. Before Don Jr. was born, he'd tell friends that he wanted at least five kids. Not to mirror his own nuclear family growing up. Not as a status symbol, as some families use it, a point of pride in Manhattan (to this day, having a fourth kid—with all the square footage and tuition money and second taxis that necessitates—remains the ultimate New York status symbol, more than any home in the Hamptons or rare-skinned Birkin bag in the closet). He wanted more kids because that would mean a greater probability one would turn out just like him.

"I want five children, like in my own family, because with five, then I will know that one will be guaranteed to turn out like me," he'd say. It is common for narcissistic parents to view their children as mirrors. Their children's gifts and flaws reflect back onto their mother and father, and so they often demand perfection in their offspring. Donald often refers to himself as the smartest guy with the highest IQ, the ultimate dealmaker with the best genes, a storied athlete with an Ivy League education and a company worth more money than any detailed, well-respected calculation gives him credit for. If just one out of his five children had all of those things, well, any parents should be so lucky.

His vision didn't pan out exactly as he'd imagined. As Michael Cohen, the president's attorney, who worked closely with the family for the decade, sees it, each of his kids got one of the traits that, together, make up Donald Trump. "They're like mini super bots, Mini-Voltrons," he said. "Collectively, they make the whole."

In Ivanka, there is the hyperskilled media-savvy messenger. She works the press to serve her best, and when the camera comes on, she comes alive. In Don Jr., his father's press-me-and-I'll-hit-you-back-harder sensibility rages. In Eric is the builder, who lives and breathes construction, a natural when it comes to spatial relations and building material and working with developers and guys on a job site.

"They're so good in their zones, like the boss is," Cohen said, "but try to have them do what the other ones are good at, that's just not what they do."

Tiffany and Barron weren't initially categorized in the same way, though it is clear that both had Donald's guy-on-the-outside-looking-in passed down to them.

Consciously or otherwise, the Trump children have spent their lives settling into and perfecting their prescribed roles within their father's orbit. The degree to which they've dug into them is astounding.

CHAPTER 6

Ivanka—Voltron Number One

The Media Mastermind

Rain pattered down on the hood of the town car and clung to its windows all the way through Midtown Manhattan, down into the Lincoln Tunnel, and then winding through the sleepy, slick roads in a New Jersey commuter town as one of Donald Trump's former associates made his way home for the evening. It was 1997, and car phones were plastic bricks, but they worked well enough to telegraph a yammering Donald for the twenty-minute commute home. Mercifully for the associate, Donald got off the line as the driver turned onto his street.

He hadn't yet put his briefcase down before his wife told him that Donald had called for him.

"But I just hung up with him," he told her.

Donald, in the years he'd known him, was an infinite pit of need—a time-sucking vampire who fed off those around him to sustain his own vanity. To work with him was to be telephoned or summoned and shouted for, sometimes all at once, to handle non-crises, or actual crises, to stroke his ego or tamp down a rage or puff up an insecurity, or simply, most commonly, to entertain the ever bored and constantly unfocused mind of the man in Trump Tower.

They implemented little tricks, ways in which they could get him off the phone quicker or brush him off more readily. Take, for instance, when Donald would not stop calling lawyers and advisers around the time he was taking his Atlantic City casino public. The financials were a disaster and time was crunched, and technically, they were in the quiet period—the time in which a company preparing to go public cannot make statements or news or say much of anything—but Donald just couldn't shut up. Concerned about the way the press would write about him, he called and called and called with every suggestion and question and thought bubble bursting in his brain. At this point, the ink was well dry on his divorce with Ivana and he had settled in with Marla, who at that moment was sunning herself at Mar-a-Lago.

"I need to wipe this makeup off my face," he said into the receiver. There were two people on the line, both of whom asked why he was made up in the middle of the week. It was the mid-1990s, predating *The Apprentice*, and surely they would have had to clear any preplanned press for the IPO.

"I shot a commercial for Pizza Hut with Ivana, but it's not going to air until the weekend," he said. (The commercial, now rather infamously, features the estranged couple, in diamonds and black tie, delivering innuendo-laden dialogue: "It feels so wrong, doesn't it?" "But it feels so right." "Then it's a deal?" "Yes! We eat our pizza the wrong way, crust first.") Of course, that violated the quiet period, but looking for some quiet of his own, one person on the line saw an opportunity.

"I sure hope you told Marla," he told Donald. "You better call her right now, because if she doesn't hear it from you first . . ."

Donald called back shortly after. "The poor girl," he told them. "She's sick. She told me, 'I'm going to puke my fucking brains out.'"

"She's not sick, Donald," one associate told him. "She's sick of you. You better go and get on a plane to Palm Beach right now." That bought them a few hours of time without a phone call.

So when the associate asked his wife how he could be calling again, she shrugged and pointed him toward the telephone by the precariously stacked mail on the table. He dialed Donald's private line in his Trump Tower triplex, waiting for the rings to be replaced by the breathy baritone he'd just hung up with a few minutes before.

Ivanka, in her own husk, answered.

"Oh, I know he was trying to talk to you, but he'll be a few minutes." So they made small talk about the things you can with your friend's teenage child; she hated math class but school was fine otherwise. He flicked through the mail, biding time.

"You'll never believe this," he told her. "I just got a postcard for a store here called Ivanka's." A woman named Ivanka Eror had opened Ivanka's Country Barn, a home furnishing store that, to this day, sells a collection of antiques, reproductions, and accessories in Wyckoff, New Jersey, twenty-eight miles from Trump Tower. That Ivanka posed, smiling from ear to ear, for a photographer from the local paper, cutting a red ribbon with her husband and the town's mayor in the summer of 1996.

On the phone, the line went silent. "I told my dad we needed to trademark my name," Ivanka gritted through her teeth. "He never listens to me. He never listens, but I told him." The associate smiled to himself. Donald didn't need to get on the line. The mini version of him had already picked up.

By September 17, 1997, Ivana filed a trademark application for the name "Ivanka." The document, marked from Ivana's home on Sixty-Fourth Street, stated the intention to use the name for international trademark classifications 3, 14, and 25: cosmetics (namely lipstick, lip gloss, lip liner, eye shadow, eyeliner, brow liner, mascara, concealer, foundation, pressed powder, loose powder, blusher, bronzer, nonmedicated skin preparations, namely day crème, night crème, mini-lift scrub mask, moisturizer, skin brightener, repair lotion, skin cleaner, astringent, skin toner, eye crème, wrinkle crème, eye gel, spot treatment; body crème, body lotion, bubble-bath oil), jewelry and watches, and clothing (pants, shorts, skorts, skirts, dresses, blouses, T-shirts, shirts, sweaters, sweat shirts, sweat pants, jeans, leggings, bodysuits, socks, hosiery, jackets, coats, anaraks, windbreakers, hats, shoes, boots, slippers, nightgowns, nightshirts, bathrobes, lingerie, intimate apparel, namely brassieres, panties, slips, camisoles, and tap pants).

THERE IS a distinct genetic quality to Ivanka's preternatural ability to self-promote. Her father, after all, built his real estate empire on a million-dollar head start from his own father and a whole lot of bluster. He spent years making phony phone calls to reporters under different pseudonyms, acting as his own spokesman to plant favorable stories about himself in the New York press, and just as often called them as himself. For a time, reporters at the *New York Post* put a self-imposed ban on quoting him in stories. Because he was willing to be quoted, all the time and about anything, it was almost too easy to get him on the line agreeing to appear in the story. Readers would tire of it. But there was an American appetite for the particular brand of gaudiness with a New York City address and a one-syllable name on all those buildings—in gold. He's the poor person's idea of a rich person, as Fran Lebowitz says, and so his name on polyester ties made in China or mattresses or hotels or water or steak or any of the now-defunct products he licensed his name to over the years had a certain appeal. "All that stuff he shows you in his house—the gold faucets—if you won the lottery, that's what you'd buy."

It translated to viewership, too. *The Apprentice*, built on this foundation, aired for fifteen seasons, later adding a celebrity version. Many have said that its most recent iteration—the presidential one—was an extension of Donald's brand. Of course, dozens of factors led to his surprise electoral victory, which will be debated and investigated for decades to come. But unquestionably, the ease with which he knew how to market himself and manipulate the media will be among them.

Ivanka is the true second-generation version of that salesman. She has all of that self-promotional ease without all the brash. She is the spoonful of sugar to her father's acerbic "You're fired" and "Nasty woman." Where the key to her father's marketing ethos may have been "All press is good press," Ivanka's, honed since she was a child, has been "Control all press so that it is as good as possible."

The psychology here is a gimme. The narcissism is hereditary, though muted in its inheritance. A full wall in Ivanka's office was plastered with magazine covers bearing her image from her brief years as a professional model while she was in high school, and subsequent turn into businesswoman with crap to sell to the masses.

"That's what she was born for! She is a Trump!," her close friend since childhood, Christina Floyd, told *Vogue* a decade ago. "The girl knew how to be in front of a camera since she started speaking."

Part of it was her natural predilection for attention. "I think part of the reason is that she is a beautiful woman, but she's like me," Donald once said of his daughter. "She loves the public. She loves to be out there."

That's why some of her friends and associates think she'll run for president one day. "I'm a hundred percent sure it will happen, though maybe when her kids are older," an associate said after she moved to Washington. "The attention, she loves it. She's like, addicted." Part of it, too, made good business sense. Posing for magazine covers and appearing with her father on *The Apprentice* was cheap mass exposure. "What other developer could generate that sort of publicity for free?" she asked the *New York Times* when she first came back to the Trump Organization and posed for the cover of *Elle* Mexico.

A big chunk of this is the fact that much of Ivanka's life was not only out of her control, but also documented and determined by the press. She was a preteen when she saw her media-obsessed father leave her, her mother, and her brothers for Marla, and witness how he lit up or blew up depending on how the press depicted him. She carried the burden of wondering if her father would leave again or love her still, and knew full well that one way to endear herself to him forever was for him to read about her in the paper, particularly if she could make him money while getting her name in print at the same time.

This idea played out in steroidal proportions during the presidential campaign, which was not Ivanka's idea for what she wanted at that point in her life. She was an executive in her father's company, at the helm of her own eponymous fashion line, and had just inked a deal on a book about being a working woman and mother (at the time, her publisher thought of it as a C-list celebrity self-help book that might appeal to a coastal audience). She and Jared had just bought another apartment in the Trump building where they lived on Park Avenue, and she was about a minute pregnant, if that, with her third child when her father announced his candidacy in June 2015. She had invitations to the annual Met Gala, vacations planned aboard David Geffen's yacht, small kids who were happily settled in their schools and classes in the city. Their schedules were already so packed that she had to schedule time to play cars with her son Joseph and designate a day to bring her daughter to the office. Her trainer had begun bringing a notebook and pen to sessions so that Ivanka could write down what she had to do after their workout. Otherwise, she would be too overwhelmed to focus.

Ivanka's life didn't have room for a presidential campaign, especially one that required her to be both a second-string campaign spouse, since her stepmother largely sat out, and a proof point that her father did respect women, despite the things he'd said about their appearance or the behavior he'd been accused by two dozen women over the years. But there was no question that if her father decided to run, she would do what he needed her to do, even if it

wasn't what she herself wanted, or what would be best for her own life and business and family. That's how their dynamic worked.

Still, Ivanka found control in a situation that seemed, in every way, beyond her grasp. In all her public statements—the stump speeches, the television interviews, the phone calls to reporters—she stuck to one issue. She used her speech introducing her father at the Republican National Convention to talk about paid family leave; she stumped about affordable childcare; she told interviewers about all the times her father had told her she could be anything she wanted to be if she worked hard enough. She avoided any political discussions that didn't mesh with her personal brand and the vision she'd already been marketing to customers for years. Her role helped her father's cause, sure, but even more, it set her up for her life after the campaign.

That level of messaging mastery doesn't appear out of thin air for adult children of presidential candidates to harness during a campaign. As Chelsea Clinton, an acquaintance Ivanka ran into at dinner parties before the presidential campaign cut off the oxygen between them, once remarked to *Vogue*, Ivanka was "always aware of everyone around her and insuring that everyone is enjoying the moment. It's an awareness that in some ways reminds me of my dad."

This quality would serve as perhaps Donald's greatest political asset, and, in an unintentional political turn, Ivanka's too. Without knowing it, she'd been preparing for this moment all of her life—learning to contain the uncontainable, and steer it in her favor. "I'm always known as kind of a control freak," she admitted on *Good Morning America* when she was sixteen. "I like to be in control of everything and not be vulnerable." At twenty-three she told *W Magazine*, "There are very few things we can control in life, but how we project ourselves is one of them." And so she used what her father gave her, fueled by the childhood innocence and privacy he'd stripped away, and crafted for herself an image she thought

would suit her best: an ambitious heiress, privileged but not spoiled, beautiful but not dim. This Ivanka did not dance on tables, or drink, or smoke, or stay out late. She didn't want the attention, but if she could use it for the good of the family, then she'd just have to take it on. She worked constantly, and was in on the jokes people made about her being born on third base or a vacuous blonde with a big bank account. For years, those around her watched her put a calculated strategy in place, making certain that this was the image of Ivanka Trump that stuck.

ONE THING she must have picked up from her father: a half dozen points she wanted to make about herself, which she repeated, and repeated, and repeated again, over the years. They made her sound strained to many people who interviewed her. "Speaking with her was like talking to a very carefully-crafted press release," a reporter from the *National Post* noted in 2009. "She allows access into her professional world to further both the family legacy and her independent business ventures and restricts access into personal details to guard her interior life." Reporters noted that she ate big meals in front of them to ward off the impression that she was hyperconcerned with her figure, and took out her own trash lest she appear in print as overindulged.

"I had been feeling that I was getting only her work face, a kind of tough, boss-lady character that she plays to overcompensate," a *New York Times* reporter wrote two years earlier. "She did not really break character."

This kind of strategic repetition is a tell. The things people choose to emphasize reveal the things they wish to be, that they believe best serve their ambition. It just so happens to actually work.

In no particular order, and over the better part of two decades, Ivanka constantly made the point that she was a hermetic, unentitled goodie-goodie who worked her ass off, had no interest in television or modeling as a career, and enjoyed the simpler things in life.

Paris Hilton served as a constant foil. The two both grew up up-town in the same era; both were bleached-blond real estate heir-esses born the same year to rich parents who wanted the best for their daughters, even if they may have diverged in their definitions of "best." Donald had publicly said he found both of them attrac-tive. When Paris's reality show, *The Simple Life*, premiered, in 2003, the show was a hit. The era of the celebutante was reborn, and sud-denly the real-life Eloises and Little Lord Fauntleroys spilling out of nightclubs routinely made Page Six, and populated the entire home page of TMZ. It is not the image most conventional parents would choose for their children, but Donald was not a conventional parent. Friends of Ivanka at the time remember Donald constantly talking in front of his daughter about how famous and attractive Paris was, and urging her to have her own reality show like *The Simple Life*.

Instead, Ivanka repeatedly made a point of setting herself apart from her peers who were behaving badly. "It makes me sad," she said of Paris in 2004. "One of the easiest stereotypes of kids with money is that they're the same—they were raised with the same val-ues, they behave the same way." Later that year, on *20/20*, she said, "When people say, 'You know, why aren't you wild and, you know, out and very ostentatious and partying all the time?' And I think the difference is, we wouldn't be allowed to. It's really as simple as that." Two years later she made it clear that "Paris and I don't hang out," though they know each other. "We both come from wealthy families, but that's all that links us. I think there's something more accessible about me," she said, adding that it's annoying to her when she is lumped into "that heiress category" because she "works her ass off."

It didn't take an interviewer asking about Paris for her to bring up how hard she worked and how little she socialized. "I know her wardrobe might tell another story, but she's really a homebody," said Alexis Zimbalist, her roommate after she transferred to the Uni-versity of Pennsylvania for junior and senior years. They shared an apartment at a building called the Left Bank, overlooking the Schuylkill River in Philadelphia, which was both far enough away from the fraternity and sorority houses and expensive enough to insulate them from the typical college scene. "She'll rent whole seasons of shows on DVD. She's a *Law & Order* slut." Ivanka responded to her friend's comments by joking that that would be the last interview she'd let her give, yet doubled down on it by calling herself "hermetic." She gave interviews to local papers in Palm Beach and New York gushing about her version of fun—walks on the beach, which serve as both exercise and a chance to catch up with friends; dinners with six to ten friends; golf, tennis, a roller rink in Staten Island, a bar where she could beat her friends at Big Buck Hunter because she stuck to soda while they drank more than enough alcohol to make up for her. Had she ever done anything rebellious? a reporter asked in 1999. "Oh god, no. I've never smoked or taken drugs or drunk alcohol." Well, she admitted to trying it once, but she didn't like it.

Unlike Paris, a club rat in diamond chokers who built a brand on being unaware of her privilege and lacking the most basic understanding of actual labor, Ivanka branded herself as the heiress who understood the value of a dollar. She flew commercial, for one. She blogged about saving money on lunch, and when she got stuck on an unexpected layover in Salt Lake City on her way to Aspen in 2006, she slept at a Quality Inn and ate dinner at Little Caesars with the $18 voucher the airline handed out—a fact that found its way onto Page Six.

It wasn't as easy to square her teenage modeling career—the pouty poses, the scantily clad magazine cover photos, the midriff-baring runway walks—with this teetotaling, work-obsessed homebody image. But there was real value in her modeling work. It fed the Trump ego, creating around her the buzz that her father craved, and that would ultimately benefit the family business by making her a household name. "I've wanted to be a model since I was ten or eleven or so," she said just before her fifteenth birthday. "I'd be like, 'There's Cindy! There's Claudia!' And I guess I always wanted people to say that about me." Modeling had the added benefit of requiring frequent travel, which provided an escape from some of the doldrums through which normal high school kids just have to suffer.

Ivanka used her natural good PR sense to manipulate what could have been a deviation from her message. That she was nearly six feet tall and had been a front-row regular at fashion shows alongside her mother since before she could read made her modeling an easier mental leap. Repeatedly, she described it as a means to an end, not a destination. "Modeling was never an endgame for me," she said in her twenties, a sentiment she spun time and time again. "It was never what I wanted to do. I just wanted out of boarding school, where I was bored to death."

It was also a real paid job, which meant years of being able to talk about just how unspoiled the self-described unspoiled heiress really was, and how much blood and sweat her work cost her, and how many fashion show tears she'd shed. Her parents, she would say, weren't like all the other rich-kid parents who gave their kids credit cards and couture and wads of cash on demand, no questions asked. One story in her arsenal was that she bristled when she noticed her parents were flying first class on a trip to Europe, but she and her brothers were in coach. Her mother, she said, told her that if she wanted the more expensive ticket, then she could use her modeling money and pay for it herself.

It is true that Ivanka was the original template for today's version of the young top model with a famous last name. Sure, the Kendall Jenners and Kaia Gerbers of the second decade of the twenty-first century are far more successful—critically and financially—as models than Ivanka ever was. But Ivanka pioneered the idea of parlaying a family brand into a career on magazine covers and runways across the world. The notion she tested was whether designers and brands would put fashion-with-a-capital-F second to the publicity a celebrity offspring could bring. It was worth more to Thierry Mugler to have Donald and Ivana at his show in the 1990s—at the height of their notoriety—than to stick with a more typical model (as critics noted at the time, one without hips who actually knew how to walk in heels). Soon after, Ivanka posed in Versace for a spread in *Elle*, got tapped by Tommy Hilfiger to promote a line of jeans, and appeared on the covers of *Seventeen* and British *GQ*. The latter was racier than the rest, describing her as a "nymphet" with "a passion for big erections, architecturally speaking." Her father said these photos, in which she wore a see-through top and bikini bottoms, weren't his "favorite pictures in the world," but he defended them as "a job for a highly reputable magazine."

She mostly quit modeling once she got to Wharton. The real estate world was closer on the horizon, and she'd soon start posing for photo shoots about the Trump Organization and, later, *The Apprentice*. "I've known, basically since I was cognizant, that I would go into real estate. There's never been any ambiguity about that."

She says she hardly even flinched when Anna Wintour called her early one morning in the midst of finals during her senior year at Penn. As she tells it, she had stayed up late studying the night before, only to be woken up by the phone at eight o'clock the following day. Ivanka had met the *Vogue* editor years earlier through her parents, and they'd run across one another during her modeling years. Wintour, she says, was calling to offer her a job at the magazine after she graduated. She declined the offer on the spot; she had already given her word that she would work for Forest City Realty Trust, another family-owned real estate company in New York. The idea was to spend a few years in the business with a boss who was not her father in order to do some grunt work and get in the swing of things before she inevitably left to join the Trump Organization at an executive level—all before she hit her mid-to-late twenties. She told Wintour how grateful she was for the opportunity, but as much as she liked fashion, there was never another option for her than real estate.

She called her father as soon as she hung up to tell him about the offer she had just turned down. "I think you should consider it," he told her. "Working at *Vogue* sounds very exciting." Her father's word was gospel to her. She spiraled: Did he not think she was good enough to join the Trump Organization? Was she not smart enough or tough enough or in some way not cut out for the business? In the moralistic way she tells it, she realized that it was all a clever trick set up by her father. He wanted her to go into real estate because that was what *she* wanted to do, not because she thought he wanted it for her. "He wanted to make sure it was my passion—that I didn't have blinders on to other incredible opportunities for personal and professional growth," she wrote in her most recent self-help book, with characteristic starch.

The reality show was another opportunity for Ivanka to deny wanting publicity, and paint herself instead as a team player, lending a hand to the family. "I was asked to be on the show and for a while I chose not to," she said. "But when I joined my father in the company, I realized the power of television as a medium." It was an hour, in prime time, highlighting their projects around the world, she'd say; if it weren't essential to the business, she wouldn't be involved. She was interested in buildings, for goodness' sake! She liked to go to roller rinks and walk on the beach with six to ten friends for fun! None of that involved prime-time national television! But it was too good a vehicle for their brand to turn it down.

She was natural at it, though. She and Jared made a cameo appearance on the hit show *Gossip Girl* in 2010, hosting an *Observer* party. "They did it for the money," the show's creator recently said of their appearance, though he regrets not giving Jared more of a speaking role, since his voice is usually so seldom heard.

Ivanka would often go on various business shows to talk real estate. She met with executives at CNBC to ask how she could appear more frequently as an expert on real estate markets. She spent a fair amount of time on other networks, too. The audience ate her up as a guest on Fox Business Network's *Happy Hour*. "We get a tremendous response whenever she's on," Roger Ailes said of her. "For someone so young, she has quite a following. She's going to have [the opportunity to turn from real estate to news or entertainment] there."

IVANKA DID dabble on the film side early on. In 2003 she starred in *Born Rich*, a documentary by her friend Jamie Johnson, heir to the Johnson & Johnson fortune, alongside a cavalcade of überbrats like Georgina Bloomberg, Si Newhouse IV, Stephanie Ercklentz, and Luke Weil. Many of them appeared unencumbered and unaware of their privilege. And even more of their circle had known that's the way they'd come off on film should they open up to Johnson, which is why about fifty or so of the young heirs he asked to participate turned him down. Those who said yes were the ones who saw the film as an opportunity, or were confident that they could control the situation.

Ivanka's interview is partly filmed in her sixty-eighth-floor Trump Tower bedroom, where the whole of Central Park stretches north from the wall of windows at the foot of her lavender canopy bed. Twenty-one at the time, she wears a silver cross around her neck. She gives Johnson a tour of the room—the Madonna clock, the Motley Crew and Bon Jovi and *90210* posters on her wall—and tells him that she is "absolutely proud to be a Trump" because of how hard her parents have worked for all they have. She tells a story she's repeated in the press since she was a kid, and still uses today, about how she preferred Legos and blocks to Barbies and always wanted to be a builder. "I love looking at the New York skyline and being able to figure out what I'm going to add to that and what patch of the sky one of my buildings will be in."

When the film premiered at Sundance, reviewers praised Ivanka as "poised," "well-bred," and grateful for her position. "I can't say I know anybody our age who comes from that kind of background who is operating on that level, or anywhere close," Johnson said of his friend's ability to work hard and stick to a coherent message.

THE PROBLEM with this branding is it leaves out one whole side of Ivanka, the realer one. Much of her young life was a tale of two Ivankas—the one she painstakingly narrated to the public to project the image she thought best served her brand, and the true version. The two are sometimes completely at odds. For example, the veneer of Ivanka as a champion for women who work—a defining pillar of her image as a private business owner and throughout her new political life—chips slightly when it comes to light that her eponymous brand had a meager parental leave policy and relied on subcontractors whose policies were worse. Sometimes, though, when she lets herself be herself—and this is something her friends say privately all the time—Ivanka reveals herself as a much more nuanced, relatable, aspirational person than the version of herself she's crafted, with a delicious rebellious bent.

The truth, for most famous people, is quite a bit closer to earth than the shiny version they want other people to see. That is certainly the case with Ivanka. In reality she was a relatively normal teenager and young adult within the confines of first the prestigious Chapin School on the Upper East Side, and later Choate, the boarding school in Wallingford, Connecticut. Her parents were splashy, and she was modeling while she went to school, which automatically puts her in a different category than most of her rich-kid classmates. As much as she talked about eating at McDonald's and preferring to hail taxis rather than taking her father's limousines, she grew up, when she wasn't shuttling between their Greenwich home and private club in Palm Beach, sleeping in her family's gilded Manhattan triplex on a pillow embroidered "When a woman is tired of the Plaza, she is tired with life." (The Plaza, which her father owned in the 1990s and her mother ran, was her own expansive playground.)

Her friends at Chapin nicknamed themselves the Funny Pink Bunnies Club, a meaningless, self-formed little clique, not unlike their more studious classmates' group, the Eraser Club; another clique went by the moniker the Fearsome Five. Later, outsiders referred to Ivanka's friends as the Lindseys, a name given quite literally: all of them other than Ivanka were named Lindsey.

She did have an uncommonly kind side. There was a homeless man she'd pass on her way to Chapin. He looked as though he couldn't walk, and he asked passersby for spare change to help him get a bite to eat or take care of his legs. For years, as often as she could, she would give him whatever change or dollar bills she could scrounge up. One night, it was later than usual. The Midtown scrum had already cleared out, and when the man thought no one was looking, he handily got up and walked away. For years, Ivanka would tell friends how disheartening that moment was, to see someone she'd believed needed her help deceive her, deceive everyone. He had just been putting on a show this whole time, and she'd fallen for it.

And she could be as unfailingly polite as she often portrayed. When Ivanka was in college, she visited a Chapin friend who'd gone on to college at Emory. The friend arranged for her to stay in the dorm room of a classmate who was off campus for the weekend. The rooms were so tiny that adding an extra body, let alone a suitcase full of stuff, to the dorm room made it almost uninhabitable, so the extra space was appreciated. As Ivanka packed up her things to leave after her few days in Atlanta, she made sure to leave the girl whose room she'd borrowed a thank-you note.

IT IS true that Ivanka was no Paris Hilton, as she frequently pointed out, but she was not entirely immune to temptation. She once went missing on a family vacation in Aspen, sending her parents into a frenzy. After the police had been called, she turned up with a ski instructor.

Several people at Chapin recall a "scandale" in her last year as a student there. The all-girls school, founded by a suffragette in 1901, sits on Eighty-Fourth Street and East End Avenue, separated from the East River only by Carl Schurz Park. Its motto is *Fortiter et recte*, "Bravely and rightly." The future Jackie Kennedy went there, along with the daughters of other uptown socialites. Girls in the school's uniform of green pleated skirt and white collared shirt tend to plants in the greenhouse and get placed on one of two teams in elementary school, green or gold, which will compete against each other throughout their time there. This still being Manhattan, a hot-dog vendor, a kind older man, set up his cart outside the park, right across from the school. A few classrooms directly faced him, in one of which Ivanka happened to be one day during eighth grade. That's where she and a friend decided to flash the hot-dog vendor, out a school window.

The school didn't kick her out for that. That same year, she traveled to Mar-a-Lago to put together her modeling portfolio and lied to administrators about why she was missing school, which irked them far more than the *scandale du hot dog*. At Chapin, the school uses the period between eighth and ninth grades to pull students who, for various reasons, they don't want at the school aside. "I'm sure you'd be happier somewhere else" is the standard line.

Ivanka enrolled for high school at Choate, where she was immediately recognizable but seemingly normal. Some of what people remember about her in school is so distinctly normal teenage behavior that it's easy to imagine Ivanka and a few girls gathered in a friend's dorm room during her sophomore year so that one of them could teach her how to give a blow job, using a banana. She invited other girls in her dorm into her room to watch *90210* episodes.

Her class had its typical cliques—the exchange students, the day students who didn't board in the dorms, the jocks—which meant that there were only about thirty or forty kids in her more social circle on campus, in which Trump wasn't the only notable last name.

Ivanka would strut down the path between buildings, linked arm in arm with other girls. "That was kind of her runway," one former classmate told me. Because she was so tall, taller than most boys on campus, and her legs were so long, she propelled herself at a rather brisk pace as she walked from building to building and class to class. "Maybe that contributed to the perception of her being out of reach to people who didn't really know her as well," another classmate remembered. "It wasn't that she was dodging them. She was just long-limbed. But people maybe saw her as sort of out of their world and kind of untouchable."

At least some of this untouchable aura had to do with the fact that she built her modeling career primarily while she was at Choate. She would get permission to leave campus to go on photo shoots. Ivanka said it was a way to quell her endless boredom; her classmates have said it was a special perk, extended to her only because of her famous last name. What most students did not know was that when she was out of town, she would keep up with her homework and do assignments on the road. She faxed homework to the school on time for teachers to review. If she missed a class, she still did all the required reading, which is more than most students not working jobs at the same time did. She had made a pact with her parents: they would let her model and skip out on some classes in order to do so, as long as she kept her grades up. The deal was that she needed to hold onto a 3.9 grade-point average. If it slipped from there, her modeling privileges would immediately be revoked.

When she wasn't out of town, modeling, she was going back to New York most weekends, sometimes taking Choate friends with her. Sometimes they would take the train. It was a quick trip through Grand Central, not far from Trump Tower, but sometimes her father would send her an SUV with a member of his security team to drive her home.

One of her classmates who took a few trips back to New York

with her remembered walking into Ivana's house to see the dining room table covered in jewels. "Oh, Tiffany's must have brought stuff by for my mom to try on," she told her friends. They'd pop in at her father's office to say hi, and he'd sometimes comment on the way she looked. "She had dyed her hair brown for a modeling shoot, and he told her she needed to bleach it back," one friend remembered. "It was the first time I'd ever heard a parent so pointedly comment on their kid's appearance like that." In fairness to Donald, she'd caused a stir on campus, too, when she came back as a brunette. Blond was her thing, and she gave no one any warning or real explanation for the change.

She would go to dinner with her New York friends, where they'd talk about not eating fruit because it had too much sugar, and take limousines to nightclubs where, despite the fact that they were fifteen, they got plucked out of line and ushered right in. One friend, after seeing the way she interacted with her parents' staff, told her that she was like Eloise, the naughty little blond children's book heroine who lived and wreaked havoc in the Plaza, with her absentee parents and doting nanny. "When she'd go home, we would go into normal family life, which wasn't normal family like the way I knew it," the friend remembered. Ivanka would run errands for her modeling and get her hair cut or nails done, sure. But she always made time to say hi to all of the people who worked around her parents, whom she was obviously very, very close to—the elevator man, the cleaning people, her nanny. "With them, it was always a very warm, loving relationship." Was it as warm and loving with her parents? "I wouldn't call it loving in the traditional sense," the friend recalled. "They'd talk a lot. They'd tell her she needed to get a better grade in this class, pick at her for something else or advise her how to handle something else. Her mother had her own life, as a very unique woman, and her dad worked a lot."

Donald didn't call Ivanka much while she was at school, but he did send her mail a few times a week. Almost always, they were newspaper clippings—about him, or her, mostly—with notes scribbled in Sharpie on them. Rarely did he put any note or message in the envelopes, but the frequency with which they came stood out to other students on campus.

When she did stay in Wallingford, she'd head into town with her classmates to a café where the owners would let kids buy cigarettes and smoke them inside. (Once she got to Wharton, she would use the fifteen-minute break in her 9:00 a.m. statistics class to step outside Huntsman Hall and suck down two cigarettes. She wore a full face of makeup, flat-front khakis, and a Burberry trench coat all the time.) Her father turned heads at graduation for bringing not only a bodyguard, but also his new wife, Melania, whom many of Ivanka's male classmates (and their fathers) couldn't stop looking at during the ceremony. "I just remember all of our heads slowly turning as we walked by her," one male member of the class recalled. "My dad had a good chuckle at that."

Donald and Ivana did not make many trips up to Choate, though they made a few, eating in the dining hall with other visiting parents with little fanfare. This was at least in part because Ivanka went home so often. For a time, her parents kept both of her bedrooms—at Ivana's and in Donald's triplex—like mini–time capsules: the same Madonna poster tacked to her walls, the same frilly canopy bed and floral prints on all the furniture.

Classmates don't remember Ivanka as politically active, but she opted to take a bunch of classes in political history and one in constitutional law. She was opinionated in class, as Choate students are encouraged to be. One year she went with her classmates on a trip to Washington, DC. They met with lawmakers and toured all the monuments, and she participated in Model Congress, proposing legislation that would give free AZT to all people with HIV on welfare. Many remember her as unfailingly polite and uncommonly kind, particularly for someone from her background. "A lot of the kids there were raised by wolves, and I knew a lot of rich kids who were messed up as a result," one classmate remembers. "That wasn't her."

That she'd been raised by intensely competitive parents, however, certainly brushed off on her. Ivana was a near-professional skier, after all, and Donald was self-obsessed and possessed to make himself a name in the New York real estate world. Ivanka had her own streak of competitiveness, though less masochistically. "She herself was a really good skier, and really hated to lose or share that kind of spotlight," one friend since kindergarten said. Another longtime friend noted that she loved going to the movies as she got older, commissioning friends and later Jared, before they had kids, to join her at a theater every Sunday in New York. Invariably, she would order popcorn to chomp on, but she never wanted her companions to steal her bounty. So she developed the tactic of oversalting the popcorn so that no one would want to stick a hand her bag. "You can't even imagine what it tastes like after she's done with it," one movie companion of hers remembers.

Another of Ivanka's classmates at Choate had a condition called prosopagnosia, or facial blindness, meaning he had trouble recognizing faces. He would memorize a specific feature, like someone's hair color or the shape of their lips, and look out for that to figure out who he was interacting with. High school, and Choate, in particular, is hard enough, but with about 220 people in their class, most of them dressing in much the same way and speaking with the same East Coast rich-kid lilt, the disorder was debilitating. He felt socially awkward and isolated, and his grades slumped as he grew more frustrated.

He had a few classes with Ivanka, who made him feel like a nobody by comparison, especially in their mandatory tennis class. They both got put in the class for those who were not necessarily the most gifted of athletes, and one afternoon were assigned to play each other. She wiped the floor with him, partly because she had been playing in Palm Beach and Greenwich for years, but also because he was so intimidated by her. He walked off the court embarrassed, expecting a long, silent solo trudge back to another part of the campus. Ivanka hung back, though, made small talk about how nice the breeze felt, and asked him questions about himself. From that day on she said hello to him when nobody else did, every time she saw him in class and in the halls.

She was also polite enough to not chew out her date to Choate's version of the senior prom, called "the Last Hurrah." A Canadian jock, he was as big and handsome and clunky and heavy on his feet as one would assume of the star of the school's hockey team. The two danced much of the night, as most of the students did, with some good old-fashioned ballroom thrown in for good measure. He stepped on her feet so many times throughout the evening that she limped all the way back to her dorm, which, fortuitously, also housed the school nurse's office, where she paid a late-night post-dance visit.

Ivanka was hardly the only daughter of a well-known and wealthy family on campus. Carl Icahn's daughter Michelle was in her class. Publishing heiress Amanda Hearst also attended Choate, just a few years behind her. But classmates remember that there were never any persistent rumors about any of them other than Ivanka. There was the famous one about a party at a faculty member's house. The teacher, Charles "Chuck" Timlin, was a beloved longtime member of the staff who taught Ivanka English and coached a few teams before becoming the school's athletic director and a form dean and house adviser. Timlin's son was in Ivanka's class, though he was heavy into sports, and he and Ivanka were not particularly friendly. She was far closer to the elder Timlin, as many students were at the time. So when he invited a group of students, Ivanka included, to his house, she went. The party, as these things tend to do, got busted. Call it luck or intuition, but Ivanka left before that happened. Still, her classmates were quick to tattle that she had been there, and like the others who had been at the Timlins' gathering, she was drug-tested. She passed, and walked away with Choate's version of a slap on the wrist, put on restriction (something like detention) for a few weeks. As a Choate student, you are supposed to hold yourself to a higher standard of conduct. Even if you yourself are not doing something wrong, simply being around bad things is a violation of that standard.

Other students walked away with far worse. Some were suspended. Others, expelled. Now, of course, this could have been explained by the fact that Ivanka had not, in fact, done anything wrong other than show up to a party. She'd passed the drug test. She'd left before the party was busted. But some of her classmates saw it differently. Magically, the model daughter of a loudmouthed rich New York developer walked away from something they'd been chained to. Rumor had it that her father had called in, made a stink, and got her out of the whole mess. The truth rarely matters in the reputational meat grinder that is a secluded Connecticut boarding school; perception is the only reality. (Years later, in 2013, when two former students shared with school officials accounts of sexual misconduct they'd experienced as students, Choate's board of trustees hired an investigator to look into allegations of a pattern of sexual abuse at the school dating back to the 1960s. In 2016, the *Boston Globe's* Spotlight team published an exposé detailing the alleged abuse, prompting an independent investigation by a law firm. The report found that at least twelve former teachers had sexually molested and, in one case, raped students. One of the teachers named in the report was Timlin, the teacher who threw the party, the one Ivanka had been close to as a student. Two students had come forward; he had invited one to his home, where he kissed and groped her, and the other he had visited at the campus health center, kissing her, caressing her hand, and telling her "I wish I could make love to you right now," and "I always thought you were really sexy . . . sexiest girl in the class." He was let go in 2010.)

The rumors about Ivanka persisted beyond the one party. One had her father hiring a limo to bring her take-out from restaurants in New York City—about a two-hour drive—so that she could have her favorite meals on campus. One that came up year after year was that Donald had continually tried to get the administration to let him build a helipad on campus so Ivanka could fly home to New York on weekends. Another was about her decision not to go to the University of Pennsylvania, from which her father graduated, as did her brother Don Jr. Some classmates were convinced it was because she was rejected by the school; others thought it was because she had a boyfriend elsewhere. The truth, it turns out, had to do with Don Jr. He hosted his sister on campus for a weekend to show her around before she decided where she would apply. Donny was a partier; his buddies were preppy frat boys straight out of central casting, who relished taking part in hazing rituals long after they had been initiated into Greek life, and they drank themselves into stupors. The whole weekend left a bad taste in her mouth. It did not help that Ivanka arrived on campus worn out and already in something of a sour mood. She and a longtime friend from Chapin, whose older sister had also gone to Penn with Donny, came down for the weekend together. Ivanka drove, and they decided to make a quick detour at a rest stop somewhere along the way. Someone had to use the bathroom; they wanted a snack. They got back on the road and immediately resumed their teenage gossip. They didn't go to school together anymore, and teenage minutiae pile up quickly into mountains over which every inch must be combed, so there was a lot to catch up on. They didn't stop talking until they both saw the Twin Towers appear over the dashboard. Only then did it dawn on them that after their pit stop, Ivanka had gotten back on the highway going in the wrong direction, and that by that point, they were nearly back where they'd started in Manhattan. What should have been less than two hours in the car door-to-door ended up taking the entire day. By the time they finally arrived on campus in Philadelphia, they were hardly in the mood.

Her experience was completely different when she visited Georgetown, where she knew a few friends from Chapin, Choate, and the city more generally. The friends, who were a couple of years older, loved it there, and they offered to let her come visit for a weekend after her less-than-appealing few days with her brother at Penn. She had a much better time there. She loved Washington, too, since it was still close enough to New York. Ultimately she decided that was the school for her, and it was. She started dating Greg Hersch, a city boy who went to Buckley and Horace Mann before heading down to Georgetown. He had an apartment off campus, and the two of them got a dog, a yellow lab named Tyler who slept like a little human, all stretched out on his back. Hersch and Ivanka's older friends started to graduate while she was still an underclassman, and she realized she had done little to make friends her own age. She decided to transfer, and, at her father's urging, turned her sights back to Penn. She wanted to go into business anyway, not politics; Wharton wouldn't be so bad.

Unsurprisingly, the rumors continued after high school, all the way through college, and after she moved back to New York post-graduation. By that point, they were less about little parties and admissions scandals than Ivanka's dating life and alleged dalliances with cocaine. "It was New York City, she was doing modeling or did modeling and hanging out with a very rich, very social crew," recalls one friend who says he "partook" with her. "The idea is not totally revolutionary." Ivanka has vehemently denied ever doing cocaine, but has said she was at parties where people around her were doing it.

Those rumors did not stop once she met Jared, even after they were married, and even if the idea was not totally revolutionary. They were palling around with famous, well-heeled friends, and people gossip about celebrities hanging out with one another, doing things that they would not necessarily want splashed across headlines. There is a bit of deliciousness in hearing about stars behaving just like us, even if that behavior is mundane. It is a truth so unanimous that even *Us Weekly* devotes pages of each issue to the subject, showing celebrities hoisting their groceries into the trunks of their cars or spilling lunch on their sweaters. The delight comes not necessarily from salaciousness, though that does not hurt, but from the idea that it is both a joy and somewhat of a relief to see celebrities who seem perfect get knocked down a peg to our level.

Natalie Portman's wedding to the dancer and choreographer Benjamin Millepied late in the summer of 2012 is the perfect example. It had all the trappings of a Hollywood fairy tale: an award-winning actress met the love of her life while he choreographed her as a twisted ballerina in *Black Swan*, a role for which she nabbed an Oscar. He proposed, and then the couple had a baby boy, and later they invited their closest family members and friends to a weekend at a private home off the Pacific Coast Highway in California. Diane Sawyer and Mike Nichols were on hand, as were Macaulay Culkin and Ivanka and Jared. Ivanka and Culkin had known each other for years. As eleven-year-olds, the two went on a kiddie date. Culkin was filming *Home Alone II* at the Plaza Hotel in New York for about a month and a half, and at the time, Donald owned the joint. Ivanka turned up in a red dress and roamed the halls, taking photos and dipping into the shops set up in the hotel. As a token, Culkin gave her a signed VHS tape of his classic *Home Alone*. More recently, Jared and Portman had gone to Harvard together, and she came to their Bedminster wedding as a guest. There was no shortage of gossip for their Harvard friends to talk about when it came to the wedding years later. But what their pals talk about years later, particularly when it comes to Jared and Ivanka's presence that evening, is the fact that she smoked weed with the rest of the young people in that Harvard–meets–New York crew. A cause for celebration, and fuel for the rumor mill, indeed.

The other sort of chatter around Ivanka had less to do with her and more to do with her father. Parents at both schools famously talked about how cheap he was. At Chapin, many parents were generous with donations—time, wine, hors d'oeuvres—to the school's annual book sale. People recall Donald balking at the suggestion. "I already pay enough tuition for this place. I'm not giving more," he said. Of course, there are murmurs on the Upper East Side that Donald didn't even make good on his tuition for all the years Ivanka went there, and that she left with an outstanding balance, though there is no public record that this is so. Some Choate classmates remembered the same. Carl Icahn gave a tremendous amount to the school—a science center, a scholar's program, buildings bearing his name. When the development center called recent graduates in her class, some would joke that Trump had really done nothing.

Funnily enough, Ivanka was awarded a few superlatives in the Choate yearbook during her senior year on campus. One of them was Most Likely to Succeed, the universal common calling card every Type A overachiever brags about for decades to come, and certainly the superlative that sounds most Trumpian in its braggadocio. Classmates now say she also took Most Likely to Donate a Million Dollars to Choate—which, given the family history, now and then made classmates chuckle.

THERE WAS also talk among Ivanka's friends that her heralded performance in *Born Rich* was more than a disciplined message and good breeding. At the time, Ivanka was dating James "Bingo" Gubelmann, a square-jawed, raven-haired socialite whose family fell on the same New York–Palm Beach axis, and who happened to be the film's producer. After seeing the film, her fellow castmates were less than subtle in suggesting that at least part of her positive treatment in the film had to do with the fact that she was influential in the editing process.

While he may have spared her in the film, Gubelmann was part of one of Ivanka's most public breaks from the perfect image she crafted. In the summer of 2004, she stormed out of the Stephen Talkhouse, an East End institution where sweaty, overserved house-sharers in button-downs come to hear cover bands and do bumps in the bathroom off Route 27 in Amagansett, on Long Island. She had apparently gotten into it with Gubbelmann inside, and locals saw her dash across the street and tuck inside a nearby Mobil station, where Gubelmann chased after her. They exchanged words, and she unceremoniously slapped him across the face before they made amends and went back into the bar, where they stayed until about 2:30 in the morning.

THE REALITY of Ivanka's modeling career was slightly different, too. Donald wanted it for her, bad, to the point where he suggested to friends that breast implants might help her along. One friend recalled getting a frantic call from Maryanne Trump, Donald's sister, urging him to talk Donald out of letting her get plastic surgery that young. "It'll ruin her," she said into the phone. When his friend confronted him about it, he denied that she was getting implants. At the end of the call, he asked, "Why not, though?"

On shoots, she was abidingly well-mannered and punctual and grateful for the opportunities. But when a photographer asked her, at sixteen, to pose using a vacuum cleaner, she had no idea how to use it. On another shoot for a Saks Fifth Avenue catalog, with about forty other models on set at Chelsea Pier 59 on the Hudson River, famed photographer Patrick DeMarchelier had to reverse course on his vision. DeMarchelier had wanted a shot of the men without shirts and the women without pants. Ivanka, however, wasn't wearing any underwear—a fact she had to reveal to handlers on the set.

CHAPTER 7

"Bashert"

"IT'S BASHERT." "They're *bashert*." "*Bashert*." Their friends and colleagues and associates separately repeated the same Hebrew word when asked why Ivanka and Jared Kushner settle into one another. The word roughly translates into something being preordained, fated, inevitable, and in the case of a romantic match, a soul mate. And it makes sense that the word came up as often as it did when describing Javanka: of course this match was inevitable, fated, and preordained, particularly for two people as single-mindedly striving and media-savvy.

In some ways, all matches between especially moneyed young men and women are inevitable—good matches, anyway. There are, after all, only so many people who swim in this silver spoon of a dating pool, within this hyperspecific socioeconomic bracket, appropriate age range, metropolitan area, and post–Ivy League social set and career choices. It's a tried-and-true real-world algorithm that rarely produces happy, lasting true love, but so often creates a true arrangement. For many of these people, whose lives revolve around closing deals, and marriage—a first one, at least—is indistinguishable from the rest. On its face, Javanka's relationship was the gold standard of this sort of deal. Both are heirs to impressive real estate thrones, though, by the numbers, his far more than hers. They are the same age; both are tall and dimpled, Ivy League–educated, and work-obsessed. They are blindly loyal to their families and hell-bent on expanding their empires.

That's just the crunchy shell. Crack it slightly, and you'll see that their gooey innards have been pulverized exactly the same way, too. Both fell victim to their father's bad, selfish behaviors. Donald publicly cheated on Ivanka's mother and, in the aftermath, played their divorce out in the press. Jared's father, Charles Kushner, was convicted of eighteen counts of tax evasion, witness tampering, and illegal campaign donations and sentenced to two years in prison when Jared was twenty-four. Both Ivanka and Jared had to pick up the pieces and cover for their fathers. Jared took over the family business while his father was in federal prison, decades before most real estate scions would get to make even one major deal without holding Daddy's hand. Ever since she was a teenager, doing press for her modeling career, Ivanka had gone on the public offensive for her dad and his businesses, from defending his remarks on *The View* about how he would date her had she not been his daughter to stumping about his respect for women throughout the presidential campaign—even after the *Access Hollywood* tape came out. Donald used his daughter as a human shield in private, too. Once, when he had just started dating Melania, he told a friend that he might get into some more public hot water. He had been fooling around in the Trump Tower triplex with model Kara Young earlier that day—leaving what he described as a mess of twisted sheets in the bedroom and towels smeared with her makeup in the bathroom, forgetting that Melania already had access to the apartment. When Melania confronted him about the foundation rubbed into the towels, he told her that Ivanka had come over that day after a modeling shoot. The makeup, he said, was hers. Just ask her.

In the summer of 2006 Jared canceled a trip he'd planned to Germany to watch the World Cup so he could make a $10 million offer to buy the *New York Observer*, the salmon-tinged weekly that covered the ins and outs of Manhattan movers and shakers. After years of having their name tarnished in the press, the Kushners bought back some control and an entrée into an elite world in which Jared wanted to play. Ivanka made a less fraught brand play by joining *The Apprentice* to help bolster her family's properties.

Perhaps the deepest similarity, though, is their ability to compartmentalize. Both know the truth about their fathers—a blowhard philanderer on one side and a brutalizing convicted felon on the other—and have spent their lives trying to prove themselves and pledge their loyalty to those fathers anyway. Ivanka and Jared watched their dads tear apart their families and turn their backs on everyone. They vowed never to do that to each other or back to their fathers or to the family they would create together.

As much as Jared and Ivanka are the publicly polished, more tolerable versions of their parents, in private the roots show through. Those who have worked for or with both often have the same advice for others taking them on as clients or bosses: be aware of who they can turn into on a dime. "These people eat their young, so just understand that," one former associate recalled being advised before working with the couple. "They had internships at Goldman Sachs when they were fifteen years old. That's not a thing you and I can understand. That's just how they were raised."

If one upper-crust truism is that you unescapably marry your own mirror, the other is that you often marry your father. "Well, he's a decent, caring, hardworking man," Ivanka told an interviewer in 2006, a few years before she met Jared, when asked if she'd end up with a guy like Dad. "And since they're all desirable traits in a human being, I probably would be drawn to someone very similar."

In Jared, there are certainly shades of Donald, who was also raised by an impossible, ghoulish patriarch who wielded money like a string that kept his children inextricably tangled to him forever, despite his unambiguous brutality. They both grew up as outsiders looking into Manhattan—Donald from Queens, and Jared from

New Jersey. Led by that special blend of inexperience and consequence that only true wannabes with Daddy's wallet possess, they were both initially drawn to buildings that made a splash rather than ones that made good sense.

Where Donald and Jared differed was with the press. Donald relished seeing his name in print and his face on the cover of magazines—even fake ones, like the faux *Time* covers hung at various Trump-owned golf courses. In the days before TiVo, he'd often tell dinner companions that he would be late or have to scoot early so he could watch an interview he'd taped earlier that day (in the White House, he has what he calls a "super TiVo" so he can spend much of his day speeding through cable news coverage of his presidency). Kushner, on the other hand, is keener on controlling the industry than being covered by it. For him, it has been about glad-handing its moguls, and trying to become one of them, rather than one of their subjects.

Nowhere is this plainer than in Jared's relationship with Rupert Murdoch. After buying the *Observer*, he cold-called the News Corp executive, who is fifty years his senior, and asked him to dinner. Murdoch agreed, and at Nobu in Midtown Manhattan, Jared fawned and flattered. "I want to be you," he told Murdoch, who slurped it up, and they began talking by phone several times a week.

The two grew closer after Jared started dating Ivanka. Murdoch and his third wife, Wendi, playing billionaire versions of Cupid, intervened when the couple briefly broke up in 2008. In return, the Murdochs' two daughters, Chloe and Grace, walked down the aisle as flower girls at the Trump-Kushner wedding in 2009. A year later Jared and Ivanka were part of a small group of attendees invited to Chloe and Grace's baptism in the Jordan River, where Jesus himself is said to have undergone the ceremony. The guests—among them Tony Blair, Nicole Kidman and Keith Urban, Larry Page, Hugh Jackman, Queen Rania of Jordan, Kathy and Tom Freston, and Burt Sugarman—all wore white for the ceremony. Wendi, who is described as a "very reserved and quiet person" on the twelfth page of a nineteen-page spread about the events in *Hello* magazine, a weekly British tabloid confection, arranged the remainder of the trip, which included a tour through the ancient city of Petra, a stay in a Bedouin tent, and a dip in the Dead Sea. "Went swimming in the Dead Sea with my husband and our buoyancy was even greater than expected!" Ivanka tweeted afterward.

At home, Wendi and Ivanka grew closer. For a time, the Murdochs moved into the Trump Park Avenue building where Javanka lived while their own triplex on Fifth Avenue was undergoing renovations. With an address and taste for striving in common, the two started spending more and more time together. In the run-up to the 2008 presidential election, MySpace, which Rupert then owned, considered having Ivanka host a series of discussions with candidates on college campuses across the country at his suggestion. It didn't pan out, but Ivanka watched the election returns come in with the couple from their screening room. Ivanka stepped out on the eve of her due date with her first child to attend the premier *Snow Flower and Secret Fan*, a movie Wendi produced. The two collaborated on a bracelet inspired by the film for Ivanka's fine jewelry line—a cuff available in black resin with white diamonds or pearl resin with black diamonds, engraved with the Chinese character for friendship. They marketed it as a symbol of friendship and sisterhood, priced at $650. Wendi recommended the interior decorator for the Trump-Kushner apartment; reciprocally, after Rupert and Wendi divorced, Kushner hooked his friend up with an architect for his bachelor pad.

Wendi and Ivanka related as mothers, too. Grace and Chloe spoke Mandarin to Ivanka's children, who, with the help of their neighbors, a Chinese nanny, and tutors, began learning the language almost as early as they were taught English. Arabella Kushner's Mandarin was a particular point of pride for Wendi, who taught the girl to speak some words in front of social audiences so readily that people sometimes mistook her for one of her own daughters. Wendi and her girls would come over for Shabbat dinner all the time, as Wendi had grown particularly fond of the challah Ivanka served. "She calls it 'that bread,'" Ivanka told the *New York Times*. On one Saturday morning, Ivanka turned up at Ivana's home with her two eldest children. Since it was Shabbat, and she couldn't, as an observant Jew, exchange money, she needed her mother's help. Chloe and Grace were selling cupcakes on Fifth Avenue to raise money for a new locker room at their school for a buck apiece, so she dragged her mom outside to fork over a few dollars. They ate them standing in a circle on the street. Until she moved to Washington alongside her husband and father, Ivanka was one of five trustees for a chunk of shares belonging to Chloe and Grace in 21st Century Fox and News Corps and additional interest in Murdoch companies, worth north of $2 billion. She stepped down on December 28, 2016, as she worked with lawyers to remove herself from financial interests and positions that could be perceived as a conflict of interest.

Wendi was one of the few members of their New York social circuit who publicly stood by them during the campaign, and an even smaller circle after they started working in the White House. As Ivanka's father's campaign fell apart at the seams in August 2016, she invited Jared and Ivanka to take a break with her in Croatia on billionaire business magnate David Geffen's yacht. Before they moved to DC, she hosted a dinner for them in her penthouse, and sat beside Ivanka on the eve of her dad's inauguration, at a ball for Republican bigwigs held in Union Station. She continued to make trips down to Washington, while the rest of their social friends wagged their tongues about how she could continue to so openly support them. In January 2108, it was reported that US counterintelligence officials had warned Kushner in early 2017 that Wendi might use her friendship with them to advance the interests of the Chinese government. The news was first reported by the *Wall Street*

Journal, Rupert's crown jewel. By this point, Rupert had been telling people for years that his ex-wife was a Chinese spy.

The relationship between Jared and Rupert was far more straight-forward. They were friendly, sure, in a mentor-mentee way, with no sense that the undercurrent running between them was anything other than professional. There was never any question that it would be Jared who would soothe tensions between his father-in-law and his media godfather during the campaign. Donald and Rupert had stewed in something of a feud for years, the way two multidivorced, scandal-prone moguls do. Rupert, who actually had money, told friends that Donald was a "phony," a bloviator who greatly exaggerated his fortune. Donald once sued Murdoch, who owns Donald's beloved *New York Post*, for libel after the paper printed a story that the Trumps had been rejected from the Maidstone Club—a 126-year-old private golf club on the dunes of East Hampton that overlooks a twenty-seven-hole course on one side and the Atlantic Ocean on the other.

The campaign kicked up the heat. "When is Donald Trump going to stop embarrassing his friends, let alone the whole country?" Rupert tweeted after Donald said he didn't like Senator John McCain because he only liked service members who hadn't gotten captured (McCain, a decorated prisoner of war during the Vietnam War and a long-serving senator, had been a critic of the Trump bid. Donald, for his part, was repeatedly granted draft deferments because of bone spurs). The *Post* ran with front pages scrawled with "Don Voyage" and "Trump Is Toast," while Rupert's other paper, the *Wall Street Journal*, printed an editorial calling the candidate "a catastrophe."

"Murdoch's been very bad to me," Donald told *New York Magazine*. On the Murdoch-owned Fox News, he was mostly spared. There were a baker's dozen other more serious, likelier Republican candidates in the primary, but no one quite rated like the Donald.

At that point, Roger Ailes was still in place atop the network, before he was ousted over sexual harassment allegations, and he advised the Trump campaign behind the scenes.

It wasn't until Donald was pressed by Megyn Kelly in a primary debate that Jared was dispatched to do what he does so well—lick the wounds of aging titans and their outsize egos and work them in his favor. He cajoled Rupert into speaking with his father-in-law. By June 2016, when Donald was a shoo-in for the Republican nomination, Donald had Rupert's fourth wife, supermodel Jerry Hall, beside him in a golf cart at the Trump International Golf Links in Scotland. Murdoch was behind them in the back seat.

THE MEGYN KELLY incident was one of two moments during the campaign that Ivanka thought the media got downright wrong. The way she saw it, had reporters known the intricacies of her father's personality and tics the way she did, the stories wouldn't have been stories at all.

The first was in the first Republican primary debate in August 2015, which aired on Fox News at 9:00 p.m. Eastern Standard Time on that Thursday evening. According to Nielsen data, 24 million people tuned in to the debate, making it not only the highest-rated primary debate in television history but also the highest-rated telecast in Fox News's twenty-year history. To put those numbers in context, the first Republican primary debate in the 2012 election on the same network drew in 3.2 million viewers.

The moderators—Chris Wallace, Megyn Kelly, and Bret Baier—methodically addressed each candidate, asking them about various policy positions and prompting them to dress their opponents down. Eventually Kelly was up, and it was her turn to put a question to Donald. She buttered him up at first, telling him that one of his most appealing aspects as a candidate was his candor, before it turned. "You've called women you don't like fat pigs, dogs, slobs, and disgusting animals," she said.

Donald corrected her: "Only Rosie O'Donnell." She, in turn, corrected him, reminding him that it has not just been O'Donnell. He sniggered. "Yes, I'm sure."

She continued: "Your Twitter account has several disparaging remarks about women's looks. You once told a contestant on *Celebrity Apprentice* it would be a pretty picture to see her on her knees. Does that sound to you like the temperament of a man we should elect as president, and how will you answer the charge from Hillary Clinton, who is likely to be the Democratic nominee, that you are part of the war on women?"

"I've been challenged by so many people, and I don't frankly have time for total political correctness," he responded, in an answer that spoke directly to his supporters. "And to be honest with you, this country doesn't have time either. This country is in big trouble. We don't win anymore. We lose to China. We lose to Mexico both in trade and at the border. We lose to everybody.

"And frankly," he continued, "what I say, and oftentimes it's fun, it's kidding. We have a good time. What I say is what I say. And honestly Megyn, if you don't like it, I'm sorry. I've been very nice to you, although I could probably maybe not be, based on the way you have treated me. But I wouldn't do that."

He did do that, of course. The next night, he called in live to Don Lemon on *CNN Tonight*, which aired directly opposite Kelly's program on Fox News. Lemon mentioned that Kelly had pushed Donald, like she had pushed a lot of people onstage with him the night before. As he does, Donald took that chance to push her harder. "She gets out and starts asking me all sorts of ridiculous questions. She was, in my opinion, totally off base. In, by the way, not in my opinion—in the opinion of hundreds of thousands of people on Twitter. She's been very badly criticized."

He went on to very badly criticize her himself. "I just don't respect her as a journalist. I have no respect for her. I don't think she's very good. I think she's highly overrated. . . . She gets out and she starts asking me all sorts of ridiculous questions. You know, you could see there was blood coming out of her eyes, blood coming out of her wherever." Before the producers could even catch on to what had happened, the moment was picked up and clipped and tweeted and GIFed and aggregated thousands upon thousands of times over. The majority opinion was that Donald had insinuated that Megyn Kelly, who had asked him a question about how he speaks to and about women, had to have been menstruating. Donald denied this the next morning, tweeting that by "wherever," he meant her nose. The campaign followed up with a statement, claiming that he had said "whatever," not "wherever," but even so, it really was in reference to her nose.

This moment got to Ivanka. Not for the reasons it vexed everyone else, but because she knew her father well enough to know that he would never, not in a million years, talk about a woman's period. He was a germophobe who had never in her life made a scatological joke. She and her brothers didn't mind that kind of talk. She said they would watch *Tommy Boy* over and over again, laughing their heads off, but their father found nothing funny about those jokes. It was preposterous, then, to think that he could be referring, so publicly, to a woman *menstruating*. It wasn't that it was blatantly wrong. He finds that stuff icky.

The other moment that irked her was after a rally in South Carolina a few months later, in November 2015. At the time Donald faced backlash over his support for creating a database of Muslims in the United States. To defend his position, he doubled down on an assertion that he had watched "thousands and thousands of people" cheering in Jersey City as they watched the Twin Towers topple on September 11, 2001.

The fact checkers who furiously checked what candidates said on the trail throughout the campaign could find no evidence supporting Donald's recollection. So the candidate propped up a *Washington Post* article written on September 18 of that year by Serge

Kovaleski as proof. The article, though, did not back up his claim. Kovaleski had reported that "within hours of two jetliners' plowing into the World Trade Center, law enforcement authorities detained and questioned a number of people who were allegedly seen celebrating the attacks and holding tailgate-style parties on rooftops while they watched the devastation on the other side of the river." In a statement, Kovaleski said that his reporting didn't even show there were "hundreds" of people there, let alone thousands. And the *Washington Post* said that an extensive examination of news clips from that period turned up nothing backing up Kovaleski's claim.

A day before the South Carolina rally, Kovaleski had said as much in an interview on MSNBC, which Donald must have watched. Onstage at the rally, he mocked the reporter. "Now, the poor guy—you ought to see the guy: Uh, I don't know what I said. I don't remember,'" Trump said, contorting his arms and flailing them about in a way that many believed mirrored a physical disability that Kovaleski has.

The controversy lingered through the primaries and into the next summer. What bugged Ivanka about all of this was that the media and the outraged voters likely had it all wrong. Had they known her father as well as she did, they would have known that he wasn't mocking the reporter's disability with his hand gesture. That was the exact gesture he always used to imitate someone who was groveling, she'd explain to people. She'd seen him use it time and time again. And, as her father tweeted after the rally, he was simply "showing a person groveling to take back a statement made long ago!"

RUPERT MURDOCH was hardly the only media *macher* to get the Jared treatment during his father-in-law's run. As one Trump adviser explained, "Your media relationships are an asset to Trump." It was one of the many ways in which Jared was rich. Joe Scarborough and Mika Brzezinski got it, too. The *Morning Joe* hosts had a

long history with Donald, and a short-lived live-TV love affair with him in his early candidacy. He repeatedly called in to the MSNBC morning show, in exchanges that felt like breakfast-table chatter between old friends. Trump referred to them on air as "supporters," and if they weren't quite that, you could call them "believers." That changed once the summer of 2016 rolled around, when the duo began questioning on air whether Donald had what it took to win the election, let alone govern.

That didn't sit well with the candidate, an early riser who watched cable news for hours on end, propped up on pillows on his Trump Tower bed. He tweeted that Brzezinski was "off the wall, a neurotic and not very bright mess." He threatened that "when things calmed down," he would "tell the real story" about his friend Joe and "his very insecure long-time girlfriend, Mika. Two clowns!" Brzezinski had recently finalized her divorce, and for the sakes of both of their families they were still keeping their relationship as private as they could, though it was by that point a poorly kept secret.

The cohosts were livid. Her daughters, both in college, were bombarded with a news cycle about her mother's love life. The swipes and the fallout further entrenched Scarborough, a protective, hot-tempered colleague who'd served in Congress and understood the magnitude of the job, in his belief that Donald wasn't up for the job.

It wasn't long before Jared called, as he frequently did. Typically, he would ask for advice, or pass along bits of information from the campaign, or give a status report and ask for one in return. But this go-around, he knew he had to do damage control. He pleaded with Scarborough and Brzezinski just to meet with his father-in-law to see if they could patch things up. Initially, they resisted. What was the point? For one, they thought his behavior was growing more and more erratic and inappropriate. And second, this was becoming something of a pattern. He would insult them, time would go by, and then he would once again try to cozy up and sweep the bad stuff under the rug. If they sat down and talked, Donald would walk

away thinking they were going to be buddy-buddy once more, and then be shocked and stung all over again next time he heard them say something critical of him on their show. The mean tweets would follow, and the whole cycle would repeat itself, as it always did.

But Jared continued to ask, maybe four or five times, and eventually they relented. They agreed to sit down, the four of them, in Trump Tower. The meeting started off with Donald telling Scarborough that he was tough on him, but that Brzezinski "makes you look like a little baby, Joe," with how hard she could be. "Mika, why are you so tough on me?" he asked her.

She deflected. Instead, she explained the damage the tweets had done to her and her children and the hurt they caused to her family. In a most uncharacteristic move, Donald said he was sorry.

Jared, who was behind him, looked as though he was going to fall off his chair. "He very quickly said, 'Okay, let's end the meeting right now, because I have never heard him say that before,'" Scarborough recalled. It was a moment of levity before it got much worse between the longtime friends.

Jared didn't just clean up after her father's media messes during the campaign. He got into some skirmishes of his own. Around the time when his relationship soured with the *Morning Joe* crew, Donald's distaste for CNN deepened. One day in June 2016, Donald, in a dark mood, barked for his son-in-law to call CNN president Jeff Zucker and complain about what he thought was a barrage of biased and unfair coverage. Zucker was in the South of France, at the annual Cannes Lions festival with dozens of other network and studio heads and entertainment bigwigs, when he got Kushner's call delivering Donald's message. Zucker had put *The Apprentice* on the air when he ran NBC. But, as many of Donald's relationships do, theirs had since soured, as CNN remained critical of his campaign and Donald took credit for landing Zucker his job at CNN.

"You have to be kidding me," Zucker told Jared. "Go fuck yourself." He hung up on Donald's son-in-law.

The hard feelings brewed through the early days of summer, but lessened as the weeks went on. No one thought Donald was going to win, and Jared started talking about using the wide swaths of data collected during the campaign to start some sort of media venture targeted at the throngs of people clearly enraptured by the Trump message. The campaign was still somewhat boycotting the network, so Zucker had some incentive to smooth things over as best he could.

Plus, Jared doesn't like being in fights. He reached out to say, Let's clear the air. On the day before Donald officially nominated Mike Pence as his running mate, in mid-July, Jared crossed Central Park to CNN's offices at the Time Warner Center in Columbus Circle. Behind closed doors, in an executive office, Zucker and Jared both apologized for their tough language. They recognized that CNN needed the Trump campaign, and the Trump campaign needed CNN. Neither CNN's coverage nor the Trump campaign's opinion of it softened as a result. They would never really like each other. But Jared knew how to kiss the ring, and executives knew that Jared was willing to play reasonable—if not good—cop, when need be.

THE RELATIONSHIP between Jared Kushner and Ivanka Trump began as a business arrangement. Moshe Lax, whose family diamond business had partnered with Ivanka to start her fine jewelry collection, was also putting together a real estate deal in the mid-2000s. He invited them both to lunch at Prime Grill, a high-end kosher steakhouse on Madison Avenue in the fifties with sushi on the menu and Andy Warhol–style prints of rabbis against primary colors on its walls. "I wasn't playing *shadchan* [Hebrew for matchmaker]," Lax said in an interview. "It was a business opportunity." For Jared and Ivanka, as most things are, perhaps it was a bit of both. Ivanka emailed one of her closest friends after the lunch saying that she knew it was a work thing, but that she really kind of liked him. The friend, who had not much cared for most of the guys Ivanka had dated before, immediately bought in.

Jared had been dating Laura Englander, the daughter of billionaire hedge fund manager Israel Englander, and Ivanka's dating life became tabloid fodder. There was Bingo Gubelmann, Topher Grace, Lance Armstrong, and—in a rumor propagated by her father, who told reporters it was true—Tom Brady. Her father, she told reporters, would be happy if she dated an athlete "because he's always wanted to be an athlete." She contended she wanted someone more intellectual, smart, hardworking. "My friends always joke that I'm going to marry a 90-year-old Pulitzer Prize winner," she told an interviewer before she started dating Jared.

Jared was not exactly an intellectual. He attended Harvard as an undergraduate and New York University to get a dual law and business degree. His admission to both schools, documented by Pulitzer Prize–winning writer Daniel Golden in *The Price of Admission: How America's Ruling Class Buys Its Way into Elite Colleges—and Who Gets Left Outside the Gates*, drew some attention. The Kushners pledged $2.5 million to the university in 1998, a year before Jared started school in Cambridge. According to the book, Charlie Kushner asked Frank Lautenberg to lean on his Senate colleague Ted Kennedy to put in a good word with the school's dean of admissions. In 2001 Charlie pledged $3 million to NYU, and later he took a seat on its board of trustees. The year Jared graduated from Harvard and looked toward graduate school, Charlie leased the university a few floors of the Puck Building, a building he'd bought four years earlier, at below-market rates.

But he was kind, polite, handsome, and in the business, a power player with his own paper. His family, flawed as it was, was tight and worth billions of dollars. He, like her, prized familial loyalty above everything else, which, after her parent's divorce, outweighed intelligence in terms of what she looked for in a mate. "I could never be with someone whose motives I was constantly questioning and I certainly couldn't stand worrying about whether he'd run off with the first blonde who came along once I got my first wrinkle," she said in an interview when she was nineteen. She saw that in the man she refers to as a "great New Jersey boy." Her friends saw how happy he made her and how perfectly suited they were, and all encouraged her not to let him get away. She saw him volunteer to help his friend's parents and siblings negotiate apartment leases and find office space and appreciated that he would want to stop by the seven parties she had to make an appearance at in one evening, before spending the rest of the night answering emails and waking up the next morning before dawn to work out before heading to the office. He never got frazzled like she did. "He's unbelievably calm," she told *Redbook*. "I think he's a mutant."

Even on the campaign, he often tried to keep people around him calm. Katrina Pierson, the Tea Party activist turned national spokesperson for the Trump campaign, remembers that Jared would find people in the office or make phone calls if the media wrote something unflattering about them. "He would go out of his way to say, 'Don't worry about that, just let it go,'" she remembers. "He was cognizant that people were putting everything on the line for his father-in-law, and he wanted them to know that their work was appreciated by the family and the higher-ups in the campaign." That happened to extend to her. Pierson's fortieth birthday fell smack in the middle of the Republican National Convention in Cleveland at the end of July 2016. "I was so bummed to have to go and be in Cleveland for it," she said. "Nobody wants to spend their fortieth birthday at a convention in Cleveland." She vented to Jared, who she knew was distracted by handling a hundred different things at the time. That night's programming focused on opportunity and prosperity, under the mini theme of "Make America First Again." The campaign had to wrangle its hodgepodge list of speakers set to take the stage that evening—Jared's brother-in-law Eric, oil and gas baron Harold Hamm, Newt and Callista Gingrich, conservative radio goddess Laura Ingraham, senators Marco Rubio and Ted Cruz, Florida attorney general Pam Bondi, Wisconsin governor Scott Walker, retired astronaut Eileen Collins, and vice presidential nominee Mike Pence, to name the most notable. Still, when Pierson got back to her hotel room late that night, she had a whole slew of goodies set up for her. There were a dozen mini cupcakes, a mix of chocolate and vanilla, with red, white, and blue sprinkles and a campaign sticker slapped onto the plastic container holding them all. Then there was the black bag with the gold Trump Winery logo on it, stuffed with red, white, and blue tissue paper and some of the family's finest blends. There was a Trump Pence 2016 bumper sticker, two canvas tote bags, also stuffed with the patriotic paper, one with a Trump Make America Great Again insignia, and another with little red Republican elephants printed in horizontal lines across it, both filled with Trump-branded goodies. There was a handwritten card from Jared, as well, all exclamation points and well-wishes. "Even with all the chaos and the pressure, Jared still made sure I didn't feel like I was away from everyone on my birthday," she said.

He was as persistent after the initial lunch with Ivanka. Not long after she sent the email to her friend saying what a good time she had—the same day they met—he sent her an email. He invited her to a party his friends were throwing downtown, and instantly she knew she would say yes. "Oh my god. Oh my god. Oh my god," one of her best friends, someone she met at Penn and became closer with after she graduated, remembers her saying at the time after she read his message. "She was so clearly smitten with him from the second she met him. That he followed up so quickly, clearly he felt the same way." So she took him up on the invitation, dragging this friend down to a sweeping loft in SoHo. A band was playing, his friends were hanging around, and they all left together, going out to another bar in the neighborhood so that Ivanka and Jared could keep things going as long as they could that night. "I had seen the way she interacted with other guys she liked or even other guys she dated," the friend said, "and it was never anything like that. Things got heated and they got heated pretty quickly after that."

* * *

JARED AND Ivanka's courtship, which began in earnest in the spring of 2007, was quite public. They were spotted stealing kisses at Bowlmor Lanes; she toured the *Observer* newsroom, where, once they settled into his office, they kept the door open so that prying eyes could see them together; they holidayed in St. Barth, and tipsters sent Gawker details of them flying home to JFK airport from Nice after a trip together, with Ivanka in business class and Jared reading *The Observer* and a Michael Chabon book in coach. They met up in baggage claim once they landed.

Jared's family, observant Modern Orthodox Jews, wasn't thrilled with the match. Ivanka, though hardly raised religiously aside from the nightly prayers she said with her Irish nanny, was Presbyterian. She had worn that little silver cross around her neck when she taped the interview for *Born Rich*, after all. Seryl, Jared's mother, had a particularly hard time with the idea, and urged her son to cool his heels. The breakup in 2008 devastated Ivanka. Though the couple now insists to friends that they hadn't split because of religion, Ivana Trump wrote in her recent book that her daughter told her his family would not let Jared marry her because she wasn't Jewish.

Ivanka sobbed to a business associate on a helicopter ride to Atlantic City for a meeting at her father's casino soon after. "I told her that I knew they were going to get back together, and that I'd bet her $100 he'd come crawling back in a few months." (The associate never got her to pay up. Ivanka is like her father.) Many of her friends thought the breakup wouldn't last long; they were effortless together. But she was pragmatic and compartmentalized, as she always was. She was heartbroken, yes, but she had work to get on with, and she didn't say no when other guys asked her out on dates.

It took the highest-end, most harebrained matchmaking scheme to bring the two back together. Wendi Murdoch, then still married to Rupert Murdoch, called Jared, inviting him on their 184-foot sailing yacht, the *Rosehearty*, for a weekend. He was working too hard,

Wendi said, and could stand a weekend at sea with them. He agreed, and arrived to find Wendi had invited Ivanka too, under the same guise. (Ivanka and Jared have paid back this billionaire matchmaking in the years since. They have set up seven couples who went on to get married. Ivanka has referred to it as her "secret talent," though some friends have joked that it's a way to make sure she and Jared have a built-in circle of friends who will always be, if not loyal, grateful to them.)

Ivanka agreed to convert, though she claimed that she didn't have that far to go: "I'm a New Yorker. I'm in real estate. I'm as close to Jewish with an 'i-s-h' naturally as anyone can start off." She started working with Rabbi Haskel Lookstein of the Congregation Kehillath Jeshurun, a Modern Orthodox shul on Eighty-Fifth Street, though friends of the Kushner family said they remained unconvinced. The process is long and grueling, and hers was especially tough, since Charlie made a point to involve himself in the matter. She studied the Torah, agreed to observe Shabbat with Jared's family, and committed to learning Jewish laws and traditions. In the thick of the process, she and Jared attended the annual, and dreaded, Inner Circle dinner—a black-tie schmooze-fest at the Sheraton where New York politicos and reporters reluctantly make the rounds. An acquaintance who barely knew her at the time remembers Ivanka making small talk about how she was learning to cook. The acquaintance was, too, at the time, and asked her if she'd come across any helpful cookbooks. "Yes! I have a great one," she shared. "It's called *Kosher Cooking*." She urged her to check it out.

"That's the thing about Ivanka," an associate said of Ivanka's ability to take something like conversion on. "She's such a perfectionist and takes everything, and herself, very seriously. So when she says she's converting, she will read every book and learn every recipe and start participating with his family to do all the holidays." To her longtime friends, particularly those she cooked for or those who were Jewish, this came as a surprise. "She just could not cook.

She really could not," one remembered. "And once she was going through the conversion, she always made fun of how little we knew about the religion and traditions. I was so impressed by how much she enjoyed learning about it." That was just the way Ivanka did things, the friend noted. Plus, she was presented with a leopard-print Swarovski-crystal-encrusted mezuzah for her troubles.

The process wrapped up when Ivanka appeared before the traditional *beth din*, a three-person religious panel, and had a dip in a mikvah, a ritual bath used to cleanse oneself before major milestones and life events. She chose the Hebrew name Yael, which technically means "mountain goat." Other translations put it closer to "to ascend." It is also the name of a biblical hero who saved the Jewish people by using her feminine charms to woo an enemy general into their tent before killing him by smashing a tentpole into his temple.

Jared proposed with a 5.22-carat cushion-cut diamond ring, set in platinum, from Ivanka's signature jewelry line, which he helped design before the style was named after her in the Ivanka Trump Fine Jewelry collection. "I got engaged last night—truly the happiest day of my life!!!" she tweeted in July 2009. So started a whirlwind, and very public, few months of planning. She hired celebrity wedding planner Preston Bailey to coordinate the events, and Brian Marcus, whose family had shot over fifty family events over the years for the Kushners—as well as one of Donald's weddings, and the Murdochs', too—to do the photos. Ivana wasn't much involved with the planning, but Ivanka told friends that her mother was a nightmare throughout, sending her a new guest list and list of requests every week.

They sent out Tiffany invitations (her "something blue") to five hundred people for a traditional Jewish ceremony in October at her father's 525-acre golf club in the rolling hills of Bedminster, New Jersey (her "something borrowed"). Guests found a promotional flyer for a round of golf at one of the family properties tucked inside the envelope (her "something distinctly Trump"), though Ivanka denies slipping in marketing material. She decided on a Vera Wang gown in the style of Grace Kelly (her "something old") and turned down offers to sell the wedding photos. She wanted to do the same thing John Kennedy and Caroline Bessette had done for their wedding a decade earlier, releasing one photo after their wedding.

The couple registered for seventy-five items at Williams-Sonoma, Crate & Barrel, and Tiffany's, though their china came from elsewhere. The items were minimal—mostly sterling and glass—and reflected what they thought would be a normal young married life, with long afternoons spent in the kitchen and meals enjoyed at home together in the evening. Guests snatched up the four $10 spatulas and a set of matching lapis cotton place mats and napkins for $4.95 and $3.95 each, respectively. Sheet pans, a rolling pin, a Bundt cake pan for $34. At Tiffany's, they listed $175 bottle stoppers and $325 cake servers and sauce ladles and carving knives for about $100 less, and sterling silver picture frames for $200 more. The much-coveted registry mainstay, a KitchenAid stand mixer, made the list, but the most expensive item was a $1,350 footed bowl in sterling silver from Tiffany's; they initially asked for two of these, but scaled it back to one.

The bachelorette party consisted of a blindfolded bride on a Hudson River boat ride and late-night karaoke with champagne. The day before the wedding, the weather cleared—Ivanka thought that was a good omen—and she went for a hike on the morning of the wedding. Family photos started promptly at three in the afternoon, with the ceremony an hour later.

They erected clear-sided tents in a remote area on the expansive property's green lawn. Through them, guests could see the trees, leaves on fire at their mid-autumn peak. The auburns and yellows and reds would be a grand enough background for any couple's exchange of vows. But the Trump-Kushners went further. For the ceremony, hundreds of gilded chairs were set up for guests like Corey Booker, Russell Crowe, Andrew Cuomo, Rudy Giuliani, Jamie Johnson, Jim

McGreevey, Natalie Portman, Ed Rendell, Emmy Rossum and Adam Duritz, Barbara Walters, and Anna Wintour, between imported trees standing throughout the tent. The couple met under a thicket of greens and thousands of willowy white buds dangling to create a traditional—if ornate—chuppah. Bridesmaids Tiffany and Vanessa Trump, Don Jr.'s wife, wore dusty lavender gowns designed by Carolina Herrera; their mothers were dressed in peach. Melania, in a low-cut purple satin number, rescued Barron, the ring-bearer, when he lost his way. Chloe and Grace Murdoch sprinkled petals down the aisle as flower girls. Ivanka's Vera Wang covered her shoulders, as is customary for Orthodox women. It still managed to show a bit of her bust, as is customary for the ladies Trump. It cascaded into layer upon layer of Chantilly and Lyon lace. Ivanka had taken a group of her closest friends to try on dresses at a few bridal ateliers and shops in the city, but settled on Vera. Her friends came along to each fitting, and to the final one she invited her bridal party and a *Vogue* editor to inspect every detail. After the ceremony, a friend of Ivanka's who was gown shopping for her own wedding at Vera Wang's atelier noticed a dress hanging on a rack called "the Esther" that was startlingly similar to her own. The friend excitedly reported the news back. "You know, Vera had asked, and asked, and asked to do my wedding dress, and I paid for the dress and everything," Ivanka said, adding that she had been given a steep discount. The dress would be given a lot of publicity, after all, and the young Trump was never one to pass up a deal. Plus, all celebrities, whatever degree of stardom they possess, know that the more money you have, the less of it you actually have to use, anyway.

"We designed it exactly how I wanted it to look. I chose every detail with her. It was perfect," the friend recalled her saying. "And then after the wedding, Vera went and tweaked the dress to make a cheaper version of it, a copy with some less expensive details." The friend remembers hanging up the phone, worried that she had annoyed Ivanka about the dress all over again.

Predictably, her jewelry bore her name as well. She wore more than a quarter of a million dollars in jewelry—all of it from her own collection—including a $45,000 diamond hairpiece, a 26-carat art deco platinum and diamond estate bracelet, and 9.67-carat mixed-cut diamond cluster earrings worth $130,000, behind which her softly waved old-Hollywood hair was tucked. Jared wore a custom black tuxedo and traditional bow tie, his hair parted and swept to the left and pinned down slightly by his yarmulke.

"It was stunning. And grandiose, even by New York standards," one guest remembered. "The only weird thing was the rabbi started talking about all the Jews suffering around the world at the start of the ceremony, which did not exactly scream romance."

Their faith was at the center of much of the evening. In the reception tent, long chandeliers hung around the room over the all-white tables. As the room erupted into the traditional hora, this being an Orthodox wedding, the men were separate from the women. Later, the men did another traditional dance, and the women were asked to leave the dance floor, which confused a number of the New York society guests who had not been to a wedding quite so Orthodox. Nicole Kushner, Jared's sister, took a few of Ivanka's friends aside and explained the tradition, the roots of it, and why it was important to them. "I thought it was very kind of her to do, until she asked us to leave, and I realized she had been dispatched by the bride and groom to make sure people weren't uncomfortable and didn't scoot out early while the men were dancing about the tent."

Ivanka did not flinch at any of it. "She acted as if she was a chosen one all night," one guest remembered. "It wasn't as if she was a Jewish American Princess, even. It was as if she'd been made the Jewish American Queen."

The couple crowd sourced their wedding song on Twitter because they had trouble coming up with one on their own, and eventually landed on David Gray's weepy "This Year's Love." It's a melancholy ballad that some guests noted was fitting for the couple. "Aren't the words something about being hurt by someone lying and hurting and needing to feel safe before losing control?" one attendee chuckled. "It was perfect for them." The cake was a hulking Sylvia Weinstock confection: seventy inches and thirteen layers of lisianthus, roses, peonies, lilies of the valley, and baby's breath, crafted in sugar, encircling each tier, in whites, pinks, ivories, creams, and flesh tones.

Donald gave what guests remember as a short, sweet toast, during which he acknowledged Ivana and made a few jokes. "Be happy and enjoy your life," he offered.

"Her parents kept mostly quiet and did not speak much," one guest recalled. "Charlie's toast was the one everyone talked about." Guests recall Charlie's toast mentioning his initial hesitation to see his son marrying someone who was not Jewish, which, he said, was so important to their family. But he saw how she treated his son, and how she devoted herself to her conversion, and how in love they were, and he came around to feeling right about it.

The evening was long. With so many guests traveling about an hour from Manhattan to Bedminster, photographs, the traditional ceremony, the extended hora, the Jewish customs, the toasts, it amounted to an eight-hour affair for some. But it was not altogether unwelcome, and many of the guests took it in stride by imbibing perhaps more than they were used to doing in black tie to pass the time. What happens in Bedminster stays in Bedminster, unless it happens at a Trump wedding, where prying eyes commit it all to memory and gab about it for years to come. And everyone walked away from the evening happy. As a gift, they gave out a little Hebrew book to each guest, along with a pair of white flip-flops with the tag: "Ivanka and Jared—what a perfect pair."

BEFORE THE couple set off on a safari honeymoon in Africa, the Kushners gifted them a weekend away at the Mayflower Inn in Washington, Connecticut, which, funnily enough, was owned by

Treasury secretary Steven Mnuchin's father, Robert. They spent a weekend at the spa relaxing before they took several flights to South Africa—one delayed to Amsterdam, and a round of lost luggage on the way.

Almost a year after their wedding, they had what amounted to a second honeymoon—a vacation from a vacation, as it happened. A guest at their reception owned a hotel in Sardinia and gifted them a five-night stay. On their first day, Ivana texted her daughter, saying that she'd heard Ivanka and Jared were in town. Ivana was nearby on a friend's boat and decided to book a room at the same hotel. They spent the days of their second honeymoon with Ivanka's mother. At night, she would start partying when the newlyweds went off to sleep.

AFTER THE marriage was official, the Kushners warmed to Ivanka, who spent weekends at their beach house on the Jersey shore, unplugged like the rest of them on Shabbat, enrolled their children in Jewish day schools, and cooked and cleaned up after holiday dinners like the rest of the women in the family. They took pride in her clothing and accessories line, typically marketed to younger shoppers on a budget keen to pick through racks at mass department stores like Macy's and discount retailers like T.J.Maxx. That demographic does not include observant billionaires with real estate empires in the tristate area, yet the Kushner women have taken to wearing Ivanka-branded shoes like a badge of honor.

"These people are made of money, and they all wear Ivanka Trump shoes. Every day," one associate said. "They'll be like, 'Oh, you have to get these. They are the best.'"

Ivanka found a little familiar charm in some of the Kushner quirks, too. The family, worth billions of dollars, stocked their office on the fifteenth floor of 666 Fifth Avenue with snacks from Costco, those colossal plastic tubs of pretzels and chocolate-covered almonds. When Ivanka was a child, her mother would pile her and her brothers in their car to take them to the wholesaler, a thrill for the woman who never wore the same dress twice and gilded anything not nailed down in their triplex. "She would get so excited. You have no idea," Ivanka said of Ivana on these trips. "She'd say, 'Why would I buy something that's more expensive when I could get the same product for less?'"

That frugality is a trait that Jared and Josh both inherited. One tech entrepreneur who went to see the Kushner brothers in the midst of a fund-raising round remembers the horror on their faces when they looked over the business plan. The founder had budgeted in an executive assistant to start in the third month, once the business had got off the ground. That stopped both Kushners in their tracks. "They told me that they only invest in companies whose founders are willing to steal toilet paper from a nearby Starbucks until they start turning a profit," the entrepreneur, who went on to build an e-commerce empire without the Kushner money, said. "That was the kind of entrepreneur they were interested in."

Of course, the Kushners could spend their money more lavishly, particularly on their grandchildren. When their grandchildren were born, Charlie and Seryl bought multimillion-dollar apartments in Manhattan for each one individually, placing them in a trust called Kinderlach, the Yiddish word for "children." This means that little Arabella, Joseph, and Theodore, and all of their cousins on the Kushner side, have pieces of property waiting for them when they reach whatever age is given in the trust.

Their grandparents also started a tradition for their grandchildren when they celebrate their bar or bat mitzvahs. Each twelve- or thirteen-year-old can choose to go anywhere in the world on a trip with their grandparents. The catch is that each trip has to first start off in Novogrudok, the town of 30,000 in western Belarus where Charlie's mother, Rae, grew up and later made an unthinkably nervy escape from a Nazi ghetto. They are unfailingly giving with their children and grandchildren, who, in turn, readily express how their parents or grandparents gave them everything.

As aware as the kids are of Charlie and Seryl's generosity, they understand how depraved they can be, too. Associates refer to Charlie as a "psychopath," a "torturer," "truly the worst person in the world," someone whose temper is so fierce that people around him when he erupts ask, "How can a person be so angry?" Seryl's own darker side has earned her the nickname "Lady Macbeth" among people who have worked with the family.

Not long after Jared bought the *Observer*, Jared invited a few writers on the staff to a lunch at 666 Fifth Avenue. It was a speaker series of sorts, and a few of his editors and reporters got to mingle with the Kushners and their developer friends before the program officially began. When one of his writers met Seryl there for the first time, pleasantries were not exchanged. She did not shake the female writer's hand. She did not say a single word. She did, however, take note of a hair clinging to the reporter's black sweater. She reached over, pulled it off, and walked away.

It's not as though Jared and his siblings, Dara, Nicole, and Josh, don't see this. In meetings, when Charlie would erupt and rip into everyone around him, Jared would repeatedly tap his father on the shoulder and whisper, "Dad, stop it. Dad, stop it. Dad, stop." One associate likened Jared and Josh to the Menendez brothers, the handsome, wealthy Beverly Hills siblings who murdered their parents and then spent much of their time behind bars talking about how much they loved them. "Their parents are insane, in their brains, they know it, and yet, they say, 'I love them. They have given me everything.'"

They are blood; there is, at least, a twisted fealty born out of both nature and nurture. Relationships with in-laws tend to lack those genetic blinders, making them some of the trickiest to navigate, particularly when your married family are, by all accounts, monsters. Ivanka, though, has a deep affection for Charlie and Seryl, whom she calls "mom and dad." As one person close to the family pointed out, Ivanka was essentially neglected by her parents as a child, so having parents around who think to buy her and her children long underwear when they are going to be outside in the cold for a long time, as Seryl did for Ivanka, Jared, and their children to have for the inauguration events, is appealing.

CHAPTER 8

You Are Who You Marry

To understand why the Kushners accepted Ivanka despite their reservations about her not being a Jew is to understand both how Jared blossomed into the entwined family's golden boy and gained leverage within it through a sibling rivalry turned catastrophe that is one part Shakespearean, one part Cain and Abel, with a sprinkle of *Dallas* and *The Godfather*, only darker, on top. To get to events that resulted in Charlie spending sixteen months in a federal penitentiary in Montgomery, Alabama, you have to kick the dirt off the roots of the Kushners' bitter history, the details of which are written in ink in a hardbound book displayed in the Kushner Companies office lobby.

The Miracle of Life tells the story of Rae Kushner, Charlie's mother and the family's matriarch. The Nazis arrived in Novogrudok, where she was raised, in 1941, executing its Jewish lawyers, doctors, and intellectuals in the town square as an orchestra played. Soldiers rounded up a group of fifty teenage girls, including Rae, to scrub the blood of the dead off the soaked cobblestones, and tens of thousands of Jews were sent to a ghetto that served as a labor camp. On Pearl Harbor Day, December 7, Nazis sorted the residents into two lines. Those to the right would die; those to the left would live. Rae's sister, Esther, was one of the more than five thousand Jews killed that day, after she tried to run to a nearby building to hide. By the night before Rosh Hashanah of 1943, only a few hundred Jews remained. Months earlier, they had decided that if they were going to survive, their only hope was to tunnel out. Late at night, they'd used scrappy instruments to dig. A human chain backed up the excavators, passing bags of soil from person to person to person all the way up into a hiding place in an attic.

It stormed on the eve of the new year, and a group of the survivors, including Rae and her father, sister, and brother, decided to go. After removing the nails from metal roofs so they would rattle in the wind and drown out the noise they made, they crawled hundreds of feet through the tunnel to nearby forests. Rae and her family had waited for her father, so they climbed behind the rest. They had hoped to find a farmer who they'd heard had gathered an army of Jewish resistance fighters, hiding out on the other side. But the Germans caught on, and were waiting for them outside the tunnel. When the first Jews crawled out, they opened fire. Rae's brother Chanon, for whom Charlie is named, ran in the wrong direction. He was killed, along with fifty others.

Rae made it to the farmer in the woods, where she found others living on straw beds in bunkers. This is where she met a man named Yossel, a carpenter who'd fled from a labor camp and had been living for three years in a hole he'd dug in the woods, coming out only to rummage for food. They stayed at the Bielski camp until the Soviets arrived. Rae married Yossel, and the two walked, step by step, to Italy, where they spent more than three years in a displaced persons' camp while they waited for the visas that would allow them to immigrate to the United States.

They came to New York in 1949. Yossel became Joseph, and the family moved to Brooklyn. They had two sons—Murray first, then Charles—and two daughters, Linda and Esther. Joseph worked construction in New Jersey until he saved up enough to buy three lots of land in Union County with two partners, brothers named Harry and Joe Wilff (the Wilff family now owns the Minnesota Vikings). Joseph was part of a group of survivors known as the Holocaust Builders, and developed somewhat of a specialty building and renting garden apartments. His sons took on the trade, too. Murray was the academically gifted one, graduating summa cum laude from the University of Pennsylvania, where he went on to law school. Charlie was a passable undergrad at New York University, and got an MBA and a law degree from Hofstra at the same time.

By 1985 Joseph had built four thousand apartments, and Charlie asked him to go into business. They worked together at Kushner Companies for nine months, until Joseph had a stroke and died. Charlie, the second son, ascended to the family throne, giving his brother and sisters a stake in what he would soon turn into an empire.

THIS, WHEN the money became real, and familial resentments boiled over without the patriarch there to mind the pot, is where the darkness set in.

Charlie's business exploded. In less than a decade, the company had more than 22,000 apartments, a bank, and commercial real estate holdings, making him one of the most prominent private landlords in the country who came to be worth about a billion bucks. His drive was relentless, and his discipline bordered on bionic. He would clock double-digit runs before work, or, if he wasn't outside, swim 180 laps in the Short Hills Sheraton before heading in to his office, where he kept a closet full of crisp dress shirts, in blue and white, each hung an inch apart. Just like his own parents, he had two sons, Jared and Josh, and two daughters, Dara and Nicole.

Charlie knew how to read a room, and as many have described, he could have a room eating out of his hand if he flicked on his charm. He knew how to flip open his checkbook, which, unsurprisingly, worked just as well. He became a *macher* in the worlds of Jewish philanthropy and politics, and, in his mind, a kingmaker

and a Jewish Kennedy. In New Jersey, there was the Joseph Kushner Hebrew Academy and the Rae Kushner Yeshiva High School,
and the rabbis at each couldn't reach him fast enough to shake his
hand when he walked in the door. From the mid-1990s to the mid-
2000s, he forked over nearly $1.5 million to Democratic politicians,
from Chuck Schumer to Jon Corzine. In July 2000, Vice President
Al Gore, running for president at the time, trekked to Livingston for
a fund-raiser chez Kushner, forcing rush-hour traffic to a screech-
ing halt as police descended and the motorcade squeezed through.
Jared, a teenager, was called on by Charlie to say a few words at the
event, surprising elders in the room with his maturity and ease. Hillary Clinton paid Charlie a visit, too, after she won her Senate seat
that same year, sitting down for a Shabbat meal in the family's beach
house on the shore.

Charlie placed a bet on Jim McGreevey, first as the mayor of
Woodbridge Township and then, later, in 2002, in his bid for governor of New Jersey. McGreevey made good on all of Charlie's years
of support by nominating him to be the chairman of the Port Authority of New York and New Jersey, a few months after his inauguration. It was a plum job for a number of reasons, one that would
make any developer in the tristate area at that time drool. It would
have put him in charge of billions of dollars in state contracts as the
states rebuilt the World Trade Center after the September 11 attacks.

Charlie never got the gig. He removed himself from consider-
ation as his family grudges and business misdeeds hemorrhaged
into public view. Money and long-standing grudges were thicker
than blood, but not quite as sticky as the bile between brothers and
sister. And ultimately, it tore them all to pieces.

It had all started to unravel a few years before, in 1999. Murray
had dragged his feet and pulled out on a few business deals that
would have catapulted Charlie's business into a new stratosphere,
both in the scope of his holdings and in how much the business

would be worth. It was more personal than that, as family business matters tend to be. Charlie had never accepted Murray's wife, Lee, who he deemed not religious enough. Soon the brothers agreed they would no longer work together, after a series of public fights, and friends and associates had to choose between the brothers. Their sister Esther and her husband, Billy Schulder, sided with Murray. It was a betrayal that infuriated Charlie, only adding to his distaste for Schulder, his former business partner, who'd had an affair with one of their employees years earlier. Schulder left Charlie's office and went to work for Murray.

Murray sued his brother on the night before McGreevey's election, a coincidence too poorly timed to ignore, alleging that his brother had mismanaged the business and owed him money. Not long after, in November 2002, a Kushner Companies accountant filed his own lawsuit, followed by a second one in February, claiming that Charlie had used company money to make philanthropic and political donations, including the $125,000 speaking fee paid to Bill Clinton for delivering remarks at a Kushner Companies–owned bank.

The lawsuits were catnip for Chris Christie, then a Republican US attorney for the state of New Jersey. They also burst any chance for Charlie's Port Authority gig as Christie's investigation became public. The already fractured family split right open when Charlie thought his sister was cooperating with the attorney's office. Charlie brought in a buddy named Jimmy O'Toole, a then soon-to-be cop he'd met on the running trails in town, and floated an idea for how he could retaliate for Esther and Schulder's disloyalty. O'Toole recruited his brother to join as Charlie hatched a plan for how to exact revenge. A prostitute and a videotape would do the trick. He offered O'Toole $25,000 and slipped a chunk of it in cash to him across his desk, along with the number of a woman who went by the name Suzanna, an East European blonde who had misgivings about the whole thing but went along with it anyway. Charlie offered to pay between $7,000 and $10,000 cash if she agreed to have sex with his brother-in-law on tape.

Thanksgiving rolled around, and one cold morning, as Schulder downed his usual breakfast at the Time to Eat Diner in Bridgewater, Suzanna and the business suit that clung to every inch of her walked in. She was in town for a job interview and her car had broken down, she told Schulder. She'd need a ride back to her motel. He turned down an invitation into her room but didn't pass up taking her number. It was snowing by the next morning when he pulled back off Route 22 and into the lot outside the Red Bull Inn. He parked and walked inside, where Suzanna performed oral sex on him in full view of the miniature video camera that had been hidden inside the room's alarm clock.

The O'Tooles, who'd been surveilling the whole thing, called Charlie right away, and brought the tape to his Florham Park, New Jersey, office. He and Seryl's brother, Richard Stadmauer, who worked for him, covered the glass windows in the Kushner Companies conference room with newspaper and popped in the tape. Once he'd stopped laughing at Schulder's heat-of-the-moment exclamation that he felt "like he was in a movie," Charlie ordered copies. It worked so well that he tried to set up his former accountant, the one who'd sued him over his campaign contributions, too, but the accountant rebuffed the advances of the woman Charlie'd hired, and a couple of offers to have a drink in her motel room. She was paid $2,000 for her troubles.

Charlie held on to the tapes of his brother-in-law until May, when investigators began targeting members of his inner circle. Then, he ordered the tape and still photos sent to Esther in a padded envelope that left no trace of where it came from. Murray was her first call; she told her brother not to go home. Both Esther and Lee were convinced they were going to be killed. Esther took the envelope and its contents to federal law enforcement agents and turned them all over.

In July 2004, the FBI caught Charlie on a wire talking about the setup, a few days before he walked his daughter Nicole down the aisle for her two-hundred-person wedding at their home on the shore. Within a week, he'd caught wind of the fact that he was going to be arrested. One morning soon after, Josh Kushner texted his brother Jared when their dad didn't show up for their company's usual meeting. Jared was interning for a Manhattan district attorney, and had just gotten off a subway on his way to work. He called his father to make sure he was okay. Less than an hour after Charlie broke it to him that he was going to be arrested, Jared walked out of work and into a car home to New Jersey. By the time he got there, his father had turned himself in.

Charlie pleaded guilty to the eighteen counts levied against him, from tax evasion to witness tampering to improper campaign donations—or, more succinctly, as Christie called them, "crimes of greed, power, and excess." They sentenced him to two years, during which his son visited him every weekend. Jared would fly down every Sunday, then spent the rest of the week taking the reins of a company he didn't yet know how to lead.

Both Charlie and Jared painted the other Kushners as the true villains in this story. "I don't believe God and my parents will ever forgive my brother and sister for instigating a criminal investigation and being cheerleaders for the government and putting their brother in jail because of jealousy, hatred and spite," Charlie said in an interview with *The Real Deal*. Jared too thought of his father as the victim of lazy siblings who'd milked their father for all he was worth and then twisted their silver spoon in his back. "His siblings stole every piece of paper from his office and they took it to the government, siblings that he literally made wealthy for doing nothing," he told *New York Magazine*. "All he did was put the tape together and send it. Was it the right thing to do? At the end of the day, it was a function of saying, 'You're trying to make my life miserable? Well, I'm doing the same.'"

*   *   *

WHAT LAY in front of Jared was both an unbelievable shot and an insurmountably Herculean task. He was fresh out of graduate school and running a multibillion-dollar company that his family now needed him to use to avenge their name. So he looked beyond garden apartments in the Garden State and toward Manhattan. And he waited for the day in the near future when his father would be back home, beside him in their weekly meetings.

The day didn't come as soon as Jared and the rest of the Kushners had thought. Charlie was set to be released twenty-eight days early. In the scheme of things, twenty-eight days is a blip—just four weeks, shorter than any month other than February, shorter than the period between Thanksgiving and Christmas, most years, at least. But for a family who believed their patriarch to be the victim in all of this, every day that he was there was a nightmare. It was an injustice. And so those extra days were not just a silver lining but a great white hope, bringing them closer to a new, rightful beginning.

Chris Christie, though, had another plan. He insisted that Kushner serve out those twenty-eight days, making sure he would not serve a week or a day or a minute less. This was gasoline on the Kushners' wounds. As a friend of Jared explained, it was so painful at the time that he carries it with him, even to this day: "He just can't let go of that part of it."

Charlie was released to a halfway house in Newark, from which Jared consulted him on his great big bet in the big city. By the time Charlie was released, Jared had put a bid on 666 Fifth Avenue, the forty-one-story skyscraper between Fifty-Second and Fifty-Third Streets in Midtown Manhattan. All beige blocks and aluminum panels, the tower was built in 1957, and designed by the same architects who worked on Rockefeller Center, just a few blocks away. Jared had brokered the deal to pay $1.8 billion for it, which at the time made it the most expensive office building in all of the United States. The Kushners financed it with very little money of their own, financing the rest by taking on a load of debt. Jared and Charlie had a name to rebuild, and an empire to get on with. It was a deal not unlike Donald Trump's redo of the Commodore Hotel, thirty years earlier and a dozen blocks downtown. Both brought their dad's real estate dreams across rivers, from Queens and from Jersey, respectively. Both signaled that the bridge-and-tunnel crowd was making an entrance. For the Kushners, the family's real estate wunderkind and his newly released felon father had arrived.

The problem was that they arrived at the most spectacularly wrong time. It was 2007, and the real estate market, particularly in New York City, was teetering on the edge of the cliff that would soon crumble into itself and take the rest of financial market with it. By 2008, the building was bleeding so much money that it could not keep up with its debt payments. To keep afloat, the company sold off the building's retail space. Vornado Realty Trust, a public company, took on 49.5 percent of its equity.

BEFORE JARED picked up and moved to Washington to work in his father-in-law's West Wing, he worked out of a corner office on the fifteenth floor of 666, within spitting distance of his mom, dad, and sister Nicole's offices (Nicole's husband, Joseph Meyer, is the chief executive of Observer Media). Josh, who has a venture capital firm, Thrive Capital, of his own, and Dara live in Livingston with her family. Charlie insisted that Jared take the south-facing office, with a view of St. Patrick's Cathedral's spirals piercing the sky over the city, a gesture that signaled his deep appreciation for the way his son had shouldered much of the burden while he was away, and a passing of the torch. The family operates under the principle of "Whatever Jared needs." He's the golden child who made the business survive, associates say. But golden child doesn't begin to do his status justice.

At the company's weekly meeting for principals, held at 8:00 a.m. on Tuesday mornings in a vast conference room with a table that seats at least two dozen people, Jared sits in the middle of the table, sandwiched by Charlie on one side and Seryl on the other, as they make their way through the three-hour agenda, during which they go over acquisitions, financing, and construction. If a family member walks into the meeting, no matter how late, or who is in the room, or how into a discussion they are, each Kushner stands up and greets them with a hug and a kiss. In fact, they do this whenever they enter or exit a room.

There had been much to talk about at these meetings since Jared took over. The company went on a tear acquiring properties up and down the East Coast, including a deal for 733,000 square feet of the former Jehovah's Witness headquarters on the water in Brooklyn—a developer's fever dream that they paid $340 million to make come true.

The deal came through when Brooklyn had already been a *thing* for years. There was a Whole Foods on the horizon; top realtors from Manhattan descended to lord it over brownstone bidding wars, and obsessive helicopter parents hovered around private schools with endless waitlists; the HBO series *Girls* had already shot a handful of seasons there, and a few SoulCycles had already opened their grapefruit-scented studios around the borough. Jared, though, was astounded by the place. "I've been checking out my brother's company and tech companies, and people really seem to love Brooklyn," he told a real estate acquaintance a couple years back. "They *live* there." The person tried to keep his eyeballs in his socket for the rest of the conversation. "I was looking at this guy who looked all of twelve, but he was saying things that would only come out of the mouth of a baby boomer."

ALL THE Kushner kids talk to their parents every day. The grand-parents spend a great deal of time with their kids' spouses and children at their beach house, for Shabbat, on family trips over winter breaks. Josh, the baby of the family, has been dating Karlie Kloss, one of the highest-earning supermodels in the industry, for four years. Charlie and Seryl, however, have yet to meet her.

Kloss is not Jewish, though she has been taking classes and attending Jewish lectures with Josh diligently for some time. The family often says that the couple have not yet made a commitment to each other, so why would they take the time to meet her?—a barely veiled way of saying she is not Jewish, and she has not said she will convert, though friends of Charlie think he would have a hard time letting her in even if she did. To many of Josh's friends, it screams of hypocrisy. They embraced Ivanka. They helped her through the conversion. Why should it be any different for Josh and for Karlie?

"Josh is not Jared," one family friend noted. "Jared has the leverage in the family because of what he did for Charlie." There are some people who think it goes beyond this. They say that Karlie is not seen as educated in their minds, that she's a midwestern girl from a midwestern family, and that she's a model who's posed in lingerie and walked the runway at the Victoria's Secret Fashion Show nearly nude. "They care a lot about modesty," the family friend explained. "Charlie says that she's done photoshoots where she's basically naked, and that he can't be okay with."

CHAPTER 9

Don Jr.—Voltron Number Two

The Attack Dog

Tʜᴇ ᴜɴɪᴠᴇʀsɪᴛʏ of Pennsylvania's men's basketball team entered the 1999 NCAA championship as the eleventh seed in its
division. March Madness, or "The Big Dance," as it is sometimes
called, is the annual college basketball blitz in the final weeks of the
third month each year, in which college players duke it out on courts
across the country, and the rest of the country eagerly pours money
into office pools and family bets, guessing which one of the teams of
teenagers and twentysomethings will go all the way. There's a system and something of a science governing the whole thing. Champion teams from thirty-two Division 1 conferences and thirty-six
teams chosen by a selection committee and divided into four re-
gions get organized into a single-elimination bracket. Within each
region, every team is seeded and matched against another team for
the first round. It's predetermined who the winner of round one will
face in round two, who the winner of that game will face in round
three, and so on.

In 1999, sixty-four teams entered the tournament. It happened to
be a history-making year. It marked the first time that the University of Connecticut took the trophy after a tight win over Duke—77

to 74—in the championship game at Tropicana Field in St. Petersburg, Florida. It was also the year Gonzaga University first came on the scene as an NCCAA tournament superpower. The then relatively unknown team almost made its way to the finals, before UConn staged a comeback in the last minute of their Final Four game. Every year since then, Gonzaga has made the tournament.

Penn entered March Madness that year with a 21–5 record—not terrible for the Ivy League school, which is typically not a shoo-in for the tournament. The Quakers faced off against Florida, the number 6 seed, in the first round, which they played in downtown Phoenix at the NBA home of the Suns. It was the first day of the Big Dance, on March 11, a date that happened to be in the middle of Penn's spring break. So while the members of the men's basketball team sweated out the pressure in Phoenix, most of their classmates sweated out alcohol elsewhere, mostly farther south, in villas in resort towns in Mexico or on the Keys in Florida or within the walls of all-inclusives in the Caribbean. That's where Don Jr. was when his team took the court against Florida that day. He'd gone on a fairly standard—by rich-Penn-kid standards, that is—spring break trip to Jamaica, where gobs of other rich Penn kids and students from other Ivy League schools and Big Ten schools and state schools and liberal arts colleges on a similar vacation schedule migrate to get sunburns and flirt with alcohol poisoning. Who was Don Jr. to break the mold? Sure, he had grown up on vacations to Palm Beach and Aspen and summers on the Mediterranean aboard the *Trump Princess*. But a spring break trip to a crappy resort with other college kids? That wasn't his father's idea of a spring break, for which there was only ever one option, and that was Mar-a-Lago, the private club in which he was the king and his children the little princes and princesses of the castle by the sea. Don Jr. once told a *New York* magazine reporter in 2004 that his father would balk when he told him that he wanted to go fishing. "Why would you go fishing all weekend?" he'd ask his son, who he thought could just as easily play golf. "I don't get it! It's crazy!" His siblings chimed in with their own examples of their dad's contempt for activities and trips that would have him venturing outside of Trump-owned properties and Trump-approved hobbies (namely: golf) that he himself would not choose. "I went to Hawaii and he was like, 'Oh, don't go to Hawaii!' He had disdain," Eric added. "I just came back from Hawaii two weeks ago and that was exactly his reaction," Ivanka interrupted, sending all three of them into a fit of laughter. Eric broke into a spontaneous imitation of his father—an imitation dozens of late-night comics, professional and amateur alike, have perfected over the years. "Why don't you just go to Palm Beach?" he said in his father's signature rasp. "We have Mar-a-Lago!"

So Don Jr.'s Jamaican jaunt was more than a typical spring break. It was a knowing break from his father—a trip that meant more than a raucous good time, though of course Don Jr. was never one to say no to that back then, even if it stood for absolutely nothing more than an afternoon or evening of heavy drinking. Perhaps no one in Jamaica that March even noticed that the kid whose dad was rich and famous was hanging just like the rest of them. But Don Jr. knew somewhere inside it was a subtle choice that moved him away from the ideals and identity of his father—one of many such choices he'd made since he left for the Hill School nearly a decade earlier. His insistence that he not be seen with his parents at a restaurant near campus when he first moved into boarding school was one of them. That he'd arrived at Penn in a pickup truck was another. That wasn't what other kids who'd heard a Trump heir was going to be in class with them expected. A limousine, maybe. A chauffeured car, that wouldn't be out of the realm of possibility. Certainly a Mercedes or a BMW. Plenty of others on campus drove them, and this guy was a *Trump*. "We weren't the kids showing up to college with, you know, a Ferrari," Don Jr. told Barbara Walters in an interview on *20/20* in 2015, after his father entered the presidential race—a tacit admission that the pickup truck arrival was part of a collegiate rebranding strategy.

"I remember when I heard he was going to be a member of our class, there was a little bit of giddy excitement, mixed with a little bit of an 'ugh,'" one of his classmates remembers. "But I told myself, 'Okay, he is not his father. Let's give him a chance.' Whatever infamy his dad had, with the affairs, and the women, and all the money and gold everywhere and the planes and what have you, that didn't implicate him."

The way Don Jr. tried to spin it was that, sure, the world he came from was glitzy and gilded, but deep down, his parents knew the difference between rotting their children with spoils and making them appreciate what they had. "To say we weren't spoiled as kids would be asinine, right?" he told *Esquire* magazine in 2012. "We were very well traveled. We spoke multiple languages. We were around fascinating people who were making history. We got to experience things that other people didn't experience. But we were never spoiled financially." He added that "that kept us out of a lot of trouble."

The truth was, he didn't really keep himself out of a lot of trouble. And try as he might to prove that he wasn't the standard spoiled, arrogant rich kid willing to pull the Trump card, he pulled it, over and over and over. On any given night, Donny would drink himself into a stupor. He would drink to the point where he'd inevitably tussle with other drunk kids on campus who had spoils and arrogance of their own. The mix of alcohol and entitlement and raging testosterone and general lack of consequences for inappropriate behavior would lead to some pushing, some shoving, some putting their red, oily faces close enough to one another to smell on each other's breath the yeast in the beers they'd been pounding. With a lift of his square chin, Don Jr. didn't even have to say it, but he said it anyway, and he said it all the time. "Don't you know who I am?" classmates remember him saying, in so many words. "You don't know who you're dealing with."

Of course they did. Because he reminded them, for starters. And because he had already developed quite a reputation as a campus boozehound and, as one classmate bluntly put it, "undoubtedly an asshole."

"He was classist and he was messy," one person in his class remembered. "He was pretty out of control, but then again, so were a lot of people at Penn."

He was a frat boy who would willingly take part in the hazing rituals passed on in his fraternity—Phi Gamma Delta, more commonly known as FIJI—long after he'd pledged and been hazed during his freshman year. Classmates remember a belligerent Don Jr. standing outside the FIJI house dressed in a barbarian costume of sorts, yelling at the top of his lungs, as flocks of students watched outside. This was a task older brothers forced pledges to engage in. It was a trick many Greek organizations employ—humiliate the people who will later become your brothers so that they prove their loyalty and survive the kind of mortification rituals their fellow brethren have endured for decades before them. It is bonding beyond logic—a million-dollar experience no one would pay a dime for, and something only eighteen-year-olds out of their comfort zones and eager for acceptance would consider worth it. But Don Jr. had already *been* accepted. He'd already been bonded, already shared those humiliations, already paid the dues. He continued to participate, by choice, because, to him, it just seemed like a good time.

Alcohol, no doubt, had a hand in making something like that fun. His classmates remember seeing him passed out, covered in what they assumed was his own vomit, though who knows whose vomit was whose, truthfully. Not once, they recall. It was a habit. As was getting so blitzed that he'd curl up in other people's beds, passing out without knowing where he was or caring who he might displace. Clearly, he didn't have the wherewithal to consider whether he'd used the bathroom before he tucked himself in. Quickly, he earned himself the nickname Diaper Don for his proclivity for wetting the bed on these nights. Mind you, these were *other people's beds*. But mortification did not stop him. There was always more alcohol to be had the next night and the night after that. Diaper Don would wake up in some stranger's dorm room or off-campus apartment or bedroom in his frat house, covered in piss, walk back to his own room, and get blitzed that evening or the next anew. Unsurprisingly, he did not walk away with the kinds of college friends he'd really come to trust later on in life, though he has kept in touch with some and aligned with them in his new political life. "A friend of mine from college, someone I used to party with pretty hard, is now a brain surgeon—which I find very ironic," he told *Esquire* in 2012. "You go to school with someone, you party with them, and now you feel, I don't care if you're the best brain surgeon in the frickin' world, I ain't letting you operate on me."

It's hard to imagine they'd trust him much, either. "I used to drink a lot and party pretty hard, and it wasn't something that I was particularly good at," Don Jr. admitted to *New York*. "I mean, I was good at it. But I couldn't do it in moderation."

That his father showed up on campus made the connection even easier. As Scott Melker, another member of Donny's class at Penn, has publicly written, he was hanging out in a freshman dorm next door to Don Jr.'s room when Donald walked down the hall. He was taking Don Jr. to a basketball game, which, for any other father-son duo, might not have been a particularly memorable exchange. But kids on campus knew who Donny's dad was, and so when they saw Donald knocking on his son's door, a few nosy neighbors peeked their heads out of their tiny little rooms to catch a glimpse. What they saw was Don Jr. greeting his dad, all set to go watch the game in a Yankees jersey. As Melker tells it, Donald took one look at his son and slapped him across the face. Jr. flew to the ground as his classmates watched. "Put on a suit," Donald hissed, "and meet me outside."

It was a vicious cycle. That Don Jr. so desperately wanted to escape his family name and the trappings of a stereotypical rich kid led him to drink, and that he drank himself silly led everyone around him to believe he was exactly the rich-kid stereotype they'd initially expected from a Trump kid.

That was particularly true in Jamaica on March 11, when Don Jr. and a bunch of other Penn kids on break packed themselves into a bar showing the NCAA games to watch their basketball team take on March Madness. So did students from Florida, the team Penn went up against in that first round. On both sides, there was cheering, a little smack talk, and a lot of liquor going around. It was not a blowout like it could have been, but Penn didn't pull it off. Florida won 75 to 61, and Penn was eliminated almost as soon as they started. The inebriated fans on both sides erupted. Slaps on the back. Shots to celebrate or numb the pain. Sloppy high fives or consoling pats on the back. But Don Jr. took it a step further. He climbed atop a table in the bar and started a chant that he'd hoped would catch on with the rest of his fellow disgruntled Quakers in the room. "That's all right! That's okay! You're gonna work for us someday," he jeered at the Florida students.

"These were kids from a state school," one Penn student who was in the bar that day remembered. "The subtext wasn't hard for anyone to figure out. And it just came out so easy."

IF THAT sounds like something that could have come out of Donald Trump's mouth, that is because Don Jr. has spent his life emulating his father, even when he was running in the other direction. He was both abandoned by his father and given everything by him; angry with Donald to a point where they did not speak for years and obsessed with pleasing with him to a degree that he'd say anything to make his father happy. A mix of nature, nurture, and deep scars

left by wounds inflicted by his dad made Don Jr. into a yapping attack puppy, trailing wherever he went the senior attack dog with the
much bigger bark.

During the 2016 campaign, when Donald slung an insult, Don Jr.
was never far behind with a whiffle bat of his own. He called himself "the brute" to describe his own rhetorical flourish on campaign
stops (sometimes, he would include his brother Eric in the name.
"The brutes," they'd call themselves, when they spoke together). "He
was absolutely intent on showing that he had the same killer instinct
as his father," one longtime friend of the family noted. "It played
well, even though that instinct certainly was not the *same*, and certainly not as effective." The intention was so strong that it almost
made up for it. So Don Jr. crisscrossed the country in 2015 and 2016
as one his father's most effective surrogates on the campaign trail.
From the 1,300-acre bird habitat on the High Prairie Farms in Iowa
before its caucus to the Neshoba Country Fair, billed as Mississippi's
giant house party, to the Fox News studio in Midtown Manhattan,
to the dais onstage at the Western Hunting and Conservation Expo,
Donny was dispatched. He'd sling on his hunting boots, pointing
out to crowds just how well worn they were. He'd still slick back
his hair, a style, he would joke, that made him an unlikely hunter
and voice for Middle America. He'd talk about how all the county
fair food and quick fast food stocks were making it hard for him
to fit into the suits he'd donned for years as an executive in his father's real estate company. Maybe he'd even give them up for good.
A life on the trail, in flannel shirts and jeans and, sometimes, orange hunting vests or construction hats, seemed to suit him, which
is part of the reason why campaign officials wanted him out on the
road. Ivanka, in her tailored sheath dresses and stilettos, appealed
to one audience—the coastal crowd and wary women who needed
a knowing wink even to consider listening to the kind of brash
and bombast her father trumpeted throughout the campaign. Don
Jr. assured a base of people for whom the brash and bombast was

Donald's biggest draw that he wouldn't back down from that sort of rhetoric. He was a city kid bred in boarding school and Palm Beach and triplexes, but he left all of that behind. He instead laid into Hillary Clinton, lashed out about the need to drain the swamp, and served as a loyal pit bull, defending some of this father's most incendiary language. Sure, his father might tell women that they were fat and shouldn't be eating candy, but he'd say the same thing to his son. That's just the kind of guy he was. Was it politically correct to say rapists were coming over to the US from Mexico? No. But it was what the American people wanted and finally, they had someone who spoke like, and to, them when they'd felt forgotten or left out of the conversation. Finally, a politician who spoke the way they spoke, who would fight for them the way they desperately needed.

"Sometimes you have to say it like it is, and when you have the problems like we do in this country, sometimes you have to use the hammer," Don Jr. said onstage at the Western Hunting and Conservation Expo in 2016. "It's nice to be soft, when you can, but you can't be afraid to speak your mind and say things like they are."

And he said it like he saw it over, and over, and over, in interviews, and in speeches, and most often on his Twitter account. In an interview with a Philadelphia radio station in 2016, he bemoaned that the mainstream media cozied up to Hillary Clinton, giving her a pass while drilling into his father. "They've let her slide on every discrepancy," he said. "If Republicans were doing that, they'd be warming up the gas chamber right now." Not long after, he tweeted a photo of a bowl of Skittles, comparing them to Syrian refugees. "If I had a bowl of skittles and I told you just three would kill you. Would you take a handful? That's our Syrian refugee problem."

All of these instances created a swirl of outrage. Critics called Don Jr. racist, anti-Semitic, dumb, intolerant, a liability. In another campaign, his remarks would have gotten him benched for good, or at the very least temporarily sidelined. But like his father, he appeared to be Teflon Don Jr. Instead of adopting contrition, he came out combative. His actions and words weren't the problem; the outrage was. The American people wanted fighters like them, who weren't concerned with being politically correct and were unafraid to speak their minds. This is why Americans needed a leader like his father and a First Son like him. His self-defense reflexes were put to such constant use in those two years on the campaign that he went into something of a withdrawal once his father took office—though of course he continued to attack anyone he deemed in opposition of himself and his family. "I thought I'd be going back to my regular job," he told a crowd gathered to hear him speak at the Dallas County Republican Party's Reagan Day Dinner in March 2017. "But once you get a little bit of a taste of that action, it's hard to leave. You know, listen, deals are still exciting, but when you're sort of the guy out there 24/7, every day fighting in this thing—it's like a great fight, the intensity."

DON JR. had spent the two dozen years before his father threw his hat into the ring going from one great fight to the next. When Barbara Walters asked Donald who his most challenging kid was, he barely took half a breath before responding, "Don."

The fact that Don Jr. was the only one of his kids who was both old and strong-willed enough to confront his father after the Marla incident played out in Aspen and he moved out of the triplex undoubtedly factored into Donald's answer. It was Donny who shouted at him that he didn't care about his kids, and that the only thing that mattered to him was money. But Don Jr. had a sixth sense for sniffing out when someone was spoiling for a fight, and he would jump right in their path once he found them. He'd pester his father to find out when he was coming home from work, Donald wrote in *The Art of the Deal*. "I tell Donny I'll be home as soon as I can, but he insists on a time," Donald wrote. "Perhaps he's got my genes: the kid won't take no for an answer." In the height of the mayhem surrounding his parents' divorce, when paparazzi were following him to school, he beat up two boys in his Buckley class when they snick-ered about the headlines about his father's affair and his sex life with Marla. He rarely shied away from drunken skirmishes and pissing contests at Penn, and that urge didn't lessen with age. A few days shy of his twenty-fifth birthday, Don Jr. sat at a table with two women close to the stage at the Comedy Cellar, a little club on McDougal Street in Greenwich Village. On weekends, a line snakes around the block, past the holes in the wall just off NYU's campus selling falafel and bongs and booze, with people waiting to head down the few stairs and inside to watch stand-up. It was nearing two in the morning when other people around Don Jr. had had enough. He'd been loud and obnoxious and distracting for hours. Three couples had told him to pipe down, according to a *New York Post* account at the time, but he brushed them off. "People at a neighboring ta-ble thought Trump was reacting too enthusiastically to a comic's ethnic humor," the *Post* reported. It escalated from an eye-rolling annoyance to a full-on throwdown once Don Jr. raised his glass and splashed some beer on a woman at a nearby table. It is not clear if it was intentional or an accident—a malicious retaliation or a drunken mistake in the heat of the moment. It didn't much matter to the two men who watched the beer fly out of his glass and onto the woman. "You think that's funny?" one guy bellowed. Before he knew it, the man and another guy he was with had tossed their beer steins at him, which whacked him square in the head, smashing and sliding out of that slicked-back hair. Someone called the police, who turned up and took Don Jr. to St. Vincent's Hospital, where doctors closed the gash on his head with twenty-eight stitches. No charges were filed against him. But the two men who hit him with their glasses—twenty-three-year-olds from Staten Island and Brooklyn— were arrested and charged with assault before they were released on $5,000 bail.

One of the guy's family members told the *Post* that their relative was hardly hot-tempered. "He had to have been provoked," he said.

"You'd have to push his buttons hard . . . for him to fight back." A longtime friend of the Trump family, who's known Don Jr. since before Donald and Ivana got divorced, always comes back to this story when asked about Don Jr. "I've seen a lot of rough stuff in my life, and I have to tell you, I've never once seen someone break glass over a person's head," he said. "Punching a guy in the nose? Pushing him to the ground? Okay. Breaking a chair, even. Do you know what kind of a jerk you have to be to get a beer stein broken over your head? That tells you everything you need to know about a kid."

Publicly, Donald defended his son. "He was blindsided," he said of Don Jr. to the *Post*. "I'm going to sue their ass off. I'm also going to sue the club for allowing this to happen." The club's owner at the time did not sweat the threat too much. "Maybe I'll countersue Don Jr. for disrupting the club."

It wasn't the first time Don Jr. brushed with the law. Less than a year earlier, he traveled to New Orleans for a few days celebrating Mardi Gras. He reveled a bit too hard, perhaps, and on February 25, 2001, police rounded him up and arrested him on a charge of public drunkenness. The real estate heir, whose parents boasted about telling all of their children every morning before they went to school that they were never allowed to drink or do drugs or get in trouble, and who have repeatedly bragged that their kids actually listened, spent eleven hours behind bars before he was released.

The Comedy Cellar incident wasn't the first time Don Jr. had found himself worse for the wear after a scuffle. He told *Esquire* in 2012 that he's "broken probably every major bone in my body. I currently have, in my body, fifteen pins and a plate. I've broken my femur, both wrists, both ankles—my left ankle twice. My tibia. Tore my rotator cuff. And that doesn't include knuckles, noses, and don't get me started." And it wouldn't be the last. A few years later, things blew up between a twenty-eight-year-old Don Jr. and a forty-four-year-old woman who lived at 220 Riverside Boulevard, in a 420-unit high-rise on the West Side of Manhattan. In the fall of 2006,

Eugenia Kaye sent a letter to other residents living in the building, alleging that the building's board had misappropriated or misspent $500,000, stemming from a gas bill the building had not paid for six months in a row, even though gas was included in the common charges condo owners already paid each month. Her letter also alleged that the building sponsor had yet to pay back a quarter of a million dollars borrowed from building money without having gotten a green light from the board first. Kaye's letter successfully roused her neighbors to vote out seven board members, including Don Jr. At the time, Don Jr. stayed quiet about the coup, but his father stuck up for him once the *Post* caught wind of the story. As he did when news of the bar fight went public, he said that his son had been "blindsided," this time not by guys with beer steins but by "a woman with extraordinary ambition to be on a board." This go-around, instead of simply threatening legal action, Don Jr. actually filed a $50 million defamation suit against Kaye, and sought to regain his seat on the condo board. "He's a good kid and a hard worker. He did a very good job on that board," Donald added. Everything came to a head at the building's holiday party by year's end. There are two sides to how the evening unfolded. The way Kaye told it at the time, Don Jr. came in steaming mad. He found her, got in her face, and shouted at her, cursing and calling her names. Don Jr. claims it was Kaye who lost control, punching the property manager in the face in front of her neighbors. "Welcome to real estate in New York City," Donald told the *Post* in response.

Don Jr.'s attack-dog instincts manifested themselves more literally. Friends have nicknamed him "the Fifth Avenue redneck" because of his proclivity toward spending weekends and vacations fly-fishing in Alaska, moose hunting in the Canadian bush, and prairie-dog shooting in Montana. He started hunting with his grandfather during the summers he spent in Slovenia, away from his parents and the trappings of the triplex on Fifth, and picked it up again once he moved to central Pennsylvania after Donald and

Ivana's split to board at the Hill School. He started small—clay shooting at a rifle range on campus—and then began meeting other guys around town to fly-fish, venturing out into the cold, all bundled up, to meet guys at six o'clock in parking lots near campus. "I just got hooked, and then I basically read everything there was to read about all of the different forms of hunting, I just got so into it, I read every book available, I spoke to whoever would listen to me, I went with whoever would take me," he said in an interview with the online hunting publication *Bowsite* during the campaign.

That was part of the reason why Don Jr. picked up and moved to Colorado after he graduated from Wharton. "I was probably the first graduate of the Wharton School of Finance to go be a bartender," he told *Bowsite* of his decision to live in Aspen for a year after he graduated. Donald and Ivana fumed once he made the choice. His father offered him a job in the Trump Organization; Ivana told him she would give him no money if he wasted his life away as a ski bum boozehound in the middle of the woods. He turned his dad down and turned his chin up at his mom and defied them both anyway. He wanted to make sure he knew what he was getting into before entering the family business and the craziness associated there with it, he told people. He didn't want any regrets, he'd say, before settling into a life the beats of which he could plot out with his eyes closed. Plus, he was still chilly with his father, who'd just settled his divorce with Marla a year earlier and started dating Melania, and he had a lot of drinking left to do before going to work fifteen-hour days with his teetotaling, hot-tempered, impossible-to-please old man. So he left it all behind for a while, and rented a little place in Aspen on Roaring Fork Drive from a local family. It was just a mile away from the Little Nell, the hotel where he and his siblings had stayed with his parents on holidays when he was growing up, but a world away in most respects. He tended bar at the Tippler, an après-ski bar at the base of Aspen Mountain that they opened at the western edge of the Little Nell's ski run. Locals called it "the Crippler," the kind of place where vacationers and locals alike soaked their altitude-sick livers in booze and picked up equally-as-wasted singles for the night. People could come in in full snowsuits and spill out onto the enclosed sundeck, or they could come by dressed up, cozying into the maroon upholstered couches or around the built-in backgammon tables. Certainly, the crowd orbited around the oval-shaped bar, where for a year Don Jr. helped them all get drunk.

He did his fair share of drinking himself, but hunting helped him cut down a bit. "[Hunting has] been a great, great value in my life, and probably kept me out of a lot of other trouble I would have otherwise gotten into," he told *Bowsite*. "I think when you're waking up at 4:00 a.m. in the morning to get into a deer blind or to, you know, get in a stand, or to go waterfowl hunting, whatever it may be, it was a lot harder to be up at three in the morning from the night before, and so I owe the outdoors." In Colorado, he'd go out with friends he made—former members of the US ski team in far better shape than he was—who were fairly skilled bow hunters. Don knew he was at the end of his rope in Aspen by the time the three guys went out on public land to hunt elk during the month of August. His bank account was running thin, and there would be a time where his father perhaps wouldn't keep an office open for him in Trump Tower—not if he defied him for too long. As he tells it, his brain was starting to atrophy, and he was ready for something more. But there was time for one last go at it. He and his buddies spent weeks chasing the elks with no luck. They had two days left of the season—two days left before Don Jr. decided he was going to pack up and head back to New York and resign himself to being the Trump heir everyone expected him to be—when they saw hoofs through the bushes below them. They were on such a steep slope that they couldn't move up or down when the elk came into view, rounding a bend of brush seven yards in front of them. "It was just incredible," Don Jr. told *Bowsite*. "I mean, there's not many more intense experiences than that."

It did get more intense. He and Eric often went on hunting trips together, including for Eric's bachelor party ("better than a no-win trip to Vegas," Don Jr. later said, adding that he brought his young son along for the seven-mile hike with a bunch of his friends who'd never hunted before. It was not exactly Mar-a-Lago or the night out doing karaoke at Chelsea Piers that Ivanka chose for her bachelorette party years earlier). They hadn't told Donald they were going on a week-long hunting trip so far into the bush that it took days to get to the kill spot. Don Jr. had been hunting seriously for more than a decade by this point, but he had a mishap. His scope hit him smack in the head and sliced into his forehead like a hot knife into butter, nearly straight through to the bones in his skull. They were too far away from any kind of civilization for him even to get to a doctor who could stitch him up, even if he wanted to. He couldn't call Donald, because they were too far out of range. And Donald didn't know where he was anyhow. So he dug into his kit and pulled out the Krazy Glue that had languished there during his many trips. He glued the pieces of his flesh back together before they continued on, leaving a little line in the middle of his face that plastic surgeons back home would have undoubtedly easily avoided.

It would have been just as easy to avoid the public relations nightmare and blistering backlash Don Jr. and Eric got in 2012, when photos of a hunt they'd gone on in Zimbabwe two years earlier surfaced online. There was a grinning Don Jr. in a loose green jacket, dirt-stained khakis held up by a tactical belt filled with unused ammunition that would eventually end up in other wildlife, mud-caked boots, and a backward camo cap containing his jet-black hair. He leaned up against the lifeless big black buffalo he'd just shot dead, his rifle in his left hand, his right arm resting against the buffalo's horns. In another shot, Don Jr. held up a knife in one hand and the tail of an elephant he'd just killed—pink and gory at its root, where he'd sliced it off the animal's body. Don's own palms were covered in blood, his hair slicked back in the same 1980s Wall Street banker style he favored throughout his father's presidential campaign. There was another in which he and Eric, in matching khakis and toothy smirks, posed with a giant cheetah, not unlike the enormous, plush FAO Schwarz stuffed animals their little brother Barron posed with soon after he was born for a magazine spread shot in his Fifth Avenue nursery. This cheetah was real, though, and now it was dead, hanging over Eric's arm after they'd killed it a little while earlier. Eric himself posed for photos with his rifles and the kudu and buffalo he killed. In one photo, taken by the light of a raging fire, he sits on a dead buffalo he's shot like a chair, shaggy blond hair falling, half smiling like an Abercrombie model. He's leaned three guns against its body and hung his hat on one of its horns.

"It was evident from the word go that these two amazing young men are everything but the 'city slickers' you would expect!" their tour guide wrote of the two men when the photos went public. The vast majority of reactions were decidedly more negative. It was a code red for PETA and wildlife advocates. *The Apprentice* almost immediately lost one of its advertisers. The chief executive of Camping World told TMZ that its ad had already aired on NBC during an episode of that season of Donald's reality show, but he "wouldn't spend another nickel with them" after the photos came to light. Even some of their friends who were well aware of their hunting couldn't believe the tastelessness of the photos. That they would kill these animals was perhaps callous, but it was part of who they were; that they would pose with them so gleefully seemed less defensible; and that they'd do so knowing the possible press these photos could receive—coming from the Trump family media genes—was inexcusable. Donald did try to defend the photos and his sons. "They're hunters and they've become good at it," he told TMZ at the time. "I am not a believer in hunting and I'm surprised they like it." (Donald banned Don and Eric from doing interviews about their hunting until the campaign, when advisers repeatedly told him that they were in a perfect moment in which surrogates who could actually speak with authority on the Second Amendment would really help him in the race. "In the early days of the campaign, the base was terrified that Obama was going to take away all their guns, so we thought it was the perfect time for Don to do outreach," one adviser remembered.)

Don Jr. didn't need his dad's tepid response when the photos surfaced. He attacked the critics far harder this time on his own. "I am not going to apologize because some eco nuts want me 2," he wrote in one tweet. "I'm not going to run and hide because the PETA crazies don't like me," he tweeted to a critic. "I HUNT & EAT GAME," he responded to someone else. He also assured another person on Twitter offended by the photos that "it was not wasteful" because "the villagers were so happy for the meat which they don't often get to eat. Very grateful." He further defended himself against people who called him and his brother "bloodthirsty morons" in an interview with *Forbes* around the same time. Those people did not truly understand hunting, he said—and certainly they did not, and could not, understand what hunting meant to Don Jr. "If you wait through long, cold hours in the November woods with a bow in your hands hoping a buck will show or if you spend days walking in the African bush trailing Cape buffalo while listening to lions roar, you're sure to learn hunting isn't about killing," he explained. "Hunting forces a person to endure, to master themselves, even to truly get to know the wild environment. Actually, along the way, hunting and fishing makes you fall in love with the natural world."

For all the spoils and privileges and riches and comforts and opportunities and open, gilded doors dealt to Don Jr., he'd gotten some pretty rotten cards too. He was a poor little rich boy in the most classic sense. In some ways, particularly in his childhood and early adolescence, life had beaten him down. It makes sense, then, that he would grow up feeling as though he needed to always be swinging back.

Hunting gave him an outlet in which to do that. Don Jr. had so many abnormal things, but he lacked the normal securities and unconditional support systems normal children grow up without even knowing they have. Those things he lacked, he found in the sport. First, it let him be anonymous, which was something life alongside his famous parents never afforded him, as desperately as he wanted it. "When I was younger, I was very ardent about being anonymous," he told the *New York Post* in 2002. "I stayed in the background and let my parents do their thing, and didn't have a problem with it. I didn't want to get sucked in to it." He often talks about how there are men he's hunted with for years who have no idea what his last name is, and when they do find out, they already know him well enough as a normal guy in a hunting vest who knows his way around a rifle that the Trump doesn't much matter. It also was one area in his life in which he felt in control. From elementary to boarding school to Penn, his parents had decided where he would go to school. "I had the complete Ivy League résumé coming out of high school," he told *Esquire*. "I had the grades. I had the boards. I played varsity sports. I was the editor of our school newspaper, the yearbook, the literary magazine. But I thought, maybe I should go to the University of Colorado out in Boulder or to the University of Vermont and ski." But his dad thought otherwise when Don Jr. suggested that maybe Donald's alma mater was not the right place for him. "Listen, don't be a schmuck," he said. So Don Jr. went, majoring in finance and marketing in Wharton, as his dad had before him. His parents decided it was a bad decision for him to move to Aspen after college. They decided where it would be appropriate for him to work, how to work, where to vacation, and later, whom to marry. Out in the middle of nowhere, he called the shots—quite literally. It was an area his father had no expertise or interest in, so it belonged to him. For the first time in his life, he'd found a place where he was the boss, and without a dad who everyone thought knew better breathing down his neck.

The need that hunting filled most was the gaping opening left by Donald. His father, much like Donald's father before him, had spent time with Don Jr. as a child only on his terms. Donald's children would come to his office and play on his floor while he worked, until he shooed them off up the private elevator from Trump Tower's twenty-sixth floor to the triplex forty floors up. If they wanted to see him on the weekends, they'd tour construction sites with him—though they did come to love that part for themselves. If they went on trips, they were to properties their dad owned, which meant they weren't actually vacations so much as extended business meetings. A longtime associate of Donald's remembers joining Donald and a reporter from the *New York Times'* Los Angeles bureau who was working on a story about the Trump Organization and its press-courting boss for a dinner at the Atlantic City casino he owned. It was the mid-1990s, not too long after the divorce between Donald and Ivana had been settled, and Don Jr. was down there working at the Trump Marina to make spare cash. His dad insisted he come for the meal, meaning he had to sit through the tedious show his father put on for the reporter—the same braggadocio he'd likely heard a million times. He was still angry with his dad over the divorce, and he was a teenager. It was the last place Don Jr. could ever want to be on a weekend evening. He sat sullen and silent throughout the meal, rarely engaging, mostly because his father rarely acknowledged that he was even at the table, the associate remembered. Donald turned on the charm when another thirteen-year-old boy approached their table. It was his birthday, and his parents had given him the option of doing anything to celebrate—a trip to Disney World, a meal at any restaurant he could dream up—but he wanted to go to the Taj Mahal, just in case Donald Trump was in town. Donald was delighted, and warned the boy and his family not to go to the casino. "The only person who makes money in the casino is the person who owns it"—him, he told them—"so if I were you, I wouldn't go down there." The family smiled sheepishly, got a photo, and slunk away. After the meal, Donald insisted on walking through the casino floor with the reporter and his associate, knowing Don Jr. wasn't old enough to go along with them. So he sent his son down a separate staircase. "We never saw him again the rest of the night," the associate remembered. "I had to ask Donald if he wanted to make sure he got back okay. 'Eh, he'll be fine,' he told me."

Don Jr.'s grandfather, Dedo, stepped in to fill the empty space first. By the time Don Jr. was in kindergarten, Dedo would send him off into the woods for hours on end. The boy would go alone, or with Eric once he was old enough, but he knew that his grandfather was doing it for his own good, and would be there, at the wood's edge, waiting for him to return. He also knew that he would meet other boys his age playing outside, boys who grew up a world away from the mansions and private schools and jets with his last name boldly printed on their wings, kids who instead lived in then-Communist Czechoslovakia who couldn't even imagine the wealth Don Jr. took for granted. "I really learned what it was like to see the other side," Don Jr. told an audience at the Western Hunting and Conservation Expo decades later, during his father's presidential campaign. "The more and more I went back and had friends there, I learned that everything in life didn't have to do with material goods. It was about relationships."

One of those relationships was forged years later, once he arrived in Pottstown, Pennsylvania, to attend the Hill School. The dean of students on campus, who happened to be an expert shot, took a liking to Don Jr., who, he soon found out rather unexpectedly, had spent as much time as he had with his grandfather learning how to shoot a bow and handle a gun and survive for hours in the outdoors without security or maids or limos catering to him. He'd rouse him at six in the morning and bring him to meet his hunting buddies in town. "From that point on, I just fell in love with the hunting lifestyle," Don Jr. said at the expo. "I fell in love with it. There's been so many guys along the way that have been mentors."

That he quickly found out these were guys he could trust played a huge factor in his affinity for the hobby. So many people wanted something from him—his money, his family's fame and access, his business—and his parents had taught him from a young age that, because of that, there was no one whose intentions he could rely on, not even his own family. He told host Donny Deutsch in a 2008 episode of CNBC's *The Big Idea* that his father would repeat the same maxims when he'd go down at seven in the morning before school to give his dad a kiss good morning and a quick hello and goodbye before he started his day. "No smoking, no drinking, no drugs," his dad would tell him. "But then he followed up with: 'Don't. Trust. Anyone. Ever.' And, you know, he'd follow it up two seconds later with, 'So, do you trust me?' And I'd say, 'Of course, you're my dad.' He'd say, 'What did I just—.' You know, he thought I was a total failure. He goes, 'My son's a loser, I guess,' because I couldn't even understand what he meant at the time. I mean, it's not something you tell a four-year-old, right? But it really means something to him. He knows so many people who have been taken advantage of, whether it's by colleagues, but even by families." But when you're in a duck blind in the middle of nowhere, or you hear hoof steps after a month of no luck finding elk two days before you have to move back to New York but you're on a slope so steep you can't move, or a scope splits the skin of your forehead when you're too far away from any medical professional to call for help, well, you have to trust who's around you. And mostly, he could. They didn't want anything *from* him. Something sent them all out there, on a mission, fleeing the day-to-day, seeking camaraderie, searching for peace. Their reasons were all different, and Don's were certainly more unusual than most. Most of the people he hunted with weren't out there escaping anything like what he was escaping. They might not have any window into what led a rich heir who'd grown up in a glass tower covered in marble and gold deep into the bush in muddy hunting boots and ill-fitting khakis. For the most part, many of them didn't even know his last name. "I think it's the distinction between those two lives that gives me the relaxation I need," he told *Bowsite*. "I can step into the woods and out of the office and it's exactly the opposite of what I've done all week. That's my form of meditation, so to speak."

Don Jr.'s form of meditation did come to serve someone other than himself. During the campaign, then Iowa governor Terry Branstad invited Donald to his state for a hunting trip. There was no world in which Donald would have agreed to that, no matter how politically expedient it would be. So he called his son and asked him to take the trip in his place. "Don, you can finally do something useful for me," he told his son.

IN OTHER ways, Don Jr. distanced himself—however slightly—from the narrow world his father occupied. Donald had his sights set on a particular vision of success—a flashy one—in his twenties and thirties. He wanted to be on Fifth Avenue, on the water in Palm Beach, first in the Hamptons and then in Greenwich. He and Ivana went out most nights with people who also lived on Fifth or thereabouts, who wintered in Palm Beach and summered in the Hamptons or in Greenwich and took private jets or chauffeured cars to get there. Everything was the biggest, the most expensive, the goldest with the most marble, and certainly everything made its way to the press somehow. He was the cartoon version of a rich man in Manhattan, and he'd illustrated the whole thing to make sure his image fit the type to a T. Once he had all these things, he'd know he'd arrived, and thanks to the hungry press he aggressively courted, so would everyone else. That Don Jr. drew his own life in his twenties and thirties in a far less flashy fashion is a function of the fact that he'd grown up among it all. He didn't need to prove anything to anyone. He knew Palm Beach, he knew gold and marble, he knew jets and chauffeurs. Don Jr. arrived simply by being born, and so all these things weren't exciting or novel or symbols of his success. That is not atypical for a second- or third-generation rich kid, but it was even more pronounced for Don Jr., who had a bit of disdain for the choices his father made in service of his personal wealth and celebrity. So in some ways, Don's young adulthood sent him in a different direction.

"I definitely don't have his flamboyance," he said in 2005. "I am very different in my personal life. I mean, I like fly-fishing and being outdoors. He likes parties and playing golf, and he doesn't turn the work button off—ever." As for the public attention, he said, "I don't want that. That's his thing and he's really good at it."

To be sure, Don Jr. still lived a life of privilege and leisure and relative ease. His father helped him buy an apartment. He gave him an executive position within a real estate company bearing his name as soon as he returned from his lost year in Aspen, with a college degree and no other work experience than his years as a dockhand in the Trump Marina and what he'd soaked in trailing his father around job sites as a kid. He did fly commercial when he traveled for business, though, unless he was flying with his father, and he almost always flew coach, though sometimes he'd snag a business seat if it wasn't much more expensive or the travel schedule was particularly grueling. "We're too cheap," he told the *New York Times* in 2007, "and try to save money where we can. . . . I try to upgrade when I can with frequent flier miles, but that's been getting increasingly difficult." He went through security like the rest of the universe—something he'd avoided throughout his childhood on his dad's plane in private airports, where you walk right on board without so much as a wave to the guys on the tarmac. He told the *Times* that he'd missed a flight to Boston around the time of the interview because of a mishap with a $20 battery-operated Brookstone alarm clock he'd bought at an airport kiosk a few months earlier. He'd stowed it away in his carry-on, and sent it through the X-ray scanner before he made his way through the metal detector. The TSA agents screening his bag thought the clock looked suspicious, and despite the famous last name on his ticket, and his insistence that it was just a tiny little travel clock, they shut the security lane down and called in the state police. After a few minutes, they determined that it was in fact an alarm clock. Meanwhile, Don Jr. was being held, shoeless, in the security line, watching the minutes tick closer to his flight departure time. "I felt like an idiot," he told the *Times*. The plane left without him, since the whole thing took about a half hour. But he did get to keep the alarm clock in the end. "Sometimes it pays to be a Trump," he joked.

The Trump Tower triplex he grew up in is 33,000 square feet (though, like many things tied to Donald's material possessions and valuations of his assets, there is some debate over its true size versus Donald's estimation of its vastness). The first apartment he shared with his wife Vanessa was a little more than 1,500 square feet. It had two bedrooms and parquet floors, one room with sky-blue walls and one painted deep red, a zebra-print rug in the guest room. They didn't have a housekeeper to tidy up after them, at least in the early years, in contrast to the fully staffed household in which he grew up. They filled the apartment with hand-me-down furniture—an antique canopy bed Vanessa's mom had used for two decades, brown leather couches Don used in his bachelor pad. There were sentimental objects Ivana and Donald would never have had in their homes, too—oil paintings made by Vanessa's Danish grandfather, the childhood teddy bear she'd kept since she was six months old, and the "Captain Pickle" doll Don had hung on to from his child-hood. In the kitchen, where he spent a great deal of time, he kept an organized fly-fishing collection and a cast-iron skillet in which his grandmother Mary had cooked all the Trumps' family meals in their Queens home. Don Jr. and Vanessa cooked at home, too. They preferred it to going out. "I learned at a young age . . . in the single digits—8 or 9 years old . . . and was into it," he recalled of his love for cooking. He studied the chefs at Mar-a-Lago, learning how to make seafood, curries, Italian stuff that he later started whipping up for his wife. They filled their home with family photos and snapshots of their wedding and photo albums, which he said were all he'd take if the building were to go up in a blaze and they had to make a quick exit. "There wouldn't be [a fire]," he clarified, "because this is a Trump building." (In early April 2018, a fire on the fiftieth floor of Trump Tower broke out. There were no sprinklers, and one resident died in the blaze.) Their two little yappy Havanese puppies—Fraggle and Faluffa—had the run of the place, and around Christmastime their parents got them a little tree of their own, "because we're idiots," Don recalled in 2008. He was stingier when it came to presents to his siblings. "Look, I've been re-gifted presents that I've given my family," he admitted that same year. "You know, they're like, 'Oh, great, thanks!' and then you end up getting it back the next year."

AS MUCH as Don Jr.'s confrontational affect and his decision to live a lower-key lifestyle were because of and in reaction to his father, they were also, in part, inherited from him. His father passed down other traits the connection to which are harder to deny. "I think I probably got a lot of my father's natural security, or ego, or whatever," Don told *New York Magazine.* "I can be my own person and not have to live under his shadow. I definitely look up to him in many ways—I'd like to be more like him when it comes to business—but I think I'm such a different person, it's hard to even compare us. His work persona is kind of what he is. I have a work face, and then there's my private life."

Portions of Don's private life are perhaps where he and his father align most, and women seemed to be a place in which they overlap. His sister spent years distancing herself from fellow blond New York heiress Paris Hilton, making her club-rat image a foil to the squeaky clean, hardworking image Ivanka wanted to project, but Don Jr. was far softer to Hilton. In the early 2000s Chris Wilson, a rookie Page Six reporter, turned up to a party on the roof of *Playboy* headquarters on Fifth Avenue. Hilton was there, in a high-low sartorial mélange of a belly shirt and a diamond choker, and as the evening progressed Don Jr. showed up as well, his standard greasy bob looking extra greasy and bob-like for the occasion. Wilson had never

met Don Jr. before, though he had met his father a few times, once
in Trump's house, which he thought looked like a casino designed
by Saddam Hussein. Don Jr. was wasted by the time the three of
them somehow ended up sharing a cab to go home—Hilton on one
side, Don Jr. on the other, Wilson as a buffer smack in the middle
of them. Paris needed one, because Jr. continually arched himself
over Wilson to paw at the heiress, trying to rub her exposed belly
like a genie who would grant his late-night drunken wish. Paris had
no interest, clinging to Wilson and radiating a not-so-subtle "help
me" signal from all angles of her spray-tanned face. Somehow, the
three of them managed to take a photo together, which Page Six was
going to run under the caption "The Art of the Feel." It ultimately
got scrapped.

Don Jr. had more success with another model, though it took
a bit of time. He'd tagged along with his father to a fashion show
in 2003 in New York—not exactly his scene, but he obliged. This
was a more palatable parental request for the single twenty-six-year-
old, who'd settled into an executive role at his father's company by
then. It was Donald who spotted a leggy, long-haired blonde walking in the show. He approached Vanessa Haydon, a fellow Upper
East Side–raised, private-school-bred girl coming into the limelight.
Donald introduced himself and said he would like her to meet his
son, Donald Trump Jr. Before the show began, Don and Vanessa
made the uncomfortable small talk that would come from two
young people being thrust together with one's father tagging along
and prying eyes all around. At intermission, Donald approached
Vanessa again, as if the first conversation had never happened at all.
Again he introduced himself and told her that she should meet his
son, Donald Trump Jr. "Yeah, we just met," she told him, looking
toward Don Jr. as if his dad had lost his mind.

Fate—or the intensely small circle that is the twentysomething
scene on the Upper East Side, depending on your subscription
to romantic fantasies—brought the two back together again less

than two months later, at a birthday party at Butter, a downtown restaurant-cum-club that was *the* place for a New York minute. They found each other and talked for what felt like most of the night before she realized who he was, that she had met him weeks earlier at the fashion show. "Wait," she later recalled saying. "You're the one with the retarded dad!"

The way the media wrote about Vanessa—the story they created around her—was not unlike the way they described Melania when she first started dating Donald—all sunshine, success, good breeding, and no drama. The whole truth of both women's pasts was initially entirely left out. Just as Melania was described as a college graduate with two degrees, who grew up with a fashion-designer mother and thrived in an impressive modeling career, Vanessa was introduced to the world by the *Times* and other publications as a woman who grew up in a townhouse and blossomed into a tennis star at the Dwight School, "who with her athletic build, buttery tan, blond hair and sunny smile seems like a Brian Wilson fantasy." She joked and wore jeans and avoided social climbing and signed with the impressive Wilhelmina agency, even though her mother ran a modeling agency of her own. Vanessa Haydon, the *Times* wrote, was "born for the role" of becoming a newly minted Trump.

And just as it later came to light that Melania had not in fact graduated with architecture and design degrees but instead dropped out after a year, and that her mother had actually been a textile factory worker, Vanessa's fuller past didn't stay in the past for long. For as much as Vanessa might look like a Beach Boys muse, she may have actually been more of a Scorsese chick at her core. Haydon first came into the public consciousness in 1998, when she was spotted lip locked with Leonardo DiCaprio, who, at the time, was white hot in a post-*Titanic* universe, at a party in Soho. The pair dated only a few weeks, long enough for gossips to pick up on her saying how the star found dating a "down to earth" girl like her and her agents to jump on her fifteen minutes of famous flingdom by selling modeling photos of Haydon to foreign newspapers. Her romantic dalliances beyond DiCaprio captured headlines and the sharp tongues of those who knew her at Dwight, as well. For years, on and off, she dated a man who went by the name Vallantine, whom she met as a teenager. Legend had it that Vallantine, a member of the Latin Kings who lived in Astoria, was not every Upper East Side mother's dream suitor for her aspiring model daughter. But the topic was catnip for Vanessa's classmates and contemporaries and all of their parents who found out about the relationship. Rumors swirled about her briefly moving into his apartment, about her wearing starter jackets in yellow—a show of support for the Latin Kings color—and maybe stopping by a meeting for the Latin Queens. She visited Vallantine in Rikers once he was locked up on drugs and weapons charges, though the frequency of her prison visits was a subject of some debate. Her spokesman at the time told the *New York Post*, which gamely reported on all the rumors after she started dating Don Jr., that she visited Rikers only once, after she and Vallantine had already broken up, to translate for his mother, who spoke no English. Her rep also denied that she was involved with the Latin Queens or wore yellow in solidarity. "She used to be this hard-rock in leather and baggy jeans," one teenage friend said of Haydon to *New York* magazine, in a story about DiCaprio. "She was a total gangster bitch." Another friend referred to her as "an ill thug." *New York* also pointed out that in her high school yearbook, her classmates voted her Most Likely to Wind Up on Ricki Lake.

Don Jr. took a page out of his father's playbook when it came to his proposal. Donald had accepted a hefty discount from Graff Diamonds on Melania's thirteen-carat sparkler when he proposed in 2004. The jeweler, which also appeared on an episode of *The Apprentice*, noted an uptick in sales after it ingratiated itself with the Trumps, and Donald bragged to the press about how he'd knocked some money off the price of the rock. And so when it came time for Don Jr. to pop the question—only six months after his dad had asked his third wife to marry him—there was a jeweler willing to foot the bill, and a Trump willing to take advantage of it.

The difference, of course, was that Donald proposed with the discounted ring in private, before the couple walked the red carpet at the annual Met Gala. It was different for Don Jr. After a year and a half of dating, he took his girlfriend to New Jersey. The couple arrived at the Short Hills mall, where TV crews and paparazzi were waiting. They'd been invited by the real estate heir as part of an agreement made with the jeweler Bailey Banks & Biddle. If Don Jr. proposed in front of flashbulbs, and agreed to additional promotional appearances on behalf of the jewelry store, then the $100,000 four-carat emerald-cut diamond, set in platinum and surrounded by two smaller trapezoid diamonds and fifty-six others around the ring, would be his for free. So, in November 2004, right in the middle of the suburban Jersey mall, with television cameras rolling, Don Jr. got down on one knee and asked Vanessa to marry him. Yes, yes, yes, she said gamely for the cameras, though she would later admit that Don Jr. had proposed to her a couple months earlier in their apartment. Perhaps the *Times* was right when it said she was born to be a Trump.

The day after the proposal, the *Post* headlined its story "Trump Jr. Is the Cheapest Gazillionaire—Heirhead Proposes with Free 100G Ring," calling it "what has to be one of the cheesiest wedding proposals on record." Donald was not happy with the reviews. A few weeks later, he told Larry King on CNN that he "wasn't thrilled" with the way his son went about it. "I certainly don't like it with respect to a wedding ring," he said, without mentioning his own most recent wedding ring discount. "I said, 'You have a big obligation. You have a name that's hot as a pistol. You have to be very careful with things like this.'"

When it came to the wedding, Don and Vanessa again stuck close to the model Donald and Melania set for them. They chose Mar-a-Lago, where his father and stepmother had had their reception that January, setting a date in November 2005. As they registered at Bloomingdale's, and Barneys, and of course Tiffany, they began to quietly shop around the exclusive rights to photos and footage of their big day, just as Donald had with Getty and Melania with *Vogue*. Vanessa didn't hire a wedding planner, telling *OK! Magazine* that she'd spent thousands of dollars on bridal magazines, as her soon-to-be stepmother had months earlier. She threw her bachelorette party in Miami, for which Ivanka flew down to join her at the it-club Mansion in South Beach. A week before the nuptials, Hurricane Rita hit Florida, knocking out Mar-a-Lago's power for days. There was no water, either. The estate's front lawn, where the ceremony was set to take place, was ravaged by the storm. "We were going to have to have the wedding by candlelight," Donald told the *Post*. But the power came back on, as did the water, just in time for the rehearsal dinner on the Friday evening before. The couple hosted their guests for a luau, complete with a roast pig, martini bar, and a DJ Vanessa had heard at her cousin's wedding in New Jersey. On Saturday, November 12, 370 guests gathered at Mar-a-Lago to watch the eldest Trump heir say "I do."

The crowd was hardly the litany of celebrities who'd gathered for Donald and Melania's ceremony earlier that year. Joan Collins, songwriter Denise Rich, and reality TV starlet Brittny Gastineau took their seats poolside, where the couple decided to move the ceremony after Rita tore up the lawn. Donald, in a tuxedo, walked down the aisle with Melania, in a champagne strapless gown flowing out from an empire waist that barely concealed her growing baby bump (Barron would be born four months later). Ivana, in a peach satin off-the-shoulder gown that showed off a diamond necklace with honking pastel stones and fell into bell sleeves covered in ornate silk flowers, left a seat between herself and her ex-husband after depositing her son at his place by the altar, underneath an arch of white and violet flowers. Her mother, Babi, in a bubble-gum-pink dress of her own, filled the spot between them. Don Jr.'s hair was nearly long enough to reach his honking silver bow tie. He slicked it back on top and tucked his locks behind his ears—a mix of California surfer boy and Rachel Green from *Friends*. His brother Eric, in a darker gray yet equally wide bow tie, stood by his side as, one by one, all ten of Vanessa's bridesmaids, including Ivanka, made their way down the aisle in their silk pale orchid gowns, cut into deep V-necks. Several flower girls in fluffy white confections followed. Tiffany was not in the wedding party.

Vanessa's mother walked her down the aisle, as her father had passed away years earlier. The bride worked with Reem Acra to design her gown—bright white and skintight and heavily beaded on its straps and bodice. For the ceremony, a veil puffed out from the bedazzled tiara she wore atop her flowing loose curls, disguising just how low the back of her dress was cut. She carried a white bouquet filled with calla lilies and little roses, and around her neck she wore a diamond cross. The New Jersey DJ from the night earlier was also a bandleader, who'd set up a ten-piece orchestra for the ceremony and a sixteen-piece band for the reception (he charged the couple $20,000 for the evening, more than double what he typically commanded). They played a cover of Bryan Adams's "Heaven" for the couple's first dance inside the grand ballroom, where guests were served filet and a towering cake by Sylvia Weinstock, the same famed baker who'd created the masterpieces for Donald's weddings; this one was covered in red and pink flowers handcrafted from sugar and fondant. Vanessa surprised Don Jr. with a groom's cake in the shape of a fish—an outdoorsman's delight. The groom teared up when he toasted his bride, recalling that it was his father who'd set him up in the first place. "'That's the kind of girl you should be with,'" he told his guests his father urged him. The guests noted among themselves that she was exactly the kind of girl Donald himself would have been with, had Melania not been in the picture at the time. Donald toasted the couple as well, as did Ivana, who joked that the couple's future children would have to refer to her as "Glam-ma."

Ivana did not have to wait long to get her wish. Two days after their first wedding anniversary, Don and Vanessa invited a group of their closest friends and some family to their apartment. They made another round of toasts, to celebrate not just their first year of marital bliss but also the next milestone. That spring, the couple would become parents for the first time. They shared the news publicly a night later, at a party at the 460 Degrees Gallery on Fifth Avenue at which Vanessa was feted for appearing on the cover of *Hamptons Magazine*, despite the fact that the couple preferred not to go to the Hamptons, especially in season (Don Jr. would sometimes go out to Montauk to fish once the rest of Manhattan had left their second homes on Long Island in the fall). Barron Trump, Don Jr.'s littlest brother, was eight months old. By that spring, he'd be his baby's uncle. "They'll be more like brothers—or brother and sister," Vanessa joked to the press.

Barron's sister-niece arrived on May 12, 2007. On the evening of the eleventh, Vanessa made her way out to a charity event in the city, walked the red carpet with her swelling belly, and walked inside in time for her water to break at her feet. She labored for twenty-one hours, with Don Jr. there for most of them. When Kai Madison Trump arrived, at six pounds fourteen ounces, the couple named her after Vanessa's father. But she got something of Donald's. "Everyone who sees her is amazed by her hair," Vanessa told *People*, which got the exclusive first photos of Kai, as the magazine had with Barron, and published them a month after she was born. "She needed it shampooed right away!" Years later, Kai and Barron would start at the same Upper East Side preschool together, only a year apart.

In the winter of 2009, Donald J. Trump III—D3, as he came to be known—was born. Tristan Milos Trump, his middle name after Don Jr.'s beloved Dedo, followed in October 2011. Then came Spencer Frederick, *his* middle name after Don's *other* grandfather, exactly a year after Tristan. In June 2014, Chloe Sophia joined her sister and brothers. "#FullHouse," Don Jr. tweeted after she arrived.

He, like his father, and like his father's father, had five kids—three boys and two girls.

By 2017, it became clear that he would follow his father in another way. Vanessa did not accompany Don Jr. and the rest of his family to the New Year's Eve party at Mar-a-Lago, which also happened to be her husband's fortieth birthday. Tongues started wagging in their small circle, where talk was over not whether they would separate, but when. Most believed they would stick it out through the 2020 election, if they got that far. But Trump history repeated itself: in March 2018, Page Six reported that they were headed for divorce. A day later, Vanessa filed in Manhattan Supreme Court. "After twelve years of marriage, we have decided to go our separate ways," the couple said in a statement. "We will always have tremendous respect for each other and our families." It took about a minute for rumors of Don Jr.'s infidelities to whip around the press, along with stories of how his tight-wad tendencies and attack-dog nature irked her. People were claiming he repeated the very behavior he spent years freezing his father out over.

FIVE KIDS, like his father, but with only woman, and no full-time nanny, let alone two. Mothers remember Vanessa as particularly harried, with kids in a constant swirl, particularly as the kids got older and there were five individual schedules to manage. It became a thing of legend among private school moms, who told and retold one cautionary tale of a life with so many kids and so little help. It was warm enough outside that moms and nannies and assorted guardians could pleasantly stand outside Spence, an all-girls school on the easternmost block of Ninety-First Street, waiting for their little girls in their baby-blue jumpers and pleated skirts and white collared shirts and hair ribbons to burst out of the schoolhouse doors in their singsongy, chattery postschool delight. When they all burst out at once, though, the noise that came blaring out was very different. It sounded like a high-pitched siren—the school's fire alarm system. That's weird, the moms and nannies and assorted guardians thought and said to one another. Why would they do a fire drill that late in the day, as all the kids were being dismissed?

It was not, in fact, a drill. As Vanessa Trump and a couple of her younger boys showed up to Spence to pick up their eldest, Kai, who'd started at Spence in kindergarten, Vanessa started chitchatting outside. One of the boys ran into the school without her knowing and pulled the handle up on the bright red fire alarm hanging on the wall, just inside the school's entrance. "You've got to be kidding me," one of the other moms remembered thinking. Her daughter, who was in Kai's class, was terrified of loud noises at the time. "This woman had so many kids you had to feel for her. And there was no nanny. But she couldn't keep enough of an eye on the boys to stop them from disrupting the whole entire school as all the other mothers and people picked up their kids? It was chaos. Absolute chaos."

NOT LONG after, the school started a campaign to raise money, as uptown private schools so often do, and Don Jr.'s inherited stinginess started to show. At the time, Spence decided to build a brand-new athletic center to keep all of its sports programs within one building. At that point, students had to bounce around in a handful of gyms around the city for their various in-school and after-school sports programs—not exactly a draw for the crowds shelling out $50,000 a year for their daughters' elementary school educations. At the very least, that should buy their girls a proper gym. But if you're going to do it at all, why not do it the right way? And the right way, for Spence, was to build an eight-story facility on Ninetieth Street, with a hulking gymnasium taking up two floors, training and locker rooms, squash courts, classrooms, a café, and a greenhouse.

Fifty thousand dollars per pupil is a lot of money, but it does not stretch as far as an eight-story fitness megaplex on the Upper East Side. Lucky for the school, they happened to have a Rolodex of already committed families who not only had the money to afford the school but the incentive to fork that money over. It was going to their own kids' educations, after all, and maybe their kids' kids', after that. Add a little friendly parental competition within the classes over which family would give the most? They'd raise the funds, no problem.

But there is a process for this sort of thing. The school began methodically hosting a series of small dinners, asking some of its wealthiest parents to host other particularly wealthy parents along with the heads of the school to talk about the plans and about how they could contribute. Don Jr. and Vanessa made the cut for one of the dinners, held in a sweeping apartment on Fifth Avenue one evening when Kai was in her first few years at Spence. Four couples, along with the head of the school and her assistant, ate around a round table in the dining room before they moved into a living room to discuss the gym. A presentation was made, along with a pitch, and the parents were told that they would later be formally asked if they wanted to contribute in private meetings on Spence's campus in the weeks and months to come.

The rest of the parents nodded. They'd anticipated this. This is how these things were done. The nodding was interrupted by the sound of Don Jr.'s voice. "I think this sounds great," he said, loudly enough for the other parents to distinctly remember it years later. Kai loved sports, he told the group, and so he could see her benefiting from the addition, and they wanted to be involved in any way they could.

"I mean, we're not going to give money," he said in front of the group. "But I am more than happy to lend my expertise to the building process." The rest of the parents turned beet red. The head of the school thanked Don for his offer, and said the school would be grateful for a Trump perspective, but that they likely had the whole construction side of this handled. What they really needed to focus on was raising the funds. "You can think about it. You don't have to answer now," she said. "None of you do."

CHAPTER 10

Eric—Voltron Number Three

The Builder

WITH CENTRAL Park as a buffer, the Upper West Side somewhat insulated the towheaded young Eric Trump from the media chasing his older brother and sister on their way to school on the East Side as their parent's marriage unraveled. Ivana had chosen the Trinity School for her youngest child years earlier. The school, the fifth oldest in the country, first opened its doors in 1709 with classrooms in the Trinity Church bell tower and in old City Hall. Its founder, William Huddleston, pitched a missionary organization of the Church of England on the idea of a public school in New York City where poor children might be taught in the tradition of the church for free. They agreed, on the condition that the mayor and alderman prove each year that the school was, in fact, educating at least forty poor children. All of this changed after the Revolutionary War. Trinity moved out of the church and into a series of buildings built and commissioned on the very upper west corner of Manhattan, on Ninety-First Street and Columbus Avenue. Trinity shifted from public to private and, centuries later, allowed female students so that it became fully co-ed. The school founded on the ideals of a gratis education for underprivileged children has since educated the likes of Eric Schneiderman and John and Patrick McEnroe. For a time, Truman Capote, James and Lachlan Murdoch, Humphrey Bogart, Yo-Yo Ma, Ansel Elgort, and Oliver Stone also walked the Trinity halls. In the 2017–18 school year, the school charged parents $49,795 for kindergarten, though the school notes that that figure includes lunch and other required fees. Additional textbooks and field trips and the like cost extra.

The school accepted the baby Trump, which is really all that matters in that rat race. The school's motto, *Labore et virtute*—"Hard work and moral excellence"—appealed to the Trumps, as well, at least the first part of it. The lower school building—sturdy brownstone, with sweeping windows that let light flood into classrooms, bays at each end that create grass courtyards for students to play on, and a stone cross atop one of its peaks—shielded Eric during the most tumultuous period in his young life.

Divorce disorients any six-year-old. It rips apart the tiny pocket of a world they know and feel safe in. Eric benefited from the fact that his parents weren't the only adults he really knew or that ever cared for him. His father moving a few floors down within Trump Tower did not rock his day-to-day routine as it might have for most other kids. But most other kids don't have their family not only split in front of them, on top of a mountain in Aspen, but then spill onto every New York tabloid front page for weeks on end. Some children are mercifully spared the shouting matches, the curses, the insults his parents hurled at each other, and the open adultery that put his father very publicly in another woman's arms so soon. The story was so salacious and omnipresent in New York that even Eric's kindergarten classmates, who could not even read at that point, brought up the gossip to him in school.

It was not entirely surprising, then, that Eric acted out in school, and teachers soon took note. One of Trinity's traditional requirements is that students must participate in a community service program and volunteer both out of school and within the walls of Trinity. This meant that older students would take assignments alongside teachers, offering an extra hand and helping to wrangle younger kids. The year of Donald and Ivana's divorce, one Trinity high schooler got assigned to assist the dance teacher with her creative movement classes for five- and six-year-olds. One afternoon, at the end of class, she instructed all of the children to put their play mats away. It was chaos, herding the little people into some semblance of organization and coaxing them to leave the place less of a disaster than it was, but all the kids at least tried, with one exception. Eric just stood there while his classmates folded their mats and, as neatly as they could, stacked them up.

It dawned on the student teacher that perhaps Eric had never been asked to clean up for himself before, given what she knew of his family. Maybe he needed a little more of a push or an explanation. So she instructed him further, specifically, kindly, gently pointing him in the right direction and urging him to follow his classmates. "Eric, please put your mat away with the other children," she remembers telling him.

He barely paused, hardly breathed, before he looked her in the eye, in front of all the other children, and bellowed at the top of his tiny little lungs: "You're a bitch!"

She blushed, the blood rushing to her face to push down the rage boiling in her belly, unsuitable to unleash on a six-year-old. Pity quickly replaced it. Where does a six-year-old private school kid who lives in a triplex on the Upper East Side pick up that kind of language? Clearly, as a high schooler, the assistant had not been closely following Donald and Ivana's venomous split. The news was inescapable enough that she did know something about it, though. "I thought it was possible he was acting out because of the divorce," she recalled. "Or maybe," she added, "he was just an asshole."

Eric was not disciplined for the infraction. Years later, though, Trinity "counseled him out" of the school (a private school euphemism for asking a student not up to a school's academic or cultural standards to leave without pissing off the parents), as Chapin had with Ivanka and Buckley had with Don Jr. No one has ever disputed the strength of the Trump genes, and just how deeply they run throughout all of the family's lives.

ERIC TRUMP was five when Marla and Ivana shouted at each other over a spoiled mid-ski lunch on Aspen Mountain; he was six when his schoolmates started teasing him about the subsequent sex-laden headlines, and his mother pulled him out of Trinity for a few months for some space and sunshine in Palm Beach. He was nine when his father remarried for the first time. By that point, his mother had a steady boyfriend of her own. "I had a lot of resentment, especially for those people," Eric said of his feelings when his parents started dating after the divorce.

The disdain Eric felt for Marla is understandable. The way he saw it, she rocked his home life before he could even hit elementary school proper; if not for her, his father would not have moved a few floors down in Trump Tower, and a few years later, he would not have had to move out of his triplex at the tippy-top of the building for a townhouse with Ivana a few blocks north, while Marla and Tiffany moved in—albeit briefly. Of course, it was not Marla who truly broke Donald and Ivana's marriage. Marriages have to be breakable for that to happen, and there were cracks in the relationship between the first Mr. and Mrs. Trump, waiting for Marla to seep into and fill, when Eric was just a toddler.

It is not as though his parents were particularly present before the split. Workaholics and social climbers, they left it mostly to two dedicated nannies, bodyguards, drivers, hotel workers, club employees, and caretakers on various properties to look after Eric and the other Trump children, whether it was their official job or simply a role they took on out of necessity or the goodness of their hearts. "My father, I love and appreciate, but he always worked 24 hours a day," Eric told the *New York Times*. Bridget and Dorothy, the family's nannies, doted on the kids, as did Ivana's parents, Dedo and Babi. But a couple of months after Don Jr. left home for boarding school, the same year his parents separated, Dedo suddenly died, and then he and Don Jr. found their beloved nanny Bridget on the floor of their Greenwich home.

Without them, his older siblings stepped in. Don Jr., six years his senior, and Ivanka, two years older, not only looked after Eric the way all protective big brothers and sisters do the littlest member of the family, but also like a distinct Trump team. They were their own little unit, a constant for one another when everything else had turned upside down, when nothing or no one else in their world remained enduring or consistent or safe. Donny and Ivanka took their roles as team leaders taking care of the youngest member quite seriously. One of Ivanka's classmates at Choate who came back to New York on weekends away from their Connecticut boarding school remembered Eric wreaking havoc the way little boys do, and Ivanka would sweep in to calm things down. "When it came to her siblings, one of them was always upset about this or that or running around the house," the friend recalled. "Ivanka was usually the person to step in. There was no question that she was really protective of him, in a way I'd never seen a sibling who is not *that* much older be." When she was at school, she called Eric to make sure everything was okay. She would ask friends to mentor him, to give him advice about applying to schools or internships or sports or girls. "I'm definitely closer to Ivanka [because of the divorce]," he told *New York*, explaining that "she took me under her wing and raised me, took me shopping, tried to make me cool." As for Don Jr., he would take his brother off campus once Eric got to Hill himself, touring him around local spots in state parks where they could go fly-fishing or hunting. "Donny, in a way, is like a mentor. He kept tabs on everything that my grandfather taught him over the years and that I was too young to appreciate." That same year, he told the

Times that yes, Donny was his mentor, and his best friend, too—but also, he added, in a way, "he raised me."

THAT ERIC had the least amount of time with the first iteration of the Trump family, and did not get a tremendous amount of time with his father when he was little outside of visiting his office after school, did not mean he did not pick up on some of his dad's most distinctive traits. They were easy enough to pick up on. Before the divorce, when Donald and Ivana and the children would all decamp to Greenwich for the weekends, the family often went to dinner at Manero's Restaurant Steakhouse—a local joint with wood-paneled walls and white tablecloths and red vinyl chairs that long advertised under the slogan "Manero's—always bring the children." It was a six-hundred-seat joint with an illustration of its owner, Nick Manero, in a big white chef's hat on the wall, along with a sign promising that if a diner had a baby in the restaurant, she'd eat free steak there for life. Waiters served steak dinners—filets, baked potatoes, onion rings, garlic bread, a wedge salad, a dessert, and a hot drink to close out the meal—for ten bucks in the 1970s and '80s, and they'd gather around your table and sing "Happy Birthday" with a candle stuck in your cake if they knew the special day. When they were hot, they could barely keep up with the demand, despite the fact that the butcher's shop was directly connected to the restaurant outside. On a given Saturday night at its peak, Manero's served more than 1,100 dinners.

This meant that there would invariably be a line of some of Greenwich's finest out the door on a weekend evening. Andy Rooney would wait. Arnold Palmer did, too. *The Price Is Right* announcer Johnny Olson hung around biding time for his table like the rest of them. But Eric Trump, a young elementary school student no more than a few feet tall, was not about to stand in line for a table. His family came there every week. They ordered the same thing—a heaping Caesar salad, steaks for each of them, and baked potatoes topped with as much sour cream as the kitchen could muster. As one frequent diner recalled, the little blond boy zigzagged his way through people ten times his age who had been waiting for their tables three times as long. He made it up to the hostess and, without hesitation or much regard for who heard, informed her that his last name was Trump, and he expected to be seated right away. The grown-ups who overheard the youngest Trump—at that time, at least—gawked. Their utter shock and bemusement at his pure chutzpah, mixed with revulsion and their own hunger, did not end up sitting well—and this was Greenwich. These people knew from entitlement. "You can wait in line like the rest of us, dear," a frequent customer remembers telling him. He caught her eye, stared at her blankly, and promptly looked away.

THIS APPETITE—THE eagerness with which he wanted to sit and eat—was indeed a Trump trait passed down from Donald to Eric, and all of his siblings, really. As a teenager at the Hill School, Eric would constantly pick food, particularly of the fried variety, off his friend's plates. He was heavier as a kid and adolescent, which some of his classmates recall made him seem like a jolly type. During Thanksgiving break in his senior year of college, he boasted all about the family's feast and genetic appetite to a *New York Observer* reporter. The family spent the holiday at Mar-a-Lago that year, not in Greenwich, as they had for years when he was a kid, when the turkeys, "sometimes . . . wouldn't fit in the oven, they were so big." And they doused everything with sauce, whatever sauce they could get their hands on—they were "big saucers," Eric explained. So one reason for them to be thankful that year, even though it wasn't quite tradition to be in Palm Beach, was that the staff had set up the meal as a buffet at Mar-a-Lago, where they all sat down to the table in formal attire. "We were grateful that it was a buffet-style, otherwise we'd constantly have to be ordering more gravy, which would be kind of embarrassing." He was equally grateful that he didn't have to share much of the yams, stuffing, cranberry sauce, peas and carrots that the Mar-a-Lago chef prepared for them that year. Don Jr. and Vanessa were on a holiday to Mexico, celebrating their anniversary, and Ivanka was off on a trip of her own, so as for Trump kids, it was only Eric and his little brother Barron, only eight months old at the time. He boasted about the baby's ability to keep up. "He's a typical Trump," he said, with pride. "He was slamming down those mashed potatoes. We're all big eaters in our family, and I can tell that Barron's going to keep up that tradition." That tradition, he added, cost his parents a hefty sum over the years. "My mom used to joke that it was more expensive to feed me than to pay for my education."

When it came to education, Eric veered slightly from the rest of the Trumps. He chose not to go to Wharton like his father and Don Jr. and, eventually, Ivanka; instead, he opted for Georgetown, where Ivanka had started as an undergraduate before she transferred to Penn. (At the time, that Eric could get into Georgetown raised eyebrows among his classmates at the Hill School, who had a vague idea of the kind of student he was and the grades he received in class.) But he made up for it once he moved to New York after graduation. Like his siblings, he bought an apartment from his father—with his help, of course. He settled on a 1,353-square-foot, three-bedroom apartment on the fourteenth floor of a fourteen-story building at 100 Central Park South, known as Trump Park East. He shelled out $2 million for it—a price he said at the time he negotiated with his dad. "We went back and forth," he recalled. "It wouldn't be Trump if we didn't. His father was the same way to him. By the way, if I were to go into his office and not haggle, he would have thrown me out and not sold me the space." (A little more than a year after he picked up the first apartment, he snagged the one next door—a one-bedroom for $540,000, which had been listed earlier that year for $649,000. "It's probably more than I need now at this stage in my life, being a younger, single guy. I like leather couches, I like comfy couches. I like a warm atmosphere, area rugs," he said of his taste.)

Unlike Don Jr., who spent a year binge drinking in Aspen after Wharton, and Ivanka, who wanted to be able to say she did some grunt work and earned her stripes at a New York real estate company that did not bear her name before she went to work for her father, Eric skipped the whole prove-and-find-yourself gap year step. He is, after all, the baby, and in an already privileged lot, being the youngest is perhaps the most privileged spot of them all. Any hoops that the Trump children had to jump through, Don Jr. and Ivanka had already been through by the time Eric got there. Was it really all that necessary for another Trump kid to jump through them again, knowing that they didn't much matter in the first place?

So once Eric graduated from Georgetown, with a dual degree in finance and management, along with a minor in psychology, of all things, he went straight into the Trump Organization. Where Don Jr. used to squash his little brother, Eric was by then a more hulking presence. He had about three inches and a good two dozen pounds on his older brother when he first came to work with him. But Don Jr. still had more than a decade of experience working in the business by the time Eric took a glass office next to his and Ivanka's, which, for at least a time, sort of made Donny his boss. "He is," Eric responded to a *New York Observer* reporter who asked as much. "Temporarily," he added, "as I learn the ropes. Um, I'm sure we'll probably even out the work load eventually. But he is extremely intelligent, as is Ivanka, and I'm going to learn a lot from both of them."

Eric caught on quickly, and like most of the Trumps before him, he relished working with his family. One of Donald's longtime friends and business associates remembers stopping by Trump Tower to visit Donald a few years after Eric settled into his office. He was in his dad's office when the friend arrived, and for fifteen minutes the father and son, in the process of putting together plans for a new tower somewhere, sat behind Donald's paper-strewn desk, paging through a Yellow Pages–thick book of world-renowned architects together. Don Jr. walked in, which the friend thought might save him from more architect talk, but the eldest son just joined in, adding his thoughts about which architect would be most appropriate. When the phone's ring interrupted them, Donald answered on speaker. It was Ivanka, who was working with a banker to finish up another deal, and she needed her dad's sign-off on the terms. "I saw Donald's eyes light up, as they were all seeking his advice, and I thought to myself, he's got his three kids, brothers and sisters, who are working together, working for him," the friend remembered. "I really believed at the time that Donald's children had grown to a point where he had enough confidence in them, that these kids, and their unique demeanors and the same bloodline, were all three capable of running this business."

OTHER FRIENDS of Donald point out that Donald was keenly aware of these "unique demeanors" each of his kids possessed, and that is perhaps why he did not have the same level of confidence in all three of their capabilities. When Donald plunked down a reported $63 million—about £37.5 million—to buy a 111-year-old golf estate in Scotland in the spring of 2014, experts saw it as something of a bargain. Leisurecorp, the Dubai-based company that had bought it less than a decade earlier, in 2008, paid a reported £52 million for the resort, which included several golf courses, a five-star hotel along with a lodge and cottage, and a golf academy, and that was before it put in another £40 million in renovations.

The club would be a crown jewel in the Trump's collection of golf courses. The Trump Organization already owned twelve courses around the world, but Turnberry was prestigious. It was historic. It was jaw-droppingly beautiful. And it was seen as somewhat of a feat in the golf world. Built on a former World War I air force base overlooking the Irish Sea, the Isle of Arran, and a rock formation from which curling stones are made called the Ailsa Craig, the course had hosted the Open Championship four times when the Trumps agreed to buy it. "It was an opportunity as far as I was concerned," Donald said in an interview with Golf.com at the time. "Turnberry is considered one of the greatest courses in the world. It's a special place. It's an important place."

With a course this special, and a price tag that was both a bargain and still a big chunk of change for the Trumps, Donald looked to his sons to develop the property, mostly focusing on refurbishing the hotel, which had fallen into disrepair, making small tweaks to the existing course, and opening a second one on the property. Both sons, Eric and Don Jr., would be involved. The job was big enough for the both of them. But Donald knew it needed only one project leader, and he knew that only one of his sons could take that on.

On a different golf course in the midst of the Republican primaries in early spring of 2016, Donald confided in one of his friends about his two sons and sought some parental wisdom. He asked his friend what he would do if he had one son who was so much more talented than the other. The friend told him that he would give the really talented son as many challenges as he could, and the other son as many challenges as he could handle. Donald admitted that the advice was good in theory, but much harder in practice, "because they figure out that that's what you're doing."

He explained that when he put Eric in as the guy who would primarily take charge of Turnberry, Don Jr. got upset. "But how was I supposed to give the Turnberry project to Donny?" he asked his friend. "It's such an important and historic project, and it just had to be done right."

Eric, the executive vice president of development and acquisitions for the Trump Organization, took the challenge in stride. He flew to Scotland every month over the course of several years to oversee the renovation. He watched as workers took the hotel down to steel and concrete to restore it to its original splendor. He hired highly regarded golf course architects Mackenzie & Ebert to redesign the eighteen-hole course. That meant lengthening the first hole's green to create a wider landing area, pushing the fourth hole closer to the coastline, and revealing coastal views, with a result that some of the most discerning critics called "extraordinary" and "sympathetic" to the course's history. It also opened a second course named after Scottish icon Robert the Bruce.

Despite the renovation, or rather because of it, the world Eric oversaw might have been beautiful, but it bled the company nearly dry. In 2016, as his father ran his election campaign in the United States, the Trump Organization lost $23 million, or £17 million— more than double what it had lost a year earlier. The company said in a statement that this was due in part to the course closing so that renovations could be completed to its standards. "The directors believe that the resort will return to profitability in the short to me- dium term," wrote Eric in a financial filing. By that point Donald had already taken office, and technically had given up his ability to take over any such business matters, let alone talk about them to his son—perhaps one of the many perks of being in this most unusual First Family arrangement they fashioned for themselves.

FOR ERIC, and those who grew up around him, there was little ques- tion that he was built for this job. Like his siblings, he frequently mentions the elaborate Lego towers and cities he would build as a child, the frequent walk-throughs he'd made alongside his dad at any number of construction sites by the time he was in elementary school. That was in his blood, he said, the Trump gene, only made stronger from the continual exposure to building. "I think every kid wanted to fly F-14s and be a fighter pilot for a little while, but it was very soon thereafter, I was probably 10 or 11 or 12 years old, and I said, 'I want to build,'" Eric told the *Las Vegas Review Journal*. "Since I was 11, I was running wire with our guys. I was cutting rebar with torches. I was cutting down trees. I was using backhoes, and laying marble and stone, and demoing walls. It kind of taught us the building blocks of actual building. I have actual scars on my hands to prove it." Where Don Jr. grew into a love affair with the outdoors, Eric was born with a deep affection for anything that would help break things down or build things up. "I was always fascinated with tools," he recalled. "For Christmas, I want gift cards for Home Depot." He struggled to choose his favorite tool in his box when asked, veering toward something that had to do with woodworking. "I really like my chisels," he settled, after quite some time going back and forth.

Just as Don Jr. found men to fill the void his father left through hunting, Eric sought them in construction. One of them was Vincent Stellio, who worked security in the Plaza Hotel when Donald still owned it in the early 1990s. When Tiffany was born in 1993, Donald and Marla put Stellio closer to the family, hiring him to be something of a bodyguard for the little girl. Donald valued his loyalty and how hard he worked. "I have a lot of confidence in you," Donald told Stellio, calling him a "smart guy" who was "very dependable" and knew "how to get things done." He eventually extended his responsibilities to overseeing construction at all the Trump-owned golf properties. Along with his other tasks in his greatly expanded role, Stellio oversaw an eager Eric Trump, who was dying to get in on the projects and make a little money on the side.

By the time Ivana unloaded their Greenwich home, Donald had bought the Westchester property known as Seven Springs, where he and Don Jr. moved into a caretaker house when he was twelve or thirteen. Stellio had them join the rest of his guys at seven o'clock in the morning and get to work. He got them on mowers and tractors. He handed them chain saws and leaf blowers and backhoes. If he needed a hole dug, they would dig it. If he needed a road grate put in, they'd put one in. "We would sit there and cut fields all day. We would cut down trees. We would help the masons do all the patios, do all the tile work in the house, do the demolition work," he said. "We'd help them wire the entire house. . . . As a kid, you're breaking down walls with a sledge hammer for these guys, you're helping them put in marble, and you're still working on those kinds of projects together . . . It was one of the kind of the greatest lessons of my life."

Around that time, Eric went off to the Hill School, where he immediately gravitated toward the woodshop on campus. He spent hours in that room, hunched over wooden work tables between the great big rectangular windows lining the white-painted brick walls, letting light in. He'd stand on the cool concrete floor, cutting and carving into slabs of wood, sanding it, soldering it, staining it to make a bench—a picture of which he put on his senior yearbook page—and a rowing scull and a triangular structure that the school displayed on campus after Eric finished it. What he lacked in academic rigor, he made up for in that woodshop, and the school recognized that that was where his strength lay, awarding him honors for what he made several times throughout his years at Hill. Eric would often turn in his homework assignments early, which one of his former teachers noted was extremely unusual for his young male students, most of whom had to be bugged to turn assignments in at all, let alone on time. The teacher wrote Donald about this unexpected, delightful habit, and Donald asked Eric why he did his work ahead of time when he did not have to. He said he got things done early so that he'd have more time to read about things he cared about. Undoubtedly, friends at the time said, all he wanted to learn more about was craftsmanship.

That is not to say that Eric made no time to be a regular teenager at school. He had normal friends, which, for boarding school, is unusual. But Hill was not Choate, where Ivanka went. It was not St. Paul's or Phillips Exeter or Deerfield or Groton or Hotchkiss or Taft, where young heirs and barons and titans-in-waiting idle until they eventually make their way to the Ivy League and then back to their family fortunes or analyst jobs on Wall Street or whatever cushy life their parents have arranged for them. Trump was one of the most well-known names when Eric got to campus, though Don Jr. had worn down the notion that they were typical spoiled rich kids years earlier when he arrived on campus. Sometimes the school would get an Eric Trump, but far more often, the students were locals or legacy kids. Most didn't come from wealthy families or even from New York City, though of course there were some. Some came on scholarship, and some came because it was close to home and better than the public schools nearby. Their families were born and raised in Pottstown, in the shadow of steel and iron country, with its foundries and rolling mills and factories, and dairy and Christmas tree farms in between.

Donald and Ivana dropped Eric off on campus on his first day, as they had with Don Jr. years earlier, at the start of the school year in 1997. This time, they didn't forget sheets and didn't make a stop at the local Kmart, where paparazzi had met them wheeling a full cart outside. Eric heaped all his stuff into two suitcases, which he could barely zip, shoving whatever didn't fit into a hamper he carried into his room. They didn't come back to visit until he graduated in 2002, and even then, Ivana did not show up. For the ceremony, at which the school awarded Eric an award for his character and academic improvement and resolve to succeed, Ivana was on a whirlwind trip aboard her yacht, the *Ivana*, in Cannes during the fifty-fifth annual film festival there. She threw herself a belated birthday party in the VIP section of the nightclub, blowing out three candles alongside her guests, including Naomi Campbell, Sean Penn, and Harvey Weinstein. At the time, she arranged for her staff not to tell reporters her age; she did not arrange a flight home in time to see her youngest son receive his high school diploma.

That the flashiest members of his family mostly stayed away from Pottstown perhaps made it easier for Eric just to be Eric, not Eric Trump—yes, *that* Trump (in college, friends remember that he would often say no when strangers would ask if there was any relation, after they happened to see his name on a credit card or hear it called by a professor rolling through attendance). Outside the woodshop, he did some community service. He worked as an archives editor of the Hill newspaper. He fell into a rhythm with his golf swing—a skill that would come in handy later, as he tried to find common ground with his dad and, eventually, take over his father's clubs once he took office as president. He put to the test the skating skills he'd honed at the ice rink in Central Park his dad also owned, though they went only so far. He made the hockey team, albeit the JV squad. But he did earn his nickname, which immediately stuck like glue. During one game, Eric shouted out that a player on an opposing team was "a choad," a derogatory slang term for a specific shape of a certain male body part. His teammates were stunned, and flipped the name back on him. They didn't need to call him Eric Trump. To them, for the rest of his time at Hill, he was Choad. In fact, on Eric's senior year book page—which is littered with photos of his family and him posing with classmates in boxy formalwear on their way to prom and putting the finishing touches on a white bench he'd painstakingly made in woodshop—"Choad" is printed at the tippy top.

They also voted him biggest mooch on campus, because he was always asking for people to front him money to pay for little things that would come up, always skimming off their plates when they'd order food in to the dorms. According to a former classmate who interviewed Eric and several of his classmates in 2017 for an article in *City & State New York*, boys in the dorm ragged on him by doctoring photos of his sister and mom and hanging them around the dorm or setting them as the screen saver on his computer. As teenage boys at boarding school do, they wrestled it out. "Classmates remember a gangly, blonde-haired boy that most often wore an old baseball cap, a crew neck shirt under a black fleece, and well-worn khakis," the former classmate, Frank Runyeon, wrote. He was fairly quiet, sometimes awkward, mostly uncommonly kind. He was always sort of goofy and good-humored—a trait he never quite grew out of. To this day, he will tell friends and close business associates that he plans on giving them "huge noogies" the next time he sees them. He did not seek the friendships of the most popular or attractive or wealthy people on campus, Runyeon explained. In fact, when he visited one classmate's modest home nearby campus, he told his friend's mother that he'd lived in lots of places, but their house felt "really homey." As gentle as he was and as smooth of a talker as he could be, he sometimes let his not-so-stellar command of academia slip. Runyeon wrote that Eric once asked a classmate if Fidel Castro was the king of Spain.

Despite the good-humored hard time his classmates gave him, Eric was very clearly grateful for the normal way they treated him. In his yearbook, he thanked his friends for the memories and great times they had over the years. "Like you, they will never be forgotten." He praised his teachers for the wisdom and foundation they gave him. He also thanked his family, in initial form—DT (Donald), IT (Ivana), DT JR (Don Jr), IMT (Ivanka), MZ (Ivana's mother), and DC (Dorothy, his nanny) for "supporting me throughout a great five years," adding "I couldn't have done it without you." He finished it off, in true high school yearbook fashion, with a Led Zeppelin quote from "Stairway to Heaven": "There's two paths you can go by/but in the long run there's still time to change the road your on." (The high school grad on his way to Georgetown did, in fact, use the grammatically incorrect "your" in the quote.)

The path Eric chose at Georgetown led him to study what his father would have wanted him to study. He partied hard—though not as hard as Don Jr. did at Penn—and he lived in the dorms his freshman year, with a roommate who played on the football team, and stayed on campus for sophomore year too. He joined a business fraternity and took part in long-range rifle contests, and traveled to New York and to visit family on weekends. When he graduated in 2006, Donald's security reserved three rows, and he plunked down right in the middle of the blocked-off area. Ivana made it to that ceremony, as did Melania, Don Jr. and Vanessa, and Ivanka. Barron, a baby at the time, stayed back in New York, and once Eric had accepted his diploma, they flew off to Atlantic City, where Donald threw himself a party for his upcoming sixtieth birthday.

The path led Eric to a few months off to travel and resettle back into New York, but ultimately back to working for his dad. He had little by way of actual work experience outside the Trump Organization when he took on his position within the company, though he contended that he'd been working for his dad for a decade, and under his tutelage from birth. He had obviously been exposed to the construction side of things, but he would tell people that his father taught him far more about the industry growing up. "Fortunately," he told *Construction Today* in 2009, "he has done a great job exposing us to everything," adding that as he and his siblings learned the ropes on worksites, he also "would bring in the business strategy and teach us the intricacies of finance, working with the banks, and other invaluable lessons that he had learned from his father and firsthand throughout his career."

Even as he first started, his attention to detail and how hard he worked to get things right jumped out at people, even those who were used to working with other real estate scions in the business. One former employee remembers that Eric was constantly checking in on people. "He would ask how I was, what's going on, what did I need, was I on schedule, how I was feeling," the employee said. "It was almost like a tic. He was just always, always asking." One friend of the family said that Eric had both incredibly high standards and a good eye, like Ivana did, though his demeanor was far more mild-mannered and do-it-yourself (Ivana was known among her staff as ruling with an iron fist in Atlantic City, in a manner that engendered respect but also terror). His years going to clubs with his parents meant that he could see things the way members saw them, not just how owners thought they should be, which the friend said gave him a distinct advantage. "When he goes into his clubs and he sees things that aren't right or things that need to be changed, he's not above doing it himself," the friend said. "I'm sure that if he walked into a dining room and it was short-staffed, Eric would jump right in and work alongside them. He's able to just get things done where something is falling short."

That he hardly ever stopped looking for those areas stood out, too. "I would get a call from Eric at eight or nine or ten o'clock at night and he'd say, 'Let's talk about windows,'" one New York construction executive who worked with the Trump Organization on projects over the course of three years remembered. Eric would point out structural changes he wanted to make as they walked through sites, or finishes that weren't quite right. It was never too early for Eric, and he stayed at work late, too. "They were some of the hardest-working clients that I've ever worked with. It's not exactly what you'd expect from a billionaire's kid."

Undoubtedly Eric got that from his father, who got that from his father. Fred Trump used to tell Donald that to retire is to expire. He didn't get the concept of a vacation, and when he spent time with his grandchildren on the weekends, he had little understanding of how to relate or what to do with them. Work, he got. Work, he liked. So he would take his kids' kids, including Donald's, with him on the job. They would collect late rents from his tenants, driving around Queens in the back of his car, going with him to knock on doors and fight to collect checks. Donald was less hands-on, and he was able to unwind with trips to Palm Beach and Westchester and Bedminster. But he never stopped thinking of work, a habit his children picked up. "We love work," Eric told CNN's Anderson Cooper in a live televised town hall during the presidential campaign, when he was asked by a member of the assembled audience what he bonds with his father over. "It's something that really brings us together. We love building. The two of us just love machinery. We love building. We love concrete. We love jobs. We'll sit on the phone at six o'clock in the morning, and we'll talk about our favorite jobs." They both liked to golf, too, he added.

Like his dad, who polls his friends and colleagues on matters big and small, personal or business-related, and who, those close to him often remark, tends to soak up whatever the last person he spoke with said to him, Eric likes to listen. Eric, though, understands the subtle distinction between listening and hearing. When he asks someone for their opinion or their advice, particularly when it comes to a professional matter, he takes it to heart and mind. Perhaps this has to do with the fact that he is generally far quieter than his father. It may also have something to do with the reality that because he took such a senior position and its corresponding responsibilities at such a young age and with so little on-the-job experience, he actually needs answers from people much older, with more wisdom and real-world know-how, in order to do his job. One friend of the Trump family who works in the club industry remembers hitting balls with Eric at their Doral club on a Friday afternoon. He stopped dead in the middle of the swing when he thought of an issue at the club he needed advice on. "We spent ten minutes standing there as he asked my opinion on something," the friend said. "We just stood there as he asked a ton of questions, trying to see what I thought. He listened very carefully to what I had to say."

On the surface, Eric took after his father when it came to women, as well. Almost as soon as he graduated and started working at the Trump Organization, reporters started talking about Eric as the last standing Trump bachelor, ready to take on New York the way Donald and Don Jr. had before him. Donny had already settled down with Vanessa by that point, and Donald had been married to Melania for more than a year. That left only Eric, when it came to single Trump men on the prowl, of eligible age, and ascendant within the family business. "I can probably handle it," he told the *Daily News*, referring to his status and the familial reputation he had to live up to. Eric did stumble a bit on the coolness factor, despite his name. He was turned away from Light at the Bellagio while in Las Vegas to celebrate his birthday in his early twenties because he broke the cardinal rule of nightclubs: he showed up to the door with a teeming group of fifteen buddies, all of them guys. Not even "Trump" scrawled across his credit card made that an easy feat with a bouncer after midnight.

A few years later, at a nightclub in New York, he spotted a bottle blonde a head above the crowd—literally, at five feet ten inches, and in heels; the other women around her barely reached her chest. Lara Yunaska was the kind of woman Donald had dated when he was Eric's age (and, frankly, up until the time he married Melania). She grew up in Wrightsville Beach, North Carolina, an oceanfront town on the Carolina coast, where she went to the high school from which Michael Jordan graduated and lived with her mother, Linda Ann Sykes, her father, Robert, who built heavy-displacement boats, and her little brother Kyle. She studied communications—broadcast journalism, in particular, struck her—while staying close to home at North Carolina State. She interned at local news stations and took up personal training on the side to make cash. Like her future stepmothers before her and like Don Jr.'s wife Vanessa, Lara did a bit of modeling. Her old modeling site, a page on One Model Place, lists her as a model specializing in fashion, editorial, runway, sport, casual, swimwear, hair, and makeup. Her eyes, she said, were green. Her shoe size, an eleven. Her additional skills included film and television acting, music, extreme sports, and singing. "I am a very versatile model," she wrote on her profile. "I have an athletic look since I do so many sports." The five photos in her portfolio show it off—one in low-slung ripped jeans and a white undershirt shrunken enough to show her silver belly-button piercing, and four other shots in two different bikinis—one red, one black—and a collection of shell necklaces in various colors. "I am responsible and serious," she wrote. "You won't have to worry about a 'no show' from me. My time is important, and so is yours." She noted that she had won both the Hammerjax Bikini Contest in 2004 and the Aaron Chang Bikini Contest in 2005, appeared in the July 2005 issue of *Stuff* magazine and as a *Maxim* Hometown Hotties participant. She also noted that from 2000 through 2004, she had a job as a Hooters Girl.

With all the modeling, the side jobs, and the college credits on her plate, she still wanted to make sure she was the one in control of everything—not some agent who would decide on gigs for her. "I reply to all e-mails and handle all bookings and offers," she wrote. A Trump before her time.

LARA MOVED to New York City in 2007, despite her parent's urging her to stay closer to home. She kept doing personal training, and took classes for pastry arts at the Culinary Institute. Eventually, she got her résumé in front of folks at *Inside Edition*, CBS's syndicated newsmagazine show, where they hired her as a field producer and story coordinator. All of the jobs she bounced from and toggled between did not add up to a clear picture of someone with a cohesive identity or path forward. She was a personal training pastry chef Hooters girl broadcast producer Maxim model who handled all inquiries herself. The technical description for someone like that is a hustler. And so, when she spotted a tall guy with gelled, spikey blond hair from across the club one night in New York, a city boy who only ever had one job and one path to go down, she found her exact opposite. That his path happened to be lined with gold, well, that is a hustler's dream come true. It was a comparison Eric would undoubtedly cringe at, but the résumé and the meet-cute suggested a striking resemblance to Marla Maples.

The way Lara tells it, they struck up a conversation because Eric was one of the few, or perhaps only, guys in the room who was taller than she was. "I wish it was some silly, lovely scenario, but we just happened to be out in the same place at the same time in New York," she remembered. She claims she didn't know his last name until after she left with her friends that evening. They broke it to her who he was. With Eric traveling as often as he did, it took three months for them to schedule a date, a date she, frankly, was not terribly optimistic about. "I was sort of expecting it to be a bad date," she said, anticipating that he would be "sort of what you would expect from a rich guy's son." The way she saw it, she would "just go out with him to say she did it." But when they went to dinner, they talked for two hours before they got around to opening their menus and ordering something to eat. "It ended up being the best date I've ever been on."

Things moved quickly from there. By late summer of 2008, about three months after they started dating, Eric invited Lara to join him at the US Open (where Marla had made something of a splash with Donald a decade and a half earlier). He'd left out the fact that his dad and Melania would be there, too, meaning that the first time Lara would be introduced to her newish boyfriend's famous family would be a total surprise to her. She nearly melted in the August heat, under the weight of that unexpected pressure. Donald, however, made no deal of it whatsoever. He gave her a quick greeting and offered her some ice cream, which she gamely accepted. "This was normal," she breathed a sigh of relief. It wasn't some fancy showing, nor was it a series of tests. "This is what people do. There was no grilling, not a ton of questions. Just nice hellos and ice cream."

THE TRUTH was, Donald never really got to know Lara much. To his friends, he'd made snide comments about her. He thought she was in it for the wrong reasons—a lesson he had learned in his own life and through his own relationships, and become quite paranoid about, as time went on. "He'd say such nasty things about her," one very close friend of Donald's recalled. "Mostly, the sentiment was that she dropped the Trump name more than he did, and it was *his* name." The rest of the family warmed up to her with greater ease. As she continued her cake-baking business—Lara Lea Confections—

she created elaborate constructions for Don Jr. and Vanessa's children on their birthdays—a tiered blue fondant cake with an edible Elmo figure on top, alongside a number 1, and "DTJIII" cut out in red lettering, and a Dora the Explorer version for Kai's birthday. Vanessa, too, got the Lara Lea treatment, with a Tiffany box cake of her own. (Her website also showcases photos of impressive cakes shaped after Christian Louboutin pumps and Chanel purses, BlackBerry phones for a fiftieth birthday, and a tool box cake for a fortieth. There is also a woman's figure dressed up in an L.A. Lakers jersey, labeled "boob jersey cake.") Donald eventually came around to Lara, years after their wedding, once she took on a public-facing role within his presidential campaign, and particularly as she did more and more interviews on Fox News. Friends say that Donald would say he hadn't thought much of her until he watched her on cable. "He'd say, 'Have you watched her? She is *great*,'" one friend recalled. Suddenly, he started paying attention to his daughter-in-law.

Whatever hesitancy his father expressed initially, either Eric did not know about it or he decidedly ignored it. On July 4, 2013, he and Lara and her rescue dog—a beagle named Charlie—went up to Seven Springs in Westchester for the holiday. He convinced her to go on a walk across a field on the property. All she could see at first was a blanket laid out with a bottle of champagne. "Oh my gosh," she thought. "What is this?" As she got closer, she saw a little white box. Inside, there was an emerald-cut diamond ring—from Ivanka Trump's fine jewelry collection, no less. "It was a thoughtful proposal," she said. It was a yes.

THE COUPLE decided to follow in the footsteps of Eric's dad and his third wife, and his older brother and his first. They would wed in the fall of 2014 in Palm Beach, at Mar-a-Lago. They set up a wedding website to fill in the 450 people they invited to their blessed event on all the details. The wedding would take place in November at his father's estate, with a tasting of Trump Winery's finest (Eric had taken on the Virginia vineyard as one of his chief responsibilities and pet projects within the Trump Organization), a formal black-tie affair with dinner and dancing in the 118-room private club. The website winked in its description of the groom, for those guests who might not know him. Eric, it read, was "born into a relatively unknown New York Family," and early on, he "embraced his family's passion for Erector sets, Monopoly and Jenga, which ultimately led to a very successful career in construction and real estate." For those unfamiliar with the bride, Lara, the website read, is a "Southern girl" by birth, who grew into a "breaking news guru and baker extraordinaire." Despite Eric's "successful career," something was missing. "Bored with world domination, however, Eric soon realized that success isn't all it's cracked up to be without someone to love by your side."

They hired both a wedding planner and an event designer—the same designer who worked on Ivanka and Jared's wedding—who worked with the couple to strike a balance between what Eric described as "formal and fun," with elegance mixed in. What they did not plan for was that Lara would have a riding accident a couple of weeks before the big day, sending her flying off a horse and straight to the X-ray machine. She broke both of her wrists, meaning she would need to cover the bottom halves of both of her arms with casts before, during, and after her wedding. Lara tried to brush it off. She initially posted a photo of herself holding up two bandaged wrists, her lips turned downward in a pout: "Wedding countdown: 2 weeks and 2 casts to go!" On October 27, less than two weeks before the nuptials, she posted a photo of her, in tan riding stirrups and boots and a black helmet, clearing a jump on the back of a horse. "There are inherent risks that we all take in life," she wrote in the caption. "When you truly love something, it's worth it. I wouldn't take back one day of riding—stuff happens. I will ride again and it will be better than ever. Most importantly, I still get to marry the love of my life on Nov 8th!"

Luckily, she was able to wear soft casts by the time her wedding day came around, meaning she could slip them off for the ceremony. The casts would go back on for the reception, at which point, she did in fact cover them with fingerless, gathered and bejeweled gloves custom made for her and her casts.

The sun fell into the horizon as Ivana, in a different pink, off-the-shoulder gown that flowed into a mermaid silhouette, accompanied her youngest child to the altar. Eric wore a black tuxedo, white bow tie, and Tiffany cuff links, his blond hair slicked back to show off his deepening widow's peak. Next to his best man, Don Jr., he walked down the aisle that Saturday evening in the mid-fall Florida heat, in front of guests like *Real Housewives of New York*'s Jill Zarin, Howard Lorber of the brokerage firm Douglas Elliman, and radio host Elvis Duran. Ivanka, dressed in a cobalt-blue gown like the rest of Lara's bridesmaids, stood off to the side. Ivanka's daughter and Don Jr.'s son followed, as flower girl and ring bearer. Eric's nephew shared the role with Lara's rescue dog Charlie, who also served as ring bearer. Lara walked down the aisle with her father and a bouquet made with baby pink roses, the petals on the skirt of the Vera Wang gown floating in the light breeze. Her simple tulle veil waved against her highlighted blond hair, which she left down for the ceremony, and the diamond earrings from Ivanka's fine jewelry collection that she'd chosen for the day.

They asked Jared to officiate the ceremony, under a sweeping white, dozens-of-feet-high chuppah. From an extended arch of hundreds of tightly bunched ivory flowers flowed a cascade of hanging crystals that fell in steps and framed the couple in front of the palm trees in the background. The couple had asked his sister's husband to officiate because "Jared knows us so well that what he had to say was heartfelt and especially meaningful," Eric said in an interview at the time. Jared spoke into the microphone arranged in front of him to help the couple exchange their vows, telling the bride, "You are not just gaining a family. You are getting 6 million Twitter followers."

Eric and the newest Mrs. Trump kissed and walked back down the aisle, past the ivory urns filled with bursting lollipop ivory florals.

The ballroom was lit in a golden hue, decorated in more golds and pale pinks and ivories, with white orchid trees with gilded branches at the center of each table. Unlike Donald and Melania, who made a spectacle out of flying in a chef for their reception, and Don Jr. and Vanessa, who served a formal meal to their guests, Eric and Lara decided on a buffet. "Our guests could eat to their hearts' content," Lara said in an interview at the time, including a nod to her southern roots with a station set up with barbecue and shrimp and grits, "but not be stuck at a table." Donald toasted the couple, while mentioning his first wife, Ivana, and thanking her for raising such a wonderful son. Don Jr.'s best man toast—or roast, rather— left the guests in stitches.

After the couple's first dance, during which Eric gave Lara a very lovely little staged dip, they hardly left the dance floor. Their siblings joined them, as did all of their kids. "All of the siblings were right smack dab in the middle dancing," one guest remembered, as a fifteen-piece band played. They eventually cut into their six-tiered cake—a confection in various shades of whites and pinks and textures. It was hardly as ornate as the Sylvia Weinstock masterpieces of Trump weddings past, but this one was, in fact, edible.

They moved onto an after-party by the pool, where a DJ followed along as Lara turned the whole thing into a karaoke party. The bride sang along to every single song he played.

CHAPTER 11

Tiffany

The Voltron from Another Universe

T IFFANY TRUMP sat alone on a couch backstage in the Quicken Loans Arena in Cleveland, Ohio, one Tuesday evening at the end of July in 2016. A little earlier in the evening, on the other side of the stage at the Republican National Convention, the party called roll to get an official delegate count. After knocking out a baker's dozen opponents in sixty-five primaries and shelling out more than $600 million in campaign dollars, at 7:12 p.m. on July 21 Donald Trump officially became the Republican nominee for president of the United States, having exceeded the threshold of 1,237 delegates. It was Don Jr., a delegate for the state of New York, who technically got his father over the line. "It is my honor to be able to throw Donald Trump over the top in the delegate count," he told the thousands and thousands of people cheering in the arena's audience that evening, and the millions more tuning in from home. "Congratulations, Dad," he said from the front row of New York's section, alongside his siblings, Ivanka, Eric, and Tiffany. "We love you." An instrumental version of Frank Sinatra's "New York, New York" played over the speakers. The rest of the red-hat-wearing crowd leaped from their seats, slapping their palms together, hugging their neighbors, taking selfies in front of an arena erupting in applause around them.

Don Jr. would speak again onstage later that evening, on a night the Republican National Committee themed "Make America Work Again!" As would Mitch McConnell, Paul Ryan, Jeff Sessions, Chris Christie, Ben Carson, the National Rifle Association's Chris Cox, golfer Natalie Gulbis, *The Bold and the Beautiful*'s Kimberlin Brown, and Ultimate Fighting Championship's president Dana White. Despite the fact that she had just graduated from college two months earlier and had never actually held a full-time job apart from a summer internship her older half sister scored for her at *Vogue*, Tiffany was also slotted in among the nineteen scheduled speeches on an evening dedicated to focusing on rebuilding and bolstering the American workforce. It didn't matter much that she couldn't speak on the theme; no one did, really. Much of the rest of the lineup used their speeches as opportunities to jab-hook Hillary Clinton and fawn over Donald, congratulating him on his official status as it happened.

The timing of Tiffany's speech had a triple misfortune. First, she was scheduled to follow Christie, a gifted orator with years of experience as a US attorney and governor and presidential candidate. His performances at the primary debates were, in fact, part of the reason Donald was so keen to have Christie on board his campaign team in the first place. Second, she would be the first member of the Trump family to go onstage after her stepmother's speech at the convention the night before. Melania had done a fine job delivering a beautifully eloquent, reflective speech. Large chunks of that beautifully eloquent, reflective speech just so happened to be plucked and pilfered from a convention speech Michelle Obama had given onstage at her husband's nominating convention in Denver in 2008. The media pounced. Melania was humiliated. Politicos on both sides of the aisle scratched their heads as to how this slipped by the many people who should have been vetting this speech down to its every adverb and punctuation mark. Those inside the Trump orbit and campaign were not entirely surprised that a gaffe of this proportion was possible, given the bare-bones, chaotic, chicken-with-its-head-cut-off nature of the operation. But many were furious that the secret of just how bare-bones, chaotic, chicken-with-its-head-cut-off the campaign was had been laid bare by the blunder. In some ways, this lowered the bar ever so slightly for Tiffany. All she needed to do was not plagiarize her speech, and it would play better than her stepmom's did. But that Melania's had now fallen so flat also meant that Tiffany's had to land, that she could not have any mishap, that it had to mean something. The campaign, and her father, couldn't handle another blow—not one at the hands of his own family, that's for certain. With his wife's sentiments all but forgotten in the chaos her speech created and its sentiments discarded because they were largely not her own, his youngest daughter then needed to humanize Donald, to portray him as a family man, to share the little details only a daughter can that would both reveal to the American people something intimate and telling about Donald Trump and evoke something familiar, universal, in their parent-child bond for the rest of the electorate to see themselves in. Jenna and Barbara Bush had done this for their father, as would Chelsea Clinton.

But that is where the third bit of trouble came in for Tiffany. The draft of the speech she was reading and rereading, rehearsing inside and out and practicing out loud, did not have any of the little illuminating gems about her dad that were needed to sprinkle some humanity on his public image. It was not that Tiffany, like Melania, had been ill served by speechwriters, or that she had wanted to keep those moments between her and her father. The truth of the matter was that she didn't have many unique, intimate moments with her dad.

Tiffany's father and mother didn't live together when she was born, two months before her parents married, after Donald gave in to mounting business pressure and Marla's ultimatum that unless he married her by Christmas, she'd take Tiffany and leave. Even after the wedding, Marla and Tiffany and Marla's mother Ann spent a healthy chunk of their time at Mar-a-Lago, or in Georgia with her family, or in California, where her mom tried to jump-start her acting career while Donald hung back in New York. For a while they lived in separate apartments in Manhattan too, before Ivana and the Trump 1.0 kids vacated the Trump Tower triplex and Donald moved his second wife and daughter in. They didn't last long. Marla and Donald separated well before Tiffany's third birthday, and before the divorce was even finalized, Marla moved her to Calabasas, California, home of the Kardashians and the span of the United States away from her father.

Tiffany would spend spring breaks with her father in Palm Beach. Sometimes her parents would force smiles together at her birthday parties. Infrequently, he would visit her in California for school events, or, if he had business in Los Angeles, Marla would drive her through the valley and into the city to make sure she got face time with her father. She would make an occasional trip to New York, too. And as he did with his older children when they went to boarding school, he would send her notes—messages scribbled in Sharpie. He would call her, too, not just to gab, but if the occasion struck and it seemed appropriate. "She'd like to get to know her father better and spend time with him like his other children did, by going to his office and watching him work," Marla told the *New York Times* in an interview during the campaign. "I had the blessing of raising her pretty much on my own."

Donald's friends would regularly hear him talk about how little he knew of his second daughter, and how impressed he was that she'd managed to emerge relatively unscathed by his absentee fathering. "He would say that Tiffany has had a really tough life. Stuff like, 'I didn't have any time to spend with her. I never spent any time with her,'" one friend recalled. "He would say, 'It's really a miracle that she is as well-adjusted as she is, and that she's accomplished *anything.'* He gets that he screwed it up when it came to Tiffany, and this is a man who doesn't ever admit that he got it wrong on anything."

The distance was apparent to any keen observer throughout the campaign, and was pointed out—constantly. Some news reports likened her to the Trump family's version of Jan Brady. When in the spring of 2016 Fox News aired an hour-long special called *Meet the Trumps*, for which Melania, Don Jr., Eric, and Ivanka all sat down with Greta Van Susteren for interviews, Tiffany was not only not interviewed but also barely mentioned. "There is also Tiffany Trump," Van Susteren said in a voiceover, "who keeps a low profile." It is true that the special ran just as Tiffany graduated from the University of Pennsylvania, and was likely put together while she was in the throes of finals and senior week festivities on campus. But the slights continued throughout the summer and into the fall, after she moved to New York with the rest of her family. In an interview on *Fox & Friends*, Donald told the hosts that he was quite proud of all of his children. "I'm very proud, because Don and Eric and Ivanka and—you know, to a lesser extent because she just got out of school, out of college—but, uh, Tiffany, who has also been so terrific." She was nowhere to be found in the biographical documentary that aired during the RNC in Cleveland.

So the only anecdotes Tiffany could throw into her speech were lacking the personal depth many wanted of a presidential candidate's own daughter, which very much reflected the nature of their relationship. Her father wrote "sweet notes" on every one of her report cards—not just on her grades, as people might expect of *The Apprentice* host, but about her behavior in and out of the classroom—and she'd kept every one. When her grandmother's fiancé passed away years earlier, her father called her. She praised such "unwavering support."

As Tiffany sat trying to breathe backstage, Marla, who had come to her ex-husband's nominating convention because she had pretty much always gone everywhere with her daughter from the day she was born, ran around trying to recruit people to keep her daughter calm. "I'm pretty nervous," Tiffany told one of Marla's recruits, who let her know that all she had to do to make her father proud was not faint onstage. "I think I can pull that off," Tiffany joked.

She made no secret of the terror she felt that evening when she walked onstage in a cobalt sheath dress with a built-in belted waist she had bought off the sales rack at Bloomingdale's the day before she flew to Cleveland, and tromped toward the dais in patent leather nude pumps. Her teased-up, big-ol'-curl Barbie hair looked more southern beauty queen than Washington establishment, which perhaps served as a nod to both her father's underlying campaign message and her mother's Georgia pageant girl history. Behind the microphone, she steadied her face—a millennialized version of a Kewpie. A Bratz doll, with the big blue eyes frosted with purple shadow and fake eyelashes as long as knuckles, puckered-up lips under a tiny ski slope of a nose, cheekbones jutting out and slathered in blush and highlighter.

"Please excuse me if I'm a little nervous," she said at the start of her speech. "When I graduated college a couple of months ago, I never expected to be here tonight addressing the nation. I've given a few speeches in front of classrooms of students, but never in an arena with more than ten million people watching."

Anyone with a pulse would be nervous in that setting. Surely any twenty-two-year-old who hadn't spent fairly odd, definitively troubling formative years touring as a pop star or getting tutored in trailers on Hollywood sound stages would be scared silly. Tiffany was terrified for all the reasons any of them would be. Unlike her siblings, who had spent their childhoods on the pages of the tabloids, chased down the street by paparazzi, and later, on the set of *The Apprentice* with their father, Tiffany had lived a relatively normal life. And she had the added pressure, as she always did, of trying to impress a famously hard-to-please father who hardly knew anything about her.

RARELY IS the argument made that a child is lucky to have her parents divorce at a very young age, particularly if it means that she will have little to no memories of life as one cohesive family unit and will know only what it is like to live all the way across the country from one of her parents, with whom she spends virtually no time. Tiffany Trump may be the exception to that line of reasoning. Like bacteria blooming under a microscope, Donald and Marla's relationship grew, in part, because of the ceaseless tabloid attention they garnered. There was the affair, which was depicted in great detail for weeks, the cover-up, the blowup, and the breakup. All of that coverage was following by their initial coming out as a couple, the messy, years-long divorce from Ivana, the blows to his business.

Every detail of their courtship, through their on-again-and-off-again engagement, Tiffany's out-of-wedlock birth, and their eventual wedding, days before Christmas in 1993, played out in the gossip pages and supermarket magazines. So did their separation at the beginning of May 1997, their subsequent squabble over the prenup, and, after a couple years, their official divorce.

When Donald and Ivana split up in such a spectacularly public fashion—calling in stories about each other themselves to the press—Don Jr., Ivanka, and Eric were twelve, eight, and six, respectively. The elder two understood what was going on. It was hard for them not to—their classmates and paparazzi made it impossible even for Eric, not yet in grade school, to avoid. He was old enough to read, and the split caused a fracture between his older brother and his dad that made it hard for Eric to avoid the fallout from the divorce.

But for Tiffany, unlike her siblings, living through her parents' divorce would not be a defining event seared into her memory, guiding many of the decisions she would make and leaving scabs to be flicked open for the rest of her life. Tiffany, at just three and a half, would not remember the headlines, or the paparazzi. She wasn't yet in real school. She couldn't read. She didn't live with her older siblings, so their reactions to Donald and Marla's split couldn't influence her own (though since they had never warmed to Marla in the first place, the split hadn't exactly kept them up at night).

She also wouldn't remember the time before her parents separated, when they were an unconventional nuclear family. Of all the lucky breaks Tiffany Trump has gotten in her life, perhaps that is the luckiest break of them all.

MARLA AND Donald and their little baby girl Tiffany, and sometimes Donny, Ivanka, and Eric, shuttled between a few homes. There was Trump Tower, Trump Park, the other Manhattan apartment Marla and Tiffany stayed in, and Mar-a-Lago. None of them were particularly happy in any of them, in the conventional, nuclear family sense. That was largely because Marla and Donald, as the heads of this very modern family, weren't particularly happy with each other. Marla—content in her New Age–iness, her mostly vegan diet, her distaste for harsh language, especially around Tiffany—stood in opposition to practically every character trait that defined her now husband. Around the time of his fiftieth birthday, Donald sat for an interview with *Playboy*, in which the reporter noted that he had lost weight on what he called the "anti-Marla diet." Most anything she served him, he would grimace at. "What the fuck is this?" he'd say. "Want it?" And he'd cast off what he'd been served on to those around him. The regime got him down twenty pounds—a change he didn't much mind on himself, but loathed on Marla. As friends recalled, he liked her with a little more meat on her bones. She, however, "felt sloppy" with extra weight, and "couldn't wait to get rid of those pounds." To her, they made her feel not much like herself. It just so happened, though, that that is the version Donald was attracted to, even if it made his wife feel dowdy and itchy in her own skin. They also fought over her spirituality. Donald didn't mind going to church; that is, after all, where the couple had sometimes met in the heat of their illicit courtship. But he liked to do his worship in churches that knew they had to worship him a bit, too, in exchange for his presence on Sundays. "I don't want to go to that hillbilly church you go to," he'd tell Marla. "If I'm going, I want to go to a church where somebody knows me."

On their way down to Mar-a-Lago one spring, on Donald's 727 out of LaGuardia with a *Playboy* reporter on board, Donald took a seat in one of the big bucket chairs covered in buttery beige leather. Marla carried food aboard for everyone, along with all of little Tiffany's things. The girl, in a plaid jumper, milled about, as if flying on a jet bearing her last name en route to her 118-room mansion on the ocean was as normal as going on a trip to the park or the zoo—as, in her very young reality, it was. Donald was in a sour mood and wanted to pop in one of the movies he kept in a cabinet on board his aircraft. Friends remember that he often settled on *Zulu*, the 1960s war flick depicting British soldiers fending off four thousand Zulu warriors in a bloody battle during the Anglo-Zulu War nearly a century earlier ("He loved the scene where the mountain in the background starts moving and you realize it's thousands of Zulus," one friend recalled). But he chose *Pulp Fiction* on that flight. Marla tore into her husband, in her gentle, southern way, of course. Surely there was a film more suitable in that cabinet for Tiffany than *Pulp Fiction*. Something with the Muppets, for instance. He popped the VHS in as if Marla hadn't said a word. She dragged her daughter toward the front of the plane, away from her father and his TV screen, when the f-bombs started flowing freely almost as soon as the movie started. (The flight back was happier; the reporter noted that Donald swept up Tiffany onto his lap and asked her to hold open her little toddler arms to show him how much she loved her daddy. Her wingspan only went so far. "Only that much?" he teased.)

At Mar-a-Lago, Marla struggled with how to blend Donald's oldest children, who made no secret of their feelings toward her, with his new family. From the get-go, the melding was fraught. In an interview with Geraldo Rivera a few days after Tiffany was born, Ivana said that she had to reassure her children that their relationship with their father was separate from his relationship with Marla and his new baby. "I sat them down and I told them there will be nothing changing in their lives," she said. "They will have their father and he will love them the same, and we have to just explain to them because they might feel threatened by a new baby."

Marla didn't always ease those concerns. *Playboy* noted that Marla bristled at the oil portrait of Ivana and Don Jr., Ivanka, and Eric hanging in his office. Donald brushed her off, so she took it upon herself to commission an oil painting of her own to replace it. None of Donald's children sat for this one, of course, but she commissioned an idealized portrait of all of his children, this time with Tiffany included, sitting on Ivanka's lap. It was a masterful trick that Donald accepted as a gift on his fiftieth birthday. The old painting was carted out, the new one hung in its place.

THERE WAS some levity, particularly when Donald viewed Marla as the starlet she came to New York to be, not as the rail-thin, hippie-dippie wife he never much intended to have in the first place. In the summer of 1992, when Marla spent a few long weeks practicing for her role on Broadway. Donald was taken by Marla's coolness around it. Marla not only faced her critics head-on, but she also gave them a performance strong enough to shut up all the people who went in practically drooling to have nasty things to say about it. As her star rose, so did his. For that time, Marla was not his mistress, or a liability, or a minder keeping him from living the bachelor life he knew he could live if not for her sticking around. Marla was a Broadway actress—a not-so-bad one, at that. She elevated him. And that one fact sometimes brightened up their more common state of gloom.

Tiffany was not yet born when her mom stepped onto the Broadway stage in the *Will Rogers' Follies* for the first time, but she was conceived during her stint in the show. In fact, her parents announced that they were expecting a little baby Trump one night before Marla went onstage to perform, to a group of hungry photographers and reporters waiting in the wings for the couple's latest publicity maneuver. It was one of the points in their relationship in which Donald took great pride in Marla.

Tiffany could not, as a baby or a toddler, have known that the one aspect of Marla that really lit Donald up was that she could be this bold, calm star. But Tiffany, in gestation and in her genetic makeup, unquestionably inherited some of her mother's showmanship. She got that from her father, too, who never met a crowd he did not like. That was the case long before he ran for president. He was the man who barely kissed Marla at the altar after their wedding ceremony at the Plaza, but smooched her four times in front of the flashbulbs and onlookers who came to catch a glimpse of the couple after the nuptials outside the hotel. He starred in a reality television show and relished every magazine cover on which he appeared, hanging them in his office and strewing them across Mar-a-Lago in silver frames Ivana bought. He's sat for countless interviews on cable TV and with Howard Stern, splashed his name across buildings and steaks and water bottles and ties and colognes and mattresses. That Tiffany would have a flair for the dramatic in her blood is hardly surprising. It would be far more surprising if she did not.

But there is a bit of nurture at play, too. She was too little to have picked up on the fact that her father praised her mother for her star power, but children are perceptive enough to pick up on when their parents are affectionate and when they are at odds. The theme was so common that it would hardly be shocking that the little girl, who for all intents and purposes grew up an only child in the Trump house, picked up on that, subconsciously or otherwise.

Tiffany never shied away from a performance, even at a very

young age, and it was a trait that never much faded away—apart from the nerves that came before she went onstage at the Republican National Convention during her father's presidential campaign. But that performance was far different. That wasn't about being a star; that was about being a political savior, and that was not the kind of secret stardust Tiffany was born with and had grown into. She made her own debut in an ad for the agency Lois/USA, in a spot for a Minolta camera they shot in Long Island City in the summer of 1995. Tiffany, just three years old, with a mop of tight, white-blond ringlets, and honking baby blues, had a giggle spread across most of her face for most of the shoot. "I can keep my little girl at any age with Minolta's Freedom Family Zoom," Marla said as she snapped a photo with the Japanese-made camera of Tiffany, who sat next to her mother, playing with a delicate little tea set. A year later Donald and Marla trotted their daughter downtown to the opening of his shiny new trophy building, 40 Wall Street, which J. P. Morgan built before anyone had an inkling that Wall Street would turn into the world's financial epicenter. Donald bragged to the crowd he had assembled that June evening in 1996, feeling ascendant, triumphant, and back on top. He had invited one hundred people, he told them, and four hundred showed up. All eyes turned toward Tiffany, three at the time, who Marla held up like a prize. Her parents let her be the one to draw a raffle ticket that would award one lucky winner a weekend at Mar-a-Lago. Undeterred by the attention, she didn't hesitate, not even for a second.

She flinched less on Donald's fiftieth birthday, when Marla invited four hundred people to the Trump Tower triplex to fete her husband and toast his half century on top. She had commissioned a statue of her husband made out of sugar, depicting him as a sickly sweet Superman with a dollar sign emblazoned across his chest. She ordered waiters to pass around champagne and strawberries, and as Eartha Kitt crooned "Happy Birthday," six hundred gold-hued balloons fell from the ceiling onto the crowd. All of that was before little Tiffany got up in front of the hundreds of people in her sweeping apartment to sing her dad a song and perform a little dance. "A little sunny and a little sad," as *Playboy* described the scene.

This became something of a habit for Tiffany. When she traveled to Nantucket with Marla for a film festival in the summer of 1997, she sat down next to a pianist playing a tune in the Chancellor's Restaurant in the Point Breeze Hotel, having him scooch over a bit so she could settle her three-year-old self right next to him. They broke into "Somewhere Over the Rainbow" from *The Wizard of Oz* together, before going into "Tomorrow" from *Annie*, and then belting out "A Whole New World" from *Aladdin*. "She has a nice pitch," the pianist, Bob Ford, told the *Boston Herald*, shortly after their duets. The mother-daughter duo left only because Marla was hungry— for caviar, in fact, and knew her daughter would want some too. The restaurant sent them home with doggie bags filled with the delicacy, enough for mom and toddler to enjoy.

By the time Tiffany turned six, she and Marla had made their first television appearance together, for the Lake Tahoe International Spring SnowFest in 2000. Marla and Tiffany appeared as part of a celebrity challenge that would air on PAX television that spring, sledding down mountains and trekking through snow and ice. At fourteen, she appeared in her first fashion show at the Beverly Hills Hotel for Anand Jon, a designer whose shows Ivanka had walked in before her, as had Nicky and Paris Hilton and Elizabeth Jagger. (At the time Tiffany was asked to strut down his runway, however, the designer was facing multiple counts of sexual assault and held on $1.2 million bail in a Los Angeles jail. "Donald is going to throw up when he hears Tiffany is doing this," one friend told the *New York Post*. In reality, until her plan appeared in the *Post*, it is hard to say if Donald would have heard about it at all.)

Marla never balked at Tiffany's star. In fact, she helped facilitate it. In 2011, when Tiffany was a senior in high school, Marla reached out to her friend Steban Demari, a songwriter who went by the name of Sprite. The two had become close nearly two decades earlier, and once Marla and Tiffany moved to Los Angeles, they would write music and go to music events together around town. In 2010, for instance, they posed for a series of photos together on a red carpet outside of the House of Blues on the Sunset Strip in West Hollywood, before an Artists for Peace and Justice and We.The.Children Project benefit for Haiti. Demari placed one hand on Marla's shimmery gold, beaded minidress, and another around her leather jacket, his nose nestled into her cheek. Marla asked him to help write a song for her daughter, and her old friend obliged. He brought on a producer Marla also knew to work on the track, and the producer recruited an Antiguan rapper, who goes by the name Logiq, to record a verse in the song. "They wanted a hip-hop verse on it 'cause I'm a hip-hop recording artist and I'm a songwriter," Logiq said in an interview of how he ended up connected to the teenage Trump and her budding music career. "[The producer] is a friend of mine and mutual friend of Marla Maples, so he called me up and was like 'Yo, I want you on this track.'" He said that he listened to the track and he liked what he heard, "so it was basically a done deal from there."

The track they came up with was "Like a Bird," a synthetic dance-pop tune featuring a voice hardly decipherable as human as a result of all of the autotune and other crafty postproduction tricks. "Like a Bird" was the only song Tiffany released, though Logiq has said in an interview that they recorded two or three others together that he hopes will someday see the light of day. The song got little attention when it first came out, apart from a mention in an appearance Tiffany and Marla made on an episode of *Oprah* filmed in 2013. Tiffany takes her cameras into the recording studio with her, and she discussed her budding music career for the first time. "I love music," she said in an interview from her childhood bedroom in Calabasas. "It's always been very dear to me. It's more of a hobby right now, but we'll see in a couple of years if I actually want to take it to the next level as a professional." It was not unlike the way Ivanka talked about her modeling career, though Tiffany's older sister pursued photo shoots and runway shows with far more vigor than Tiffany went after recording and writing songs. Ivanka, though, had an agent, and her father pushing her along to be the sort of celebrity he wanted for himself. Friends have said there is no question he would have been more than happy for Tiffany to find that sort of fame, too, though it's not likely he took as much of an interest in her career as he did with Ivanka's. Plus, becoming a full-blown pop star takes a lot more elbow grease—and, for the daughter of a billionaire, greased palms—than becoming a run-of-the-mill model.

Tiffany's pop stardom was over before it started. It stayed a hobby, and she never did take it to that next level as a professional, as she suggested to Oprah. That Tiffany's brief stint as a recording artist was done alongside her mother, aided and arranged by her, in fact, falls in line with how the mother-daughter duo operated from the time Tiffany was born. With Donald working so often, as he had with his older children during his first marriage, Marla and Tiffany were often left to their own devices. Before the split, she would take Tiffany to Central Park, trailing up a jungle gym behind her little toddler to race down a slide (a bodyguard Donald hired from his security team at the Plaza to look after his youngest daughter would trail them closely, lingering on the playground as they chased each other around). To the press, Marla painted a rosy image of a happy home, in which she and her daughter lived their own Kumbaya existence within Donald's twenty-four-karat life. "Tiffany and I rise at about 8 a.m. and give big hugs to each other while we sing 'You Are My Sunshine' or 'Oh What a Beautiful Morning,'" she told the *Guardian* in an interview, describing her daily routine with her daughter. "Most mornings I make her an organic sunshine egg. I cut out the center of a piece of wheat bread and fry an egg in organic butter. It makes an egg face inside the bread. My mom, Tiffany and I usually do a little workout. Tiffany has even got a baby tennis racket."

Of course, that was a snapshot of their day and a snippet of their lives, the cleaned-up, see-everything-is-just-fine, grin-and-bear-it veneer she'd perfected and packaged. It was the version of her life, and of her daughter's, that she wanted the press to believe; maybe she said it because she wanted to believe it, even if she knew the reality was not quite as Pollyannaish. If she projected that part and repeated that story enough, maybe she could will it to come true. Maybe, for a moment, everyone, including Marla, would buy that that was how her fractured fairy tale turned out.

It was far more fractured than she let on for years. And once she and Donald announced that they were separating in the spring of 1997, all the truths about her life and her relationship and the father of her daughter that she had shoved down deep in her stomach up-chucked right out of her. In an interview that summer, Marla said that the marriage hadn't worked because her values and concept of a partner and father differed so wildly from Donald's. Marla, as a mistress turned girlfriend turned fiancé, had a distinct advantage over Donald's early girlfriends and Ivana in that when she decided to settle down with Donald, she already had a window into the kind of father he would be, the sort of effort and attention he gave to his three older children long before Tiffany came around. And yet she either did not care or thought he would be different the second time around. To be fair, some men, who were young and still working like maniacs when they had children with their first wives, relish the opportunity for a do-over when they remarry and have a second set of children. But that wasn't Donald. "After all these years, I realized that he couldn't change who he was," Marla recalled. Who he was turned out to be exactly what she did not want for her daughter—for many reasons. "I wanted a man who would read stories with me to the baby," she said. "I absolutely wish he would have been present in all of their lives. I would have loved to have seen him be the kind of dad who would take us all to Disney World and sit around the dinner table without having the financial news on." What irked her was that Donald cared more about work than his children, and spent far more time concerned with building "the prettiest buildings all around the world" than nurturing his family within his own home. "His main priority is moneymaking and that's where we differ tremendously," she said. "I don't think that's a good life to bring a child up in. I think basic values are much more important. That's something money can't buy."

Once the divorce was filed, though, Marla fought to make sure she had enough money to buy her daughter the good life Tiffany had been born into. This was particularly true when it came to making sure that her father would take care of Tiffany the same way he'd taken care of her older siblings. She complained to friends and lawyers that in Ivana's prenup and their subsequent divorce settlement, his first wife had scored a far more generous arrangement when it came to supporting Don Jr., Ivanka, and Eric than Marla had for Tiffany. Like Ivana, Marla argued that she had signed the marital agreement under duress—just days before the wedding—relenting only under the pressure of the clock ticking closer to their big public day. "I was backed against the wall," she said in another interview with the *Daily News* in the fall of 1997. "I really felt at the time that I had no choice. I was looking out for the best for my baby." Donald contended that Tiffany was "very, very special" to him and that "she will be magnificently taken care of." When it came to whether or not he was stiffing his youngest daughter, he told the press, "I don't think there should be an issue about that." Marla responded by saying that she hoped that proved true. "I'm praying that he's fair where she's concerned. She's a famous child, and I want to give her a secure home in a good, safe neighborhood, in a good school district. That's all I want."

FOR A time after the divorce, Marla tried to give her that secure home in New York. Immediately they settled into something a bit more normal—and certainly closer to earth, less gilded, and lacking a certain balance in the checking account—outside Trump Tower. "Now we enjoy the simple things," Marla said in an interview at the time. "Being a child brought up riding in limousines all her life, [Tiffany] looks at the buses and the cabs and says, 'I want to ride in those.' We have a much more normal life now. It's about pure, unconditional love." As pared down as their lives were, they were inextricably tied to Donald in Manhattan, where the Trump name was splashed across buildings and tabloids, and stood for something Marla did not necessarily want to associate with anymore. He had already started dating Melania, which meant his name was again in the gossip pages. Marla also wanted to restart her acting career. She couldn't live off the divorce settlement, and that was not as easy to do from New York. She would bring Tiffany with her when she traveled for auditions, and at first she kept a little apartment in Hollywood where they would stay as she went out for TV gigs and movie roles. But Tiffany was getting to the age where she would need to settle into a real school, and she couldn't be traveling back and forth to Los Angeles with her mother. It wasn't as though she was going to spend half the time with her father, anyway, so Marla made the choice to move with Tiffany to California.

At first it was going to be temporary. "If I get the right parts, I'll stay," Marla said at the time. She never really landed them, but she stayed regardless. In November 1999 she bought a 5,770 square-foot home for herself and Tiffany in a gated community called Mountain View Estates. It was one of 385 Mediterranean-style homes built in the early 1990s in the private community behind stone gates and buttressed by two man-made ponds with fountains spouting water toward the sky. The grounds are meticulously kept, and the homeowners association dues go toward maintaining the tennis courts, funding security, and keeping access to hiking trails in the surrounding Santa Monica National Recreation Area open.

Marla paid $1.349 million for the sunny yellow five-bedroom, six-bathroom home with a terra-cotta roof and views of the mountains, built on a lot big enough for a basketball court and a swimming pool with a custom water slide and swim-up bar with several stools built into the water. Inside the house's double doors, a double-height rotunda with a double wrought-iron staircase led to Marla's bedroom, with a stone fireplace and balcony, and Tiffany's, outfitted with a fluffy pink carpet and frilly drapes.

It was lavish, certainly, but it was nearer to earth than the triplex or Mar-a-Lago. Marla stuck her in the $30,000-a-year Viewpoint School in Calabasas, where she was a fairly standard rich kid with a recognizable last name. Once she got her license, she drove a black Audi A5; in her senior year, she went to Coachella to see Rihanna and Calvin Harris with her friends, and to senior prom in a hot pink floor-length gown. Donald paid for most of it, but that's about where his daily involvement stopped, and where the Trump side of her ended. "She [hasn't] grown up in the Trumpdom," Marla said in an interview when Tiffany was a teenager. "She's grown up really a kid playing soccer, playing basketball, playing her sports. Pretty regular. I've been the soccer mom, I've driven the SUV." Tiffany said that the move to California let her have a fairly normal, comfortable existence—the kind of childhood her older half siblings never got. "Since I have grown up on the West Coast, I'm definitely different from all of them growing up on the East Coast," she remarked on *Oprah*. "'It was great for me getting a chance to grow up as a normal kid just out of the spotlight, versus all of them growing up in New York. They always had that intense media and spotlight on them."

Marla had boyfriends, of course, but it was mostly her and Tiffany making dinner together, playing tennis, shuttling to sports practices, spending time in Georgia with her family. After Tiffany graduated from high school, Marla accompanied her on a European trip, through Paris, London, Vienna, and Amsterdam. "I've had a real blessing of being able to raise Tiffany as a single parent," she said. Donald, she said, took care of her school and some of her needs, "but as far as the day-to-day parenting, I've been the

one here. There's no secrets I ever kept from Tiffany." Tiffany wasn't
shy about how much her mom did for her. "We've always been very
close, since she raised me as a single mom," she told *Oprah*. "My
friends are always like, 'Wow, you guys have a really good relationship. She's with me a lot of the time and people find that kind of
shocking."

That's not to say Tiffany had no relationship with her father.
There were the Palm Beach breaks and he would fly in for occasional school events. But she didn't quite get him, nor he, her. Her
siblings spent years perfecting how to maneuver around and inter-
pret Donald—how to get a few extra bucks for a pair of jeans or a
trip they wanted to take, when the best time to ask was, what moods
to avoid. Tiffany hadn't spent years collecting that emotional data.
And so when she was in high school, about fifteen years old, she
approached Ivanka for some intel. Tiffany didn't have a credit card
linked up to her dad's account, and she didn't know how best to
ask their dad about it. As Ivanka tells it in her book, *The Trump
Card*, Tiffany's "relatively simple money needs" were not "because
she was spoiled," but because she wanted to keep up with her friends
at school. Tiffany had come up with a strategy; she shared with her
sister, who told her it was no big deal and to make the ask. Tiffany
couldn't quite work up the courage, though. She couldn't pull the
trigger. "I didn't tell her of course," Ivanka wrote, ostensibly telling
her and anyone who would read her book, "but I went to our father
and suggested he think about surprising Tiffany with a credit card
for Christmas, with a small monthly allowance on it. Sure enough,
he did just that. Tiffany was thrilled and relieved. And so appreciative." (Donald never had to worry about Tiffany taking advantage
of the card. Like her father, she developed a reputation among her
friends for her thriftiness. A certain set of Penn students follow a
social schedule that repeats itself each week. On Thursday evenings,
big groups of friends go out to dinner—usually a bring-your-own
restaurant blocks downtown from campus—before heading to a

club rented out by a different fraternity each week for Penn students, where they each pay $10 at the door and party with people they could just as easily party with in their frat houses. Tiffany sometimes went along with this, and friends remember that when she did, she had a habit that stuck out to the other well-off Ivy League students. Typically, the check would come and someone would divide the total by however many people came to dinner that night, regardless of who ordered the more expensive entrée, who just got a salad, who requested a soda or a side dish. When Tiffany would go out to dinner, she became somewhat notorious for scrutinizing the bill, tallying up what she owed, down to the penny, and only agreeing to pay exactly that amount. She would explain that her father provided her with a budget of $500 each month.)

Tiffany was clear about how living on the opposite coast from her father gave her cover. That all but disappeared when she left California on August 27, 2012, and moved east to Philadelphia for school. For the first time, she got a sense of what it was like to live life in a place where people treated her as they had treated her siblings when they heard the Trump name. As many students do in their freshman year, Tiffany went along with her friends as they felt out Greek life and other social clubs on campus. Formal sorority rush would not start until her second semester, but she started going to events during the fall of her first year at Penn for the Tabard Society, a semi-secret all-women's group on campus. Unlike official sororities, Tabard was off campus and not recognized by the university. It has no national chapter or other branches on other campuses. So its selection process began months earlier than the sororities' did, and dragged out for months, unlike the sorority "rush," which wraps up tidily within about a week. The group of girls looking to join Tabard usually hovers well about two hundred, though the group ultimately offers spots—or "bids," as they call them—to just ten to twenty girls. Tabard's early events in the fall are open to any girl on campus who wants to join, but once the girls have mingled for a few evenings, they become invitation-only, and the number of girls invited to each event gets smaller and smaller as the process moves along. Tiffany Trump attended the first event or two, along with her friends, but by the time it got to the first invitation-only event, she did not make the list. People in the group thought she was perfectly nice, but feared that having someone with her last name would turn off other girls looking to join the house. That risk outweighed the reward.

The risk was due, in large part, to the fact that Tiffany arrived on campus at a time when her father was more than just a recognizable Manhattan real estate developer known for his science experiment of a hairdo, his Cheeto-hued skin, his string of high-profile divorces and supermodel wives, and the oft-imitated "you're fired" he made famous in prime time on his reality TV show. In 2011, a year before Tiffany started at Penn, he started publicly questioning the validity of President Barack Obama's birth certificate. Obama was such a popular figure on campus at the time that students still hung Shepard Fairey's "Hope" posters in their dorm rooms. On the eve of his first presidential election, students poured out of their apartments and study rooms and the Van Pelt Library, cheering and hugging and banging on cars blaring music through open windows, despite the November chill in the air. Hundreds of them started walking down Walnut Street toward Center City, not because there was an organized celebration waiting for them farther downtown but because they were buzzing inside, bursting with so much exuberance that they couldn't stay inside or keep it to themselves. They needed to move. They knew they had been witness to history, and they almost had to see the scores of people out there reveling in this moment to believe it. So to many of Tiffany's classmates, the fact that the man bearing her last name repeatedly went on cable news and tweeted to claim that Obama's birth certificate was "a fraud" and urged him to debase himself and his office by providing proof did not engender a lot of goodwill.

That the Trump name hadn't stung Tiffany sooner is a testament to Marla's decision to move her out of New York and far away from Donald. By the time Tiffany's siblings were in college, they had spent so many years under public scrutiny, treated differently—both positively and negatively—because of their last name, that they consciously ran away from it. For Don Jr., that meant showing up to Penn in a pickup truck to prove a point (though he did find himself in the occasional "Don't you know who I am?" fights). Ivanka made a calculated effort to portray herself as the anti–Paris Hilton, constantly stressing what a hardworking homebody she was, content to skip the clubs for a movie and ice skating and hours at the office. Eric would actually deny it when people asked if he was, in fact, *that* Trump. They had lived through people trying to take advantage of their family, so they learned to turn away from it entirely in their social lives, keeping in touch with old friends they knew they could trust or those who couldn't care less about their last name or how they grew up.

Tiffany, though, hadn't grown sick of the association, because she hadn't really been associated with it much before. Sure, she lived a cushy life in Calabasas with Marla, but it was largely private, mostly normal, and well shielded from the incessant life on camera Marla bemoaned after she divorced Donald. She hadn't yet had people use her, or burn her, the way her siblings had. And unlike Don Jr., Ivanka, and Eric, she was too young to remember the firestorm around her parent's divorce, so she hadn't learned how that sort of attention can turn on a person on a dime.

Beyond that, she was the very definition of a privileged millennial, keen on posting every aspect of her life, as if it were a contest: who could share the most, get the most likes, attract the most followers. She quickly found how to do that, posting photos of her on her dad's jet or poolside at Mar-a-Lago, in a glittery gown in front of a towering Christmas tree, surrounded by dozens of presents, in the front row at a fashion show, behind the scenes at a photo shoot, or dancing in a lace bikini by a Southampton pools, wearing a tiara and a fur hood and munching from pool-deep soup bowls filled to the top with caviar.

The gossip pages quickly caught on. The *New York Post* ran an item in 2013 about spotting her in a sparkly blue sailor costume at the Boom Boom Room's Halloween party, given by *V Magazine*. That summer, *Newsday* placed her at 1 Oak in Southampton on a Saturday evening in June. That fall, the *Post* detailed her twenty-first birthday celebration, which started out with dinner hosted by her father at—where else?—Trump Soho, followed by a night at the meatpacking district club Up & Down. A year later, at the end of the summer of 2015, MailOnline posted a story about Tiffany dancing so wildly at a Jason Derulo concert that a bouncer told her and her friends to calm down their moves.

Around that time, the magazine *DuJour* did a feature on Tiffany and the group of other rich kids she was palling around with, who incessantly posed in photos subsequently posted on their Instagram and Snapchat accounts. Collectively, they became known as "the rich kids of Instagram" or "the Snap Pack," for their tendency to share images across social media almost admirable in their brazen ostentatiousness. There was a blonde with a hard-earned tan chugging a $200 bottle of Cristal, captioned "Water shortage on the island so we have to improvise." There were chilled rosé glasses sipped in front of sprawling pools, poses in front of jumbo jets or atop penthouses that overlooked the Eiffel Tower, stacks of Cartier "Love" bracelets and diamond-encrusted Rolexes. Their feeds became a delicious guilty pleasure, with other millennials and lookie-loos far older hate-watching their every stomach-turning move. Surely it was a new phenomenon: hundreds of thousands of people following these kids' accounts, just to both loathe and envy them—kids who hadn't worked a day, unabashedly, fliply bragging about all the unthinkably grand things they were conspicuously consuming. If their parents had grown up subscribing to the maxim "Money talks, wealth whispers," this new generation of rich kids bought into the idea that wealth shouted itself from the rooftops, and prayed that hundreds of thousands of people would hear.

This new media-savvy silk-stocking posse included Andrew Warren, the grandson of 1970s fashion mogul David Warren; Gaïa Jacquet-Matisse, the great-great-granddaughter of French artist Henri Matisse; Peter Brant Jr., the son of model Stephanie Seymour and art collector Peter Brant; Kyra Kennedy, Robert Kennedy Jr.'s daughter; and Reya Benitez, the daughter of Studio 54 DJ John "Jellybean" Benitez.

Because they emerged in the middle of the second decade of the twenty-first century, when the Kardashians and *Real Housewives* got far more attention than the war in Iraq and the upcoming presidential election (before that turned into a reality show–like spectacle of its own, that is), this group received quite a bit of infamy. In fact, producers looking to turn their social feeds into a reality show of their own approached the crew with a variety of opportunities. In aggregate, they shied away from it. "You have to think long term. It's easy money, but . . . ," Tiffany told *DuJour*. Matisse interrupted her: "But it conflicts so much with all of our different personal goals. Besides, it's not about money or fame. It's about our friendships. It's about us being fucking amazing people and loving each other." To the *New York Times*, which interviewed the crew in a piece of its own a few months later, Matisse added that their posting had another, simpler raison d'être. "I look good in pictures I take of myself."

In the many stories written about the Snap Pack—and there are many—Tiffany was often absent or in the background. "Perhaps unexpectedly, considering her pedigree, Trump—who has just graduated from the University of Pennsylvania—is the least showy of all of them," the *Evening Standard* wrote in 2016. *DuJour* reported that she had an Ivy League degree and "a Southern gentility, using expressions like 'goodness gracious'" and that, unlike her friends, she was debating whether or not to go into business or apply to law school. It was not unlike the way Ivanka was talked about as a teenager in comparison to her more ostentatious pals when they all appeared in that documentary *Born Rich*. They might not have grown up spending much time together, but their genetic propensity to use their friends as foils, casting themselves in the best light, shone through in both of them.

Tiffany's friends distanced themselves a bit once the campaign wore on. "With Tiffany Trump, there is too much going on," Warren told the *Times* in 2016. "It was great press, but it was a distraction from the designs. I don't want to mix with politics." Some of them were threatened, harassed, and barraged by negative comments whenever they posted photos with Tiffany during the election cycle. But they did not knock Tiffany out of their posse completely. In August 2016, months before the election, the official Rich Kids of Instagram account posted that photo of Tiffany and Warren dancing poolside at a Southampton club with the caption: "Hamptons last Summer. White House this Fall!"

Author's Note

I WOULD imagine that the idea for this book, and my initial attitude toward it, was not entirely unlike those of the First Family when Donald Trump decided to launch a bid to become the president of the United States of America. To start, like the Trump kids, none of this was my idea. I got a cold e-mail one afternoon at the end of September 2016 from Jane von Mehren, a literary agent (and in my estimation a patient patron saint), with the subject line: "Might you be interested in talking books?" She introduced herself and pitched an idea for a "dish-y" but "really well-reported book" about Trump, and his kids in particular. By that point, I had been closely, compulsively covering the Trump family as a reporter for *Vanity Fair*. Like the Trump kids, I was sick of it all by that point (little did I know!), but intrigued enough to take the meeting.

We met on a sunny Monday afternoon during the first week in October, and I told her that I would take the week to think about it and get back to her. The truth is that after the meeting, I ghosted her. Everyone thought Donald Trump was going to lose, and that in a month his family would go back to selling themselves with a slightly elevated or denigrated brand, depending on where you sat; I didn't know how interesting this man, who captivated and aggravated the world for a minute, would be post–November 8. Frankly, I didn't know how interesting this would be to me. They were a famous New York family with a questionable level of wealth who lived life so publicly that I didn't know if there was anything left to know about them. These people were scrawled across Page Six since they were in diapers. Everything worth knowing about them was probably already out there. Like the Trump kids, I liked my life the way it was. I had enough on my plate that the idea of taking on something else on top of everything also struck me as unnecessary.

That Friday, the *Access Hollywood* tapes broke, and on Sunday, Donald looked as if he were stalking Hillary Clinton onstage at a presidential debate. I dodged Jane and went back to checking the countdown clock I'd set up on my phone to tick down the days, hours, minutes, seconds, until the election would be over.

About a week before the election, I began reporting a story for *Vanity Fair*'s "The Hive," about what Ivanka Trump was planning to do to get her brand back on track, and how she would transition back to life on earth after her dad conceded. I was later to the conversation than the Trump kids were, but it was one they were having at that moment, too. I made a bunch of calls to people who worked with her, who would work with her as she readjusted come November 9. Their general sentiment was that she would have to let everyone breathe and calm themselves down. She would keep her head down and focus on the business, and maybe quietly, privately, start talking to reporters. These people said Ivanka had been very strategic about what she said and when she said it, and throughout the campaign, she talked only about issues related to women and families, and in the general support of her father. It was what one person called an impressive, calculated business decision executed over the course of eighteen months, knowing that it would serve her well after the election. Would some people hold her accountable for what her father said and for not speaking up about it? Sure. "But what will they be holding her accountable for once Hillary wins?" one person connected to the campaign told me on the Friday afternoon before Election Day. "Policies her father never got to enact?"

The story never ran. An entirely different one was written. On the evening of November 9, as the world woke up from its collective coma and realized that Donald Trump had been elected the forty-fifth president, I sent Jane an e-mail. The subject line read: "Let's do this."

My hesitation faded a week later, when *60 Minutes* aired its interview with the new First Family. "I think it's impossible to go through this journey and not change," Ivanka whispered. Two days later, early on a weekday morning, my phone buzzed with an incoming call from an unknown number. I was still in my pajamas when that same voice came through my receiver. The call was off the record, so I can't report what she said. But, while Ivanka was still insisting at that point that she would not take on an official or unofficial role in her father's administration, she was going to take advantage of an opportunity she never imagined now splayed out in front of her.

So for the next fifteen months, I set off to figure out who they were and where they came from and what shaped them, in order to understand how they'd changed and where they might go from there. There was no political agenda or bent. These would soon be some of the most powerful people in the world, and I wanted to give a view into their past as a way to preview what their future might look like, too.

I dove deep into their groups of friends, former classmates, colleagues, and business associates to learn the ins-and-outs of the First Family—the intense privilege and the damage left by a very public divorce, periods of rebellion and public mastery of the media, the engagements and weddings and reality shows and rotten business deals that make up the life of a family. I interviewed hundreds of people, many of them multiple times, for hours. I culled through thousands upon thousands of what I think are just about every press clipping that mentioned the Trump kids back to the 1980s. Do you know how many times they've been written about since they were children? The sheer volume is staggering.

I faced two main issues in my reporting. The first was Don Jr.'s name. Since there are so many ways in which to refer to him—Don, Don Jr., Donald Trump Jr., Donny—the effort to find old press clippings about him was a complicated one. And the second was that there was an endless number of people who wanted to talk about them. The talk didn't stop. This person knew that person who had gone to boarding school with one of them. That person's friend taught one of their preschool classes, and their former colleague partnered with them on a real estate deal. At lunch with them, a well-known flak who'd worked for the family or a publisher who worked on one of their books would be eating across the room. Would they want to be interviewed for a book I'm working on? Most often, the answer was yes. Sometimes, it was less kind. And for every yes, I tried to figure out their motivation for wanting to speak to a reporter.

By now, it is no secret that this is a First Family with no equivalent. President Donald Trump is in the White House with a First Lady who is his third wife and two senior West Wing advisers to whom he is related. His two adult sons are back in New York running the family business from which the president opted not to divest, despite a constant barrage of ethical concerns. He has five children from three women and a string of products from water to wine, hotels to cologne, all of whom and which bear his last name.

But it is a First Family so uniquely suited for the second decade of the twenty-first century and its fame-obsessed, money-hungry, voracious twenty-four-hour cycle of a culture. They are *Gossip Girl* meets *The West Wing*. The Kardashianification of the Kennedys. And they're just dying for you to tune in, and we're all just dying to watch, even if the dirty laundry they end up airing, intentionally or otherwise, stinks.

combed through property records, and managed always to find an answer to whatever question I threw her way. My life, and this book, would have been significantly worse without her (and a thank-you to my colleague Nick Bilton for introducing me to her).

I never would have found myself writing about the First Family, or in a position to author this book, had it not been for Jon Kelly, my editor at *Vanity Fair*, who saw the story in them long before I did. He always sees the story, which is why he is the gold standard for any reporter trying to find the bigger picture or smaller victories along the way. He pushed my reporting and gave me the space and platform to start telling their stories the way people actually wanted to read them. Everything I write, he makes better, smarter, more interesting, and certainly more fun. I've been humbled by the encouragement for my reporting and for this project across *Vanity Fair*. I am especially grateful to Graydon Carter, Radhika Jones, Ben Landy, John Homans, Mike Hogan, Doug Stumpf, and Krista Smith for their advice and many boosts along the way.

I am deeply indebted to the generous, tireless, talented reporters and authors who shared notes, insights, and bits of reporting, and their stories on which I leaned to fill out this book. I am grateful for the years of shoe-leather reporting that helped inform my understanding of the family and pointed me toward key players and events I might have otherwise missed.

I have to thank the many people who agreed to speak with me for this book, who dug deep in their memories for little anecdotes and offered their time and gossip and insights. They put up with my follow-ups and follow-ups on follow-ups without hesitation. One of the best parts of this book was getting to speak with such a vast array of people, who were all united by three things: they all knew the Trumps, they all wanted me to get this right, and they all loved to gossip.

My WME family, Bradley Singer, Jason Hodes, Jon Rosen, and Eve Atterman, have been touchstones and sounding boards throughout.

Acknowledgments

THIS BOOK would not exist without Jane von Mehren, who planted the seed and then nurtured the hell out of it—and me—from the beginning. I would not have said yes to anyone else, nor would I have been able to get through this process without her wisdom, reassurance, kindness, and very gentle, much-needed shoves in the right direction. If I had any lingering doubts about the whole thing, they evaporated when she brought this—and me—to Jonathan Jao. When I worried that many might not be interested in some of the softer sides of this story, I'd remember the raw way he reacted to the more human aspects the same way I did. He got it—and me—and proved to be a light post, a whip-smart wordsmith, and an endlessly patient ally. Jonathan Burnham and Doug Jones at HarperCollins took this—and me—under their wings from the get-go, giving this the kind of support and time any author would dream of. I feel beyond lucky to have worked with Sofia Groopman, Tina Andreadis, and Tracy Locke, who put this together and made it happen, and promoted with such efficiency, savvy, and attention.

This book is filled with many stories from many people and many articles I would never have even known existed without my researcher, Nicole Landset Blank. She is both an absolute wizard with her work and my soul sister. She received as many tough reactions from people not supportive of the reporting as I did; she read through all of the articles, listened to many hours of interviews,

I would be remiss not to apologize for all of the birthdays, holidays, dinners, lunches, coffees, calls, and appointments I had to reschedule or miss or cancel over the course of a year and a half. My friends, who all received many "I'm so sorry to do this" messages, were not only patient and understanding but also so overwhelmingly supportive that I somehow wound up feeling even guiltier. I owe you all a great deal of thanks and drinks. I also owe appreciation to the many pairs of running shoes I wore through to clear my head as I worked. Fleetwood Mac helped, too.

Naturally, this book took a great deal of reflection about families, and boy, do I feel fortunate to have been born into mine. My grandparents, aunts, uncles, and cousins all put up with my absence, checked in for proof of life, and delighted in this project. My sister, Becca, is a stunningly gifted writer (the better writer, surely) who commiserated and willed me along this process. It was not just because she had recently finished a gorgeous book of her own; my sister has always been my greatest cheerleader, my first call for any kind of commiseration, and the most empathetic, sympathetic, deeply kind soul I've ever met. She is maybe only matched by her husband, Kenny, who puts the "brother" in brother-in-law and shows up for all of us every day. My niece and nephew, Annabelle and Beau, are my heart. Knowing that I would go back to seeing them more often once this was all done with was my pot of gold. My parents, Robb and Nancy, joked that I would dedicate this book to my childhood stuffed animal (thank you, Pinkie) and our dead family dog (RIP Lucy). There was never any question that this was for, and because of, my parents. They felt every disappointment, reporting win, setback, leap forward, stress, deadline, as their own, partly because I called them to share each one immediately, but mostly because that's the kind of parents they are. They are nurturing and smart and present and the best people I know. I don't know what I did to win this familial jackpot, but I am so stinkin' lucky that I did.

ABOUT THE AUTHOR

EMILY JANE FOX is a senior reporter at *Vanity Fair*. A former White House intern, she is also a graduate of Columbia School of Journalism and the University of Pennsylvania.